A Publication of
The AAFRC Trust for Philanthropy

Critical Issues in American Philanthropy is a publication of the AAFRC Trust for Philanthropy, a foundation that was established in 1985 both to advance research and education in philanthropy and to increase public recognition of philanthropy for its pervasive and beneficial influence in shaping the life and character of the nation.

Among other programs, the Trust publishes *Giving USA*, the annual report on philanthropy, and *Giving USA Update*, a companion bimonthly newsletter of legal, economic, and social developments that are affecting the voluntary sector. The yearbook, which provides the most comprehensive data on charitable contributions, has been issued by the Trust since 1985; previously, it was issued by the American Association of Fund-Raising Counsel since 1956.

The Trust was established by the American Association of Fund-Raising Counsel, which represents the nation's premier philanthropic fund-raising consulting firms. The Association was founded in 1935 to promote ethical and professional standards in the field.

For the most part, the Trust's operations and programs are supported by the annual contributions of its directors and the officers and personnel of the member firms of the American Association of Fund-Raising Counsel. Other foundations, organizations, and individuals have provided support for Trust programs in which they had a particular interest.

Information on Trust programs and publications is available from:

The AAFRC Trust for Philanthropy
25 West 43rd Street
New York, NY   10036

Critical Issues in American Philanthropy

Jon Van Til
and Associates

Critical Issues in American Philanthropy

Strengthening Theory and Practice

Jossey-Bass Publishers
San Francisco • Oxford • 1990

CRITICAL ISSUES IN AMERICAN PHILANTHROPY
Strengthening Theory and Practice
by Jon Van Til and Associates

Copyright © 1990 by: Jossey-Bass Inc., Publishers
350 Sansome Street
San Francisco, California 94104
&
Jossey-Bass Limited
Headington Hill Hall
Oxford OX3 0BW

Library of Congress Cataloging-in-Publication Data

Critical issues in American philanthropy : strengthening theory and
practice / Jon Van Til and associates.—1st ed.
p.   cm.—(The Jossey-Bass nonprofit sector series)
"A Publication of the AAFRC Trust for Philanthropy"—T.p. verso.
Includes bibliographical references (p.   ) and index.
ISBN 1-55542-278-0 (alk. paper)
1. Charities—United States.   2. Voluntarism—United States.
3. Fund raising—United States.   I. Van Til, Jon.   II. Series.
HV91.C75   1990
361.7'0973—dc20   90-4877
                                                      CIP

Manufactured in the United States of America

The paper in this book meets the guidelines for
permanence and durability of the Committee on
Production Guidelines for Book Longevity of the
Council on Library Resources.

FIRST EDITION

Code 9072

A Publication of the AAFRC Trust for Philanthropy
25 West 43rd Street, New York, NY 10036

The Jossey-Bass Nonprofit Sector Series

To Beatrice Blaha Van Til,
mother, volunteer, and teacher:
a dedication from the younger generation

Contents

Contents

Foreword

Several years ago an organization that promotes giving and volunteering published a brochure whose cover carried a quotation from Thoreau. This was surprising because Thoreau was more a critic than an advocate of philanthropy. In the original passage in *Walden* the quoted phrase "Philanthropy is almost the only virtue which is sufficiently appreciated by mankind" is immediately followed by the sentence "Nay, it is greatly overrated."

One could substitute quotations from Emerson, Mencken, and a host of others to show the presence of a critical, even hostile attitude toward philanthropy in American thought. One of the challenges facing efforts to promote study of and research in philanthropy is to come to terms with this negative attitude, which is not confined to, but is certainly prevalent among, students and teachers.

In the case of Emerson, Thoreau, and many other writers, dislike of philanthropy and philanthropists is an expression of the belief that people can and should take care of themselves and tend strictly to their own business. Individualists not only distrust people who seek help but are scornful of do-gooders and reformers.

Because philanthropy is so often identified exclusively with the rich and powerful, it is often regarded with hostility by people who do not have wealth or power and are suspicious of those who do. Between 1965 and about 1980 many graduate students and historians writing about American philanthropy routinely interpreted it as "social control" of the poor by the well-to-do.

As far as scholars are concerned, if philanthropy is sufficiently appreciated by humankind, there is no point in dealing with it in an appreciative way. All the challenge and fun come in pointing out its failures, discrepancies, and insignificance.

Thoreau said, "There is no odor so bad as that which arises from goodness tainted." Students take particular pleasure in sniffing out and calling attention to the terrific stench of "tainted goodness." I think that is why they seem so preoccupied with motivation in philanthropy. The canons of scholarship do not allow us to accept the donor's word on his or her motivation. We have to try to discover what we think was the motive and if we decide, often quite arbitrarily, that the motive was self-serving or not entirely altruistic, that decision brings the inquiry to a close.

The contributors to this volume demonstrate that motives for giving are much more complex than many observers or students of philanthropy have assumed. They also remind us that many questions other than the motivation of the donor should concern us in research on philanthropy. The response of recipients is no less important than the motive of the donor. The purpose of the gift, the conditions it was intended to alter, and the results—often completely unexpected and unpredictable—are what count.

Although it is impossible to deal with philanthropy without considering the benefactions of rich men and women, the subject is not limited to the disposal of surplus wealth by the rich. Support of small donors is crucially important to philanthropic enterprise and makes possible its range and diversity. Because Americans have long sought to achieve the goals of individualism through voluntary associations, a necessary part of the study of philanthropy is the effort of mutual-aid and self-help organizations to provide practical assistance and emotional support to members and to protect members and their families from dependence on public relief or private charity. Similarly, because helping others to become able to take care of themselves looms large in the American—and human—tradition, advocacy for the young and friendless, and empowerment for the handicapped and disadvantaged, continue to be essential for the health both of philanthropy and of its study.

July 1990   Robert H. Bremner

Preface

It is probably presumptuous to ask readers to pause for a brief word about the birth of this book before they dip into its provocative chapters. Our only excuse is that it could help set the stage for those chapters and explain how they happen to have been written.

The daunting notion of bringing scholars into agreement on a comprehensive definition of philanthropy was entertained in mid-1986 by the AAFRC Trust for Philanthropy, a foundation that only the year before had been established by the American Association of Fund-Raising Counsel as a vehicle for expanding and enriching its half-century tradition of public service.

The directors of the Trust, mainly fund-raising consultants who headed the AAFRC member firms, assumed that a generally accepted, comprehensive definition of philanthropy did not exist and that achieving one would be no easy task. Yet they recognized that a clear and comprehensive set of defining characteristics could have very practical uses for all of American society:

- It could give the AAFRC and other professional organizations in the fund-raising field an informed basis for evaluating the many new, nontraditional concepts and practices that are being developed, and it could provide similar guidance to the trustees, other volunteers, and the professional staffs of gift-supported organizations.

- It could assist government in furthering its historical partnership with philanthropy, including the uses it makes of philanthropic organizations to channel public funds to the disadvantaged. It could clarify for business the differences between
corporate philanthropy and the sharing of profits through
cause-related marketing arrangements.
- It could furnish to journalists and other writers who are critically assessing the support of philanthropic causes a sound basis
for judging fund-raising concepts and practices, and it could—
for all segments of the community—correct the many miscon-
ceptions that exist and adversely affect American philanthropy.

In checking their assumptions with a handful of the foremost
scholars in the field, Trust directors confirmed that a generally accepted, comprehensive definition did not exist and that it is not
realistic to expect to achieve one.

As we directors continued to refine our interests, we came to
recognize that, as useful as such a definition of philanthropy could
be, our eventual concern was to gain scholarly guidance in analyzing and dealing with the increasing, and increasingly troublesome,
issues that confront contemporary philanthropy.

And so we accepted the possibility that it could be true of
philanthropy, as former Supreme Court Justice Potter Stewart observed of pornography, "I can't define it, but I know it when I see
it." Defining philanthropy became for us a secondary objective for
the study we had in mind.

One of the scholars, while recognizing the difficulty of the
task, was interested enough to want to discuss our proposed study.
He was Jon Van Til, associate professor in the departments of Public Policy (graduate) and Urban Studies at the Rutgers University
Camden College. In discussions with Van Til, we identified more
than twenty-five cutting-edge issues in contemporary philanthropy;
he provided additional ones. At our request, he also submitted a
proposal for a study that he was prepared to conduct for the Trust.
It was enthusiastically accepted.

Because of Van Til's broad academic contacts, he was able to
enlist sixteen other scholars in the field and assign them issues in
which they had done research or had some special competence.

These scholars, who are among the foremost investigators in the field, are at the leading edge of philanthropic research. Their participation alone is enough to ensure the study's significance.

Charles E. Lawson, the founding chairman of the Trust, was presiding over the foundation when the study was proposed; he was quick to grasp its significance and enthusiastically endorse it. The other Trust directors did not hesitate in expressing their approval. They recognized that the book the study would produce could provide the insights and guidance so urgently needed today by gift-supported organizations and institutions and by the sources of their support: the government, foundations, corporations, and individuals. The book could be not only a seminal work but a very practical guide to understanding and dealing with the troublesome issues besetting the philanthropic sector.

Despite its modest resources, the Trust provided the lion's share of the funds the study required. Significant contributions were made by the Indiana University Center on Philanthropy and the Gannett Foundation, and they are acknowledged with gratitude. The Trust is also indebted to the Center on Philanthropy for hosting two conferences of the participating scholars.

It is one thing to come up with an idea; it is quite another to witness its implementation. As the AAFRC Trust's program officer for the study, I had the privilege of relating to Van Til as he advanced the work on the study. I can attest that, for him, the study was not just an assignment—it was a labor of love.

July 1990   Maurice G. Gurin
                         Chairman,
                         The AAFRC Trust for Philanthropy

Introduction

Philanthropy is in the midst of rapid change and some turmoil. Identified by recent public policy as an increasingly important source of support for the resolution of societal problems, its practice has nonetheless not been clearly encouraged by recent and wide-ranging changes in federal tax and spending policies.

Disarray in the field has become the stuff of daily headlines. On the day this study was proposed, April 30, 1987, the *New York Times'* lead story concerned a tax-exempt organization's support of the illegal arming of a foreign rebellion, apparently with the support of White House staff. On the same day, *USA Today's* headline followed its interest in an unraveling scandal: "Falwell Pleads to Keep Ailing PTL Afloat."

At the same time, however, voluntary associations have stepped forward with bold and dramatic programs designed to increase the scale of responsible philanthropy in society. United Way has set the goal of doubling its contributions over the next several years, and INDEPENDENT SECTOR has announced a campaign to establish a standard for all Americans of donating 5 percent of individual income and volunteering five hours per week.

In many communities throughout the nation, voluntary and nonprofit organizations, with augmented philanthropic support, have struggled against prevailing odds both to offer a wide range of needed services to disadvantaged individuals and to sustain a level of programs in the arts, culture, and recreation.

Internally, the field of philanthropy is nothing if not diverse. The perspectives of donors, philanthropic organizations, donees, fund raisers, and the broader community all bear on the process of giving and receiving. And these perspectives often clash with each other dramatically. A primary goal of *Critical Issues in American Philanthropy* is to illuminate these different perspectives and thereby illuminate the choices that face those directly involved in philanthropic activities.

No single comprehensive definition of philanthropy has emerged from this book, though the field requires as much clarification in its theory, conceptualization, and practice as can humanly and reasonably be expected. A second goal for this book is to advance that process of clarification.

Audience

This book has been written for a broad audience: those who are concerned with the state of giving and volunteering in America. We address the interests of students enrolled in courses in philanthropy or nonprofit organization management and those who seek to find a place for themselves in the world of philanthropic giving and organization. We address the concerns of citizens in our democratic society, whose giving of time and money makes it possible for us to study what they do. We address the concerns of staffers of nonprofit organizations, whose efforts are sustained by the support of philanthropic giving. We address the interests of policymakers, whose actions regulate and oversee the workings of American philanthropy through the vehicle of tax exemption. And we address the interests of philanthropists themselves, persons who donate resources to the common good that they might have used for their own personal consumption.

We have sought to write in a language that is broadly communicative and to draw implications for the daily work of citizens and professionals alike. It is our hope that our effort will assist in the critical evaluation of philanthropic practice and a closer squaring of its lofty aims to its everyday applications.

The Critical Issues

Critical Issues in American Philanthropy seeks to identify and illuminate the most pressing and important issues in philanthropy's practice. Some of these issues are

- How the rules of the philanthropy "game" are changing, and how the principal players—big givers, small givers, donees, potential donees, foundation and corporate staffers, fund raisers, media, and citizens at large—understand these rules. Do all play by the same set of rules?
- The possibility and desirability of achieving a comprehensive and widely accepted definition for philanthropy. What definitions presently prevail? Is a "consensus" definition a realistic goal?
- How an internationalizing economy, with its many mergers and the predominance of the transnational corporation, affects patterns of giving, and what this implies for the philanthropic community.
- What new roles citizens and donees should assume in the contemporary development of philanthropy. What will be major sources of conflict as philanthropy develops? How are processes of giving and patterns of donor motivation changing?
- What the role of philanthropy in religion is, in terms of the giving of both time and money.
- Whether philanthropy will remain true to its traditional goal of aiding those most cruelly situated in society in light of the uneven turf of the contemporary welfare state. Do givers favor large organizations that benefit persons like themselves over smaller groups that seek to challenge existing structures of meaning and power?
- What ethical and legal standards voluntary organizations should be held to in their fund raising, and whether philanthropy will be an "active" rather than a "reactive" force in society. How fully active should it be? And from what sources might it further develop its leadership capacity in society?
- The implications of the increasing role of staff, rather than volunteers, acting as fund-raising solicitors for voluntary orga-

nizations. Has the cost of fund-raising risen as a result of the increasing role of such "middle-persons"?

- The role of the volunteer board member: has it been reduced by fears of litigation and the rising price of liability insurance?
- What mix of in-service training, reading, and college- or university-based curricula will prove most useful in educating volunteers and professional leaders in philanthropic endeavors?
- How can we keep alive the commitment to give and serve in American society in the years ahead?

Organization of the Book

Part One opens *Critical Issues in American Philanthropy* with three chapters that set philanthropy in its historical, definitional, and socioeconomic context. In Chapter One, "Philanthropy in Its Historical Context," Maurice G. Gurin and I note that philanthropy is a long and well-established tradition in many cultural and historical experiences. This chapter reviews that history and places it in the context of today's "third sector." In Chapter Two, "Defining Philanthropy," I review the major conceptions of this term and argue that philanthropy has never been easy to define. I conclude the chapter with my own definition of philanthropy. In Chapter Three, "Changing Conditions for Fund Raising and Philanthropy," James W. Harvey and Kevin F. McCrohan observe that the development of a closely integrated world economy has meant that philanthropy has become internationalized as well. The authors describe specific strategies that emphasize fund-raising efficiency and service and urge philanthropists and recipients alike to adopt practices of environmental scanning and strategic management.

In Part Two of the book, issues pertaining to the workings of philanthropy in society are examined. In Chapter Four, "Giving and Getting: Philanthropy as a Social Relation," Susan A. Ostrander and Paul G. Schervish observe that, in philanthropy, the giver and the gift are no better than the recipient and the uses to which the gift is put. These authors develop a framework within which the subtle and complex exchanges of philanthropy may be considered. In Chapter Five, "The Role of Religion in Philanthropy," James R. Wood and James G. Hougland, Jr., argue that

the entire religious experience, because it seeks to embody universalistic values, should be seen as central to philanthropy and the
third sector. In Chapter Six, "Philanthropy and the Community,"
Justin Fink notes that philanthropy is only as good as its actions,
and nowhere are these actions more important than on the level of
the local community. In this chapter Fink takes the perspective of
the community toward philanthropy and examines the strengths
and weaknesses of the American traditions of giving.

Part Three focuses on ways of strengthening philanthropic
practice. In Chapter Seven, "Teaching Philanthropy, Teaching
About Philanthropy," Robert L. Payton builds on the reality that
courses on philanthropy are increasingly common in American
universities and describes how such courses might best be organized.
In Chapter Eight, "Ethical Issues in Fund Raising and Philanthropy," Elizabeth T. Boris and Teresa J. Odendahl build on the
fact that as practitioners within the third sector increasingly come
to view their work as embodied in a professional context, the cod-
ification of ethical standards becomes more widely attempted. They
identify the issues of governance, fund raising, and accountability
as centrally involved in ethical considerations. In Chapter Nine,
"Legal Issues in Fund Raising and Philanthropy," Bruce R. Hopkins notes that philanthropy and the law have a long and intertwined tradition in American life. Tax code definitions importantly
influence the field, and tax regulations importantly affect the levels
of support philanthropists make available to donees. In this chapter, Hopkins explains how the tax code affects philanthropy and
how recent and impending changes in the law, both federal and
state, will affect nonprofit organizations.

In Chapter Ten, "The Board's Crucial Role in Fund Raising," Robert D. Herman and Stephen R. Block begin with the observation that the practice of philanthropy is increasingly becoming
the role of paid organizational staff members. Despite this shift
from volunteers to paid staff, the board of directors retains a crucial
role in advancing the funding needs of the nonprofit organization.
In Chapter Eleven, "The Dilemmas of Research on Philanthropy,"
Peter Dobkin Hall shows that as the practice of philanthropy becomes more reflective, it also increasingly becomes an arena open
to research, by both internal staff and external scholars. How to

organize and support that research are problems that confront both national organizations and individual scholars. In Chapter Twelve, "Preparing for Philanthropy's Future," I claim that philanthropy's future, like other futures, can best be understood as a series of potentials. I develop images of four possible philanthropic futures and advise the reader to choose one that seems agreeable and work for its achievement.

A concluding chapter, "Toward Guidelines for Effective Philanthropic Practice," presents eleven specific guidelines for those who practice and support philanthropic activities. These guidelines, drawn from the preceding pages of this book, suggest that the most productive philanthropic work will be done by reflective practitioners who are capable of seeing the relationship between their work and that of others in society.

July 1990   Jon Van Til
                                                          Swarthmore, Pennsylvania

The Authors

Stephen R. Block is executive officer of the Institute for Nonprofit Organization Management in Englewood, Colorado. A public administrator and social worker, Block is the author of *The Academic Discipline of Nonprofit Management* (1980) and coeditor (with R. Leduc and J. Van Til) of *The Effective Practice of Nonprofit Management* (1990).

Elizabeth T. Boris is vice-president for research at the Council on Foundations in Washington, D.C. A political scientist, Boris is the coauthor (with T. Odendahl and A. K. Daniels) of *Working in Foundations* (1985) and (with T. Odendahl and others) of *America's Wealthy and the Future of Foundations* (1987).

Robert H. Bremner is professor emeritus of history at the Ohio State University. His books include *From the Depths: The Discovery of Poverty in the United States* (1956), *The Public Good: Philanthropy and Welfare in the Civil War Era* (1980), and *American Philanthropy* (1960, 1988).

Justin Fink is the principal of Community Nonprofit Services, a Philadelphia-based consulting firm that supports the work of community based organizations. A doctoral candidate in social work at Bryn Mawr College, Fink also serves as associate editor of the *Nonprofit and Voluntary Sector Quarterly*.

Maurice G. Gurin is the principal of the Gurin Group, in New York City, which offers fund-raising counsel. Formerly a reporter, he has long been a leader within the American Association of Fund-Raising Counsel and its philanthropic arm, the AAFRC Trust for Philanthropy. Among his books are *Confessions of a Fund-Raiser* (1985).

Peter Dobkin Hall is senior research associate with the Program on Non-Profit Organizations at Yale University and has recently completed a term as visiting fellow at the Rockefeller Archives Center. His books include *The Organization of American Culture, 1700–1900* (1982) and *Inventing the Nonprofit Sector* (forthcoming).

James W. Harvey is associate professor of marketing at George Mason University. He has participated in numerous studies, marketing task forces, and executive development programs for professionals in philanthropy. His work has been published in the *Journal of Consumer Research, Journal of Public Policy and Marketing, Long Range Planning, Business and Society,* and the *Journal of Economic Psychology.*

Robert D. Herman is professor of public administration at the L. P. Cookingham Institute at the University of Missouri, Kansas City. He is coeditor (with J. Van Til) of *Nonprofit Boards of Directors* (1988) and currently serves as president of the Association of Voluntary Action Scholars.

Bruce R. Hopkins is counselor at law with the firm of Baker & Hostettler in Washington, D.C. A frequent writer on nonprofit law, his books include *Charity Under Siege: Government Regulation of Fundraising* (1980) and *The Law of Tax-Exempt Organizations,* 4th ed. (1983).

James G. Hougland, Jr., is professor of sociology at the University of Kentucky. He has published a series of papers on the value of volunteers and their place in the social structure, including (with J. M. Shepard) "Voluntarism and the Manager: The Impacts of

Structural Pressure and Personal Interest on Community Participation" (1985).

Kevin F. McCrohan is professor and chairman of the marketing department at George Mason University. He has served as chief economist at the Internal Revenue Service and was a Fulbright Scholar at Trinity College in Dublin. His work has been published in the *Journal of Marketing, California Management Review, Journal of Economic Psychology,* and *Journal of the Market Research Society.*

Teresa J. Odendahl is a frequent consultant to voluntary and philanthropic organizations and lecturer in communications at the University of California, San Diego. An anthropologist, Odendahl is the author (with E. T. Boris and A. K Daniels) of *Working in Foundations* (1985), (with E. T. Boris and others) *America's Wealthy and the Future of Foundations* (1987), and *Charity Begins at Home: Generosity and Self-Interest Among the Philanthropic Elite* (1990).

Susan A. Ostrander is associate professor of sociology and American studies at Tufts University. She is the author of *Women of the Upper Class* (1984) and senior editor (with S. Langton and J. Van Til) of *Shifting the Debate: Public/Private Sector Relations in the Modern Welfare State* (1987).

Robert L. Payton is director of the Center on Philanthropy and professor of philanthropic studies at Indiana University. He has served as president of Exxon Education Foundation, C. W. Post College, and Hofstra University, and as United States ambassador to the Republic of Cameroon. His most recent book is *Philanthropy: Voluntary Action for the Public Good* (1988).

Paul G. Schervish is associate professor of sociology and director of the Center on Culture and Economy at Boston College. His papers on wealth and philanthropy have been presented to the Spring Research Forum of INDEPENDENT SECTOR (1987) and the T. B. Murphy Foundation Charitable Trust (1988).

Jon Van Til is associate professor of urban studies and public policy at the Rutgers University Camden College. Van Til's main research interests have been in the study and development of citizen participation, voluntarism, philanthropy, and nonprofit organizations. As an applied social scientist, he has served as a board member, consultant, and executive to a number of nonprofit, voluntary, and philanthropic organizations. His books include *Living with Energy Shortfall: A Future for American Cities and Towns* (1982), which was selected by *Choice* as one of the Outstanding Academic Books of the Year. Most recently, he has authored *Mapping the Third Sector* (1988) and coedited (with S. Ostrander and S. Langton) *Shifting the Debate: Public/Private Sector Relations in the Modern Welfare State* (1988) and (with R. Herman) *Nonprofit Boards of Directors* (1989).

Van Til taught at Purdue University and Swarthmore College, and served as executive director of the Pennsylvania Law and Justice Institute before moving to Rutgers. He served as president of the Association of Voluntary Action Scholars between 1977 and 1979 and has been editor-in-chief of the *Nonprofit and Voluntary Sector Quarterly* (formerly the *Journal of Voluntary Action Research*) since 1979.

James R. Wood is professor and chair of the Department of Sociology at Indiana University. His books include (with D. Knoke) *Organized for Action: Commitment in Voluntary Organizations* (1981) and *Leadership in Voluntary Associations* (1981). Wood also serves as associate director for research at the Indiana University Center on Philanthropy.

Critical Issues
in
American Philanthropy

~~~~~~~~~~~~~~~~~~~~~~~~~~~~~~~~~~~~~~

PART ONE

Understanding Philanthropy

~~~~~~~~~~~~~~~~~~~~~~~~~~~~~~~~~~~~~~

Chapter 1   *Maurice G. Gurin*
                                            Jon Van Til

Philanthropy
in Its Historical Context

Americans have for centuries organized themselves on behalf of
worthy causes and given generously of their services and financial
resources. They inherit a long philanthropic tradition. And because
American philanthropy is so pervasive and fundamental, it is
unique in the world.

   This chapter seeks to place the study of philanthropy in its
historical context. Its aim is not to provide a comprehensive review
but rather to present an overview in which reliance is placed on
major statements that have emerged in the scholarly literature on
philanthropy.

The Concept of Philanthropy

The world *philanthropy* comes from the Greek and means "love of
mankind." A generally accepted comprehensive definition of philanthropy does not exist, and many leading scholars in the field
doubt that one can be developed. Some scholars assert that a certain
vagueness is inevitable, even desirable.

   The definition most often quoted in recent years is the one
advanced by Robert L. Payton: "Philanthropy includes voluntary
giving, voluntary service, and voluntary association, primarily for
the benefit of others; it is also the 'prudent sister' of charity, since

3

4 Critical Issues in American Philanthropy

they have been intertwined throughout most of the past 3500 years of western civilization."[1]

Charity is the religious tradition of altruism, compassion and empathy, and giving on a one-to-one basis, as Paul N. Ylvisaker has noted.[2] Philanthropy takes a more impersonal and dispassionate approach to bettering the human condition by institutionalizing giving, focusing beyond the immediate condition of people to root causes of human problems and systemic reform, recognizing a responsibility to the public interest, and helping to effect societal change.

Today, charity has come to mean serving the poor and needy. While some voluntary organizations still provide such service, the government has assumed major responsibility for it, both directly and through subvention of voluntary organizations. Contemporary philanthropy has come to be recognized as being broadly concerned with improving the quality of life for all members of the community by promoting their welfare, happiness, and culture. It therefore focuses on such interests and concerns of all income classes as protecting the environment, preventing disease, improving education, enhancing the arts, and preserving historical landmarks, as well as sustaining a continuing, if somewhat subdued, attention to the needs of charity.[3]

Today, philanthropy is viewed as a tradition, a spirit, and a sector of society. It is alternately referred to as the third sector, the independent sector, the voluntary sector, and the nonprofit sector (though not all nonprofit organizations are philanthropic in character).

Historical Roots of Philanthropy

Early evidences of philanthropy were recorded thousands of years ago.[4] The Egyptian Book of the Dead provides a good starting point. Dating from about 4000 B.C., it praises those who give bread for the hungry and water for the thirsty. The tombs of Harkhuf and Pepi-Nakht, dating from the Sixth Dynasty (2500 B.C.), offer this motivation for giving and doing good: "I desired that it might be well with me in the great god's presence."

The Hebrews' history of religiously motivated charity goes

back at least as far as the Egyptians'. The Old Testament records that the patriarch Jacob promised to give a tenth of all that God gave him; it provides the origin of the practice of tithing. The Hebrews believed in sharing what they had with the poor and doing good deeds. The thirteenth-century Spanish rabbi Maimonides defined eight levels of giving, the highest of which was to make the poor independent of charity.

In ancient Greece and Rome, giving was more in the spirit of philanthropy than of charity. The focus, for the most part, was on the general good; giving had little, if any, connection with the poor, and it was seldom motivated by pity.

Christianity set a high ethic for givers: the spirit of the giver was more important than the size of the gift, and the extent of the giver's sacrifice determined the gift's value. In the Catholic tradition, believers were asked to love God, self, and others in a holistic pattern. Beneficence, almsgiving, and fraternal association were the external manifestations that would provide the interior effects of joy, peace, and mercy.[5]

In that same tradition, a particular virtue was found to inhere in poverty, particularly if it was accompanied by a pious vocation. To be sure, the church took the lion's share of charitable giving and applied it to its own purposes, which were often political. Nevertheless, it did accept a common responsibility for the dispensing of alms and charity as part of its philanthropic monopoly.

With the Reformation, the rise of the secular state, and the growing social dislocation occasioned by the Mercantile Age, charity increasingly moved into the purview of government. The Protestant's God assumed a sterner visage toward the poor than the Catholic's deity, especially in John Calvin's conception. Poverty became a sign of exclusion from the elect rather than an indication of the absence of worldliness; it did not take long to reach the conclusion that many poor people could be rightly blamed for their own poverty.

It was thus in a climate of suspicion of the poor, urbanization of the work force, and decentralization of religious authority that England, mother to America and its institutions, began to develop charitable trusts and endowments for schools, poor relief, and general civic purposes. In the flurry of legislation in 1601 that gave

rise to the famous Elizabethan "Poor Laws," Parliament enacted
the Statute of Charitable Uses to create, control, and protect such
funds. That statute is the cornerstone of our American laws concerning charitable giving and a forerunner of our present-day American foundations.

The Poor Laws themselves provided for the collection of public funds to relieve the poor by outright taxation; it marked the very
beginning of governmental responsibility for charitable activities.

American philanthropy dates from the earliest colonists.
While it owed much to its English origins, it was marked from the
beginning by a pervading voluntarism that made it decisively different. As the country was settled, historian Daniel Boorstin observed, "communities existed before governments were there to care
for public needs."[6] The result was that "voluntary collaborative
activities" were set up to provide basic social services.

The practice of meeting community needs outside of government has profoundly shaped American society and its institutional
framework. In most other countries, major social institutions (such
as hospitals, libraries, museums, universities, and social welfare
agencies) are operated and funded by government; in the United
States, many of these institutions are organized, governed, and supported by volunteers.

Mapping the Third Sector

Institutionally, American society is divided into four major sectors:
(1) business (or for-profit), (2) government, (3) not-for-profit (or
voluntary), and (4) household (or informal).[7] Philanthropy's home
is within the not-for-profit sector, though it has links to the other
three sectors. Contributions to support nonprofit organizations are
provided from household budgets drawn from income received from
private employment or ownership. Support also comes from corporate contributions and government grants.

The realm of philanthropy in the United States is often de-
lineated by its laws of taxation.[8] Seen in that light, the realm includes organizations of two major types: (1) those that enjoy tax-
exempt status and to which contributions are tax deductible (this
includes churches and synagogues, as well as social service orga-

nizations) and (2) activist organizations, some of which enjoy tax-exempt status, such as neighborhood groups, advocacy organizations, and public interest agencies.

Philanthropy does not include such organizations as trade associations, which cannot receive tax-deductible gifts and exist primarily for the economic or membership interests of their groups. These associations include labor unions, real estate boards, chambers of commerce, and professional and fraternal societies.

Tax-exempt organizations, according to the Internal Revenue Service figures in 1987, numbered 850,000; however, some of them may be local chapters of national organizations. But the IRS figure does not include many religious organizations that have automatic tax exemption and many small organizations that do not need to file tax returns.

Voluntary contributions in 1988 to gift-supported organizations, institutions, and agencies totaled $104.37 billion, according to estimates in *Giving USA*, the annual report of the AAFRC Trust for Philanthropy, which updates these estimates every spring. In addition, a total of 80 million American adults contribute some portion of their time as volunteers in behalf of philanthropic causes, according to the results of a Gallup poll released in 1988.[9]

The sources of the voluntary contributions in 1988 were individuals ($86.70 billion), bequests ($6.79 billion), foundations ($6.13 billion), and corporations ($4.75 billion). Funds were given to the following categories of organizations: religion, $48.21 billion; education, $9.78 billion; health, $9.52 billion; human services, $10.49 billion; arts, culture, and humanities, $6.82 billion; public/society benefit (social causes), $3.02 billion; other, $16.53 billion.[10]

Total giving in 1988 of $104.37 billion does not include non-monetary contributions such as volunteer work and free corporate services. When these and government allocations to voluntary organizations are added, the amount in money and other resources increases greatly.

Rationale for a Third Sector

A persuasive rationale for the third sector has been provided by James Douglas,[11] who asserts that the sector is needed because of the limitations of business (which is ruled by market economics and the profit motive) and of government (whose democratic constraints typically permit it to support only what it believes the majority wants or would approve).

Thus, the third sector serves the values and preferences of individuals or groups whose needs are not adequately served by either government or the market. The third sector thus may be seen as a powerful force for pluralism, providing a kind of social safety net that compassionately responds to society's otherwise neglected needs.

A deeply rooted conviction in American thought holds that no single institutional structure should exercise a monopoly on filling public needs, that reliance on government alone to fill such needs not only saps the spirit of individual initiative but also risks making human values subservient to institutional ones, and individual and community purposes subordinate to bureaucratic convenience or authoritative dictates.

The third sector may thus be viewed as an addition to government, business, and the household and, in many areas, as an alternative or counterbalance to those institutions. American society is increasingly dominated by giant and impersonal institutions of business and government. Voluntary organizations enable individuals to exercise personal initiative and influence on the course of events around them.

Rationale for Tax Deductibility

Six major arguments are typically advanced to justify the granting of exemption from taxation to nonprofit organizations, according to a recent study by the Minnesota Council on Foundations:

1. *Fairness* argues that the tax exemption compensates nonprofits for the resources and opportunities that are closed to them by state and federal regulations.
2. *Market gap* argues that the tax exemption is in recognition of the fact that there are some goods and services that the market cannot supply.
3. *Subsidy* argues that nonprofits serve minority interests that are

not sufficiently served by government action and that government would have to provide if the nonprofit sector did not.

4. *Exclusion* argues that it is not an exemption (a permission not to pay a tax) but a right inherent in the sector since colonial times.

5. *Regulation* argues that the special regulatory treatment of nonprofits is in return for special tax treatment.

6. *Practicality* argues that it is less expensive and easier to treat all nonprofits alike rather than attempting case-by-case determinations of exception.[12]

In practice, the tax deductibility of philanthropic organizations is typically justified by the contention that voluntary organizations provide services that government would otherwise have to furnish. Because of the democratic constraints that limit government support, however, this contention does not hold for all voluntary organizations. Nevertheless, it is true that voluntary organizations have pioneered in offering many new services for which, when they were recognized as having public support, the government eventually assumed responsibility.

The basic philosophical rationale of the deduction is that giving should not be taxed because, unlike other uses of income, it does not enrich the disburser. Further, the deduction is an efficient inducement; econometric analyses based on tax and income data have indicated that for every dollar of taxes uncollected because of the charitable deduction, more than one dollar in giving is stimulated.

The deduction is seen as inviting the least amount of governmental involvement in influencing the direction of giving. It is also a proven mechanism familiar to donor and donee, easy to administer and less likely than credits or matching grants to run afoul of constitutional prohibitions as far as donations to religious organizations are concerned.

Broad public support exists for the charitable tax deduction. Nonetheless, it should be noted that the deduction acts as a government subsidy and that contributors taking the deduction are in effect making decisions about the use of public funds. Out of principled exception to such subsidization, as well as concerns about

public finance and public policy, some groups advocate the repeal
of the charitable deduction.

Basic Functions of Voluntary Organizations

While the purposes of voluntary organizations have evolved over
the course of American history, certain basic functions have en-
dured; and they are viewed as being as important today as they ever
were in the past. According to Gordon Manser,[13] they include the
following:[14]

1. Initiating new ideas and processes. Voluntary organizations innovate in areas where public agencies may lack knowledge
or be afraid to venture. The third sector has shown itself to be adept
at innovation and at providing the models government needs.

2. Developing public policy. Since voluntary organizations
are apart from government, they can not only try out new ideas and
initiate new services that may be too controversial for government
bodies to deal with at early stages; they can also exercise a direct
influence on shaping and advancing government policy in broad
areas in which the government is already involved.

3. Supporting minority or local interests. Because voluntary
organizations can experiment with new ideas less cautiously than
government, they can support causes and interests that may be
swept aside by majoritarian priorities or prejudices. They are also
considered better able and more sensitively structured than government to deal with small-scale activities.

4. Providing services that the government is constitutionally
barred from furnishing. The United States government is pro-
scribed from entering the broadest area of the nonprofit sector: religion. There is no alternative to this sector if religious functions
are to be filled at all in this country.

5. Overseeing government. As Robert H. Bremner has observed, "A marked tendency of American philanthropy has been to
encourage, assist, and even goad democratic government—and democratic citizens—toward better performance of civic duties and
closer attention to social requirements."[15]

6. Overseeing the marketplace. Freed from the powerful influence of economic interests, voluntary organizations can act as de-

tached overseers of the marketplace in ways that government agencies and legislators are often restrained from doing. In some areas, they provide a direct alternative to and a kind of yardstick for business firms.

7. Bringing the sectors together. Voluntary organizations can bridge the sectors because they have neither commercial interests to pursue nor governmental status to protect. They therefore are often best suited to act as intermediary coordinator of partnership activities involving government and business in the advance of public purposes.

8. Giving aid abroad. Voluntary organizations have been able to fulfill the function of giving aid abroad in situations where government help would be politically unacceptable. This has been possible even in the aftermath of the war in Vietnam.

9. Furthering active citizenship and altruism. Many voluntary organizations serve not so much beneficiaries as participants. Such organizations provide ready and accessible outlets for public-spirited initiative and altruistic action by individuals who otherwise would not be able to be involved in public causes.

Organizations That Serve the Public Interest

Under the Internal Revenue Code, twenty categories of organizations are exempt from federal income tax, but most of those that are eligible to receive tax-deductible contributions as well fall into one category of the code: Section 501(c)(3).

To qualify under this section, an organization must operate exclusively for one or more of these broad purposes: charitable, religious, scientific, literary, and educational. Two narrower aims are also specified: testing for public safety and prevention of cruelty to children or animals. The code specifies further that no "substantial" part of an organization's activities may be devoted to attempting to influence legislation and that the organization may not participate at all in candidates' political campaigns.

These specifications are both broad and vague, and considerable difference of opinion has been expressed as to what is educational rather than primarily propagandistic and to what is religious and what is a secular cult or an outright fraud. Much

litigation and administrative judgment have been devoted to an-
swering such questions.

Efforts have been made to establish a principle by which
organizations can be judged to be in the public interest and thus a
proper concern of and channel for philanthropy, but none has un-
questionably succeeded. A certain flexibility is considered desirable,
philosophically and legally, in defining the public interest.[16]

Since one of the main virtues of the private sector lies in its
very testing and extension of any definition of the public interest,
it would seem counterproductive to try to establish boundaries in
more than a general, expandable sense. Like the public interest, the
closely related concept of public needs is also fluid and shifting,
which permits new public needs to be perceived.

The Influence of the Federal Government

In the past, voluntary organizations were distinguished from their
government and business counterparts in such respects as these:[17]

- A voluntary organization came into existence in response to a
  felt need by an individual or group rather than to carry out a
  mandate of law or gain a profit.
- A voluntary organization was autonomous and controlled its
  own destiny, typically under an independent board of directors.
- A voluntary organization was free to define its own area of service, and the clientele to benefit from that service.
- A voluntary organization, it was assumed, would be financed by
  voluntary contributions.

In recent decades, the government has wielded increasing
influence on voluntary organizations in these areas:

- Existence—through granting, withholding, or withdrawing
  tax-exempt status
- Funding—through tax policy that affects incentives for voluntary giving and through contracts, grants, and purchase of
  service

- Programs—through making available government money that may or may not coincide with organizations' missions
- Operational costs—through mandates to comply with an increasing range of laws and regulations, such as equal opportunity, age discrimination, affirmative action, and occupational safety and health
- Constituency—through grants-in-aid programs for college students and health insurance programs
- Composition of boards of directors—through provisions of affirmative action programs

In recent years, it has been increasingly recognized that the third sector (philanthropy) is *interdependent* with government and business. Scholars such as Lester Salamon and Peter Dobkin Hall have noted that the interdependence of government and voluntary organizations was evident early in American history.[18]

Development of Fund Raising

The history of fund raising in the United States is distinctively American in its functional relationships to our changing social structure, notably in the shift of philanthropy from a social elite to a mass base, from the predominantly religious to the predominantly secular auspices of appeals for funds, from the amateur volunteer to the professional fund raiser, from the expansion of the original agencies of press, pulpit, bazaar, and benefit to such agencies as the United Way of America, INDEPENDENT SECTOR, Council for Advancement and Support of Education, and similar organizations concerned with stimulating philanthropic support.

Scott M. Cutlip, in his book *Fund Raising in the United States*,[19] details the development of this philanthropic activity from colonial times. Among the highlights he notes are the following:

• The first systematic effort of any kind to raise money on this continent was for Harvard College. In 1641, the Massachusetts Bay Colony sent three clergymen to England to solicit money so the college could, among other objectives, "educate the heathen Indian." Of the three, one returned with 500 pounds, one became a rector in England, and one wound up on the scaffold.

• Subsequently, Harvard and also Yale and William and Mary colleges were given grants by their provincial governments and by the king. Occasionally, bequests provided some additional funds. Harvard tried some lotteries, but they were unsuccessful; they brought in little money and tarnished its name because of squabbles and lawsuits.

• A young English evangelist, George Whitefield, began in 1739 "the most famous preaching tour in American history," assailing sin and crying out against the misery of the poor. In his seven visits to the colonies, Whitefield took up collections for poor debtors, raised money for the victims of disaster, and secured books and financial assistance for hard-pressed colleges, including Harvard, Dartmouth, Princeton, and the University of Pennsylvania.

• Benjamin Franklin undertook a number of campaigns in which he shrewdly planned his appeal and carefully catalogued his prospective donors. Asked for his advice, Franklin said: "In the first place, I advise you to apply to all those whom you know will give something; next, to those whom you are uncertain whether they will give anything or not, and show them the list of those who have given; and lastly, do not neglect those whom you are sure will give nothing, for in some of them you may be mistaken."

Fund raising in the nineteenth century consisted mainly of personal solicitation, often by paid solicitors; of passing the church plate and staging church suppers and bazaars; and of writing "begging letters." Educational fund raising was a personal search for gifts by "financial agents" who frequently were the presidents of the colleges involved.

The first attempt to stage a federated fund drive was undertaken in Philadelphia in 1829 by Matthew Carey, who sought the interest of ninety-seven "citizens of the first respectability" to sign an appeal entitled "Address to the Liberal and Humane." It sought subscriptions of $2 or $3 a year to support a number of institutions. Only $276.50 was raised by a paid collector in three weeks, and the drive was abandoned as hopeless.

About this time, two drives were undertaken to create monuments to the patriotism of the men of the American Revolution; both failed. One was attempted by the Bunker Hill Monument Society; the other, by the Washington National Monument Society.

The latter tried to raise $1 million by popular subscription. In 1883, Congress appropriated funds to complete the Washington Monument, toward which only $300,000 came from public donations.

In the 1820s, Samuel Gridley Howe started a campaign to raise money for the cause of the Greeks in their war of independence. Volunteer committees employed practically all of the methods used in charity drives today in seeking contributions for Greek relief from merchants, shippers, laborers, and schoolchildren. Thus began the almost unbroken flow of American dollars and foodstuffs to less fortunate peoples around the world.

In 1877 in Denver, two Protestant clergymen, a priest, and a rabbi joined forces to organize and promote the Associated Charities of Denver. It was the first earnest effort to centralize and correlate the financing of community charities, and it was the first federated fund.

The campaign as it is known today had its genesis in the Young Men's Christian Association in the last years of the nineteenth century and the early years of the twentieth century. Two YMCA secretaries, Charles Sumner Ward and Lyman L. Pierce, pioneered the "whirlwind campaign" approach. With Ward leading the way, the Y fund raisers, using highly organized methods, raised $60 million in capital funds from 1905 to 1906.

The Role of Foundations

In the early 1900s, Andrew Carnegie and John D. Rockefeller led the way for the march of large-scale philanthropy and the establishment of benevolent foundations. Their chief contribution to philanthropy was to found institutions and foundations capable of distributing private wealth with greater intelligence and vision than the donors themselves could have hoped to possess.

The Commission on Private Philanthropy and Public Needs, which reported in 1973, observed that "Some 25,000 private grant-making foundations exist today with combined assets, it is estimated, of around $25 billion. The great majority have modest resources and highly specialized aims. But scores operate, with wide discretionary funding powers and multimillion-dollar annual budgets, as regular, often highly visible sources of private funds for public purposes.

Most larger foundations have full-time professional staffs who are
paid to provide sophisticated analysis and management to the 'business of benevolence.'"

Waldemar Nielsen, who has examined the workings of great
American foundations in two books, writes as follows: "In the early
years of the century, when the nation had reached a certain point
in its economic development and was ready to move forward in its
educational, medical, and cultural development, the Rockefeller
and Carnegie foundations along with a few others launched the
experiments that blazed the trails that government and others subsequently followed. . . . With the vastly greater resources available
to the public sector in the 1950s, 1960s, and 1970s . . . the foundations saw their role as catalysts for the creation of new programs to
help realize the national dream of progress and equality."[20]

Nielsen notes that we have entered an "era of limits and
constraints" and that such an age requires much "rethinking and
redirection" of philanthropic approaches. He expresses a cautious
optimism that foundations can perform as well in such an age as
they did in their "golden age" at the turn of the twentieth century.

Conclusion

Brian O'Connell, president of INDEPENDENT SECTOR, has
evaluated the American tradition of voluntarism and philanthropy
as follows: "What it all comes down to is that even though philanthropic dollars are very small compared to the expenditures of government and commerce, when these dollars have been targeted
independently and creatively, the leadership value has been
tremendous."[21]

Those who take an active role in philanthropy and voluntarism will need to be ever vigilant to keep their practice attuned to
a society and a world in rapid change. The chapters that follow
present scholarly guidance with which the philanthropist and volunteer can venture forth into that world, confident of the need for
a third sector and the validity of its many missions.

Notes

1. Robert L. Payton, "Major Challenges to Philanthropy." A Discussion Paper for INDEPENDENT SECTOR, Aug. 1984.
2. Paul N. Ylvisaker, "Is Philanthropy Losing Its Soul?" *Foundation News*, May/June 1987.
3. This point, while evident to us and fully documented by Teresa Odendahl in her *Charity Begins at Home: Generosity and Self-Interest Among the Philanthropic Elite* (New York: Basic Books, 1990), is strenuously denied by some who study philanthropy. For an example, see Henry Suhrke, "Defining Philanthropy," *Philanthropy Monthly*, Nov. 1989, pp. 19–26.
4. James L. Fisher, "The Growth of Heartlessness: The Need for Studies on Philanthropy." *Educational Record*, Winter 1986.
5. Loring M. Thompson, "Different Meanings of Charity." Unpublished essay.
6. Daniel J. Boorstin, *The Decline of Radicalism: Reflections on America Today.* New York: Random House, 1963.
7. Jon Van Til, *Mapping the Third Sector: Voluntarism in a Changing Social Economy.* New York: Foundation Center, 1988.
8. There are many good reasons not to allow this legislative delineation to dominate our formal definitions of philanthropy: it excludes individual voluntarism and informal associations; it allows government, rather than those who practice philanthropy, to define the field; and it excludes a number of citizen organizations that do not choose to file for tax-exempt status. In defining philanthropy, we prefer the approaches taken by Payton (cited above in note 1) and Van Til (in Chapter Two of this volume).
9. This survey was conducted in 1987 by the Gallup Poll and reported to INDEPENDENT SECTOR (Washington, D.C.).
10. A recent work that describes these subfields of the nonprofit sector is Michael O'Neill, *The Third America: The Emergence of the Nonprofit Sector in the United States.* San Francisco: Jossey-Bass, 1989.

11. James Douglas, *Why Charity? The Case for a Third Sector.*
     Newbury Park, Calif.: Sage, 1983.
12. Nonprofit Tax Policy Study Committee of the Minnesota
     Council on Foundations, *Preserving Diversity: The Effect of
     Tax Policy on Nonprofit Organizations.* Jan. 1989, p. iv. The
     principal researcher and drafter of the report was Anthony
     Filipovich of Mankato State University.
13. Gordon Manser, *The Voluntary Sector in Brief: A Report for
     the Ford Foundation.* New York: Academy for Educational
     Development, 1979.
14. Another list of purposes is provided by Brian O'Connell, who
     suggests that two roles are key: to relieve human misery and
     to maximize human potential. O'Connell's listing serves as an
     important reminder, as we noted in summarizing the giving
     totals above, that the lion's share of voluntary effort and phil-
     anthropic giving is directed to the provision of basic service
     delivery in such fields as health, welfare, education, arts, and
     culture. Brian O'Connell, *Philanthropy in Action.* New York:
     Foundation Center, 1987, p. 8–9.
15. Robert H. Bremner, *American Philanthropy.* (Rev. ed.) Chi-
     cago: University of Chicago Press, 1988.
16. *Giving in America: Toward a Stronger Voluntary Sector.* Re-
     port of the Commission on Private Philanthropy and Public
     Needs, 1975.
17. Manser.
18. Susan Ostrander, Stuart Langton, and Jon Van Til (eds.),
     *Shifting the Debate: Public/Private Sector Relations in the
     Modern Welfare State.* New Brunswick, N.J.: Transaction
     Books, 1987.
19. Scott M. Cutlip, *Fund Raising in the United States: Its Role
     in America's Philanthropy.* New Brunswick, N.J.: Rutgers
     University Press, 1965.
20. Waldemar A. Nielsen, *The Golden Donors: A New Anatomy
     of the Great Foundations.* New York: Dutton, 1985, pp. 442–
     443. See also by the same author, *The Endangered Sector.* New
     York: Columbia University Press, 1979.
21. O'Connell, p. 279.

Chapter 2   *Jon Van Til*

Defining Philanthropy

Philanthropy is a term with many shades of meaning. Testifying in 1987 before the congressional committee investigating the Iran-Contra affair, international arms broker Albert Hakim used the concept to clarify the true nature of his motives: "As a businessman I never pretended to undertake the tasks I was asked to perform for philanthropic purposes." At the same time, fund raiser Carl "Spitz" Channell, having solicited contributions for the Iran-Contra adventure under the cloak of a tax-exempt organization, entered a guilty plea for his actions.[1]

    Hakim's candor and Channell's deception demonstrate the two major strands involved in the dictionary definition of philanthropy, which both the contemporary *Webster's* and the *Oxford English Dictionary* of a half-century earlier primarily define in terms of the love of fellow beings and "the disposition or active effort to promote [their] happiness and well-being."[2] The secondary contemporary definition (it was third, behind the love of God for

Note: The idea for this chapter developed from a suggestion by Maury Gurin that it might make a useful contribution to the field, and the present chapter benefits from both that initial suggestion and Gurin's own readings of several earlier drafts of this chapter. Elizabeth Boris and William Van Til provided detailed comments and highly useful suggestions for revisions of the first draft. Robert Bremner generously shared not only his comments at the authors' conference but also his research files. I am grateful to all these friends and colleagues for their assistance.

man, in 1933) is viewed by the current *Webster's* as the plural of the term: "**philanthropies,** something that helps mankind; philanthropic service, act, gift, institution, etc."[3]

Hakim was saying that he was in it for the money, thanks, and not because he cared about the cause that money served. Business and also politics, we might infer from this statement, are forms of human endeavor to be distinguished clearly from philanthropy. Channell, on the other hand, ran afoul of the second definition, soliciting gifts for institutions not *legally* deemed philanthropic. Unlike Gilbert and Sullivan's Mikado, neither Hakim nor Channell could claim that "To nobody second,/I'm certainly reckoned/A true philanthropist."

In the beginning, then, at least for philanthropy, there exists both the act and the institution. The act involves the intent and the subsequent ability to make good on that intent—and the act requires direction toward the melioration of the human condition. The institution involves the formal embodiment of like-minded actors, joined in a collective effort to achieve the ends of philanthropic organization. But between the act and the institution, alas, lie much ambiguity and confusion and a sense that the definitional arena of philanthropy is not in sufficient focus.

F. Emerson Andrews has noted that "it is difficult to define 'philanthropy,'" and that the "literal 'love for mankind' is not adequate." John Kekes agrees, noting that benevolence itself amounts only to a minor virtue—of less significance than the moral virtues of courage, conscientiousness, and justice. Philanthropy becomes important, Andrews observes, because it "deals with large masses" and seeks to prevent calamities.[4]

In defining philanthropy, it appears that four major issues are typically raised: (1) the range of the boundaries of philanthropy, (2) the many meanings often attached to the concept, (3) the ideological implications of the concept, and (4) the meaning of philanthropy in its interactional context. These four issues are explored in the following two sections.

The Reach of Philanthropy

The variety of issues that confound the identification of philanthropy when it is discussed focus, first, around the range of the area to be bounded by the term. Does the concept include all thoughts, words, and deeds that involve the love of fellow humans (the first dictionary definition)? Or should it be restricted to the transfer of funds from one such being to another (which raises the question of its distinction from charity)? And if the latter, should it then be further restricted to such transfers as are mediated by formal institutions (those we earlier saw identified by *Webster's* as "philanthropies")?

Historian Robert H. Bremner has asserted throughout the long corpus of his work that philanthropy should be defined broadly, following the principal dictionary definition. He reminds us that "In a sermon delivered in 1824 Henry Ware, a Unitarian minister in Boston, cited ten eminent philanthropists whose example, he said, should be kept before the public so that others might be stimulated 'to go and do likewise.' Ware used the word 'philanthropist' to cover 'those who have devoted their fortunes, or consecrated their labors, or expended their strength, or hazarded their lives, for the consolation of sufferers, the relief of the poor, the rescue of the exposed, the salvation of the perishing.'"[5]

This volume follows Ware's example and nineteenth-century practice in adopting a definition of *philanthropy* broad enough to include both givers and doers, advocates and administrators.

In staking the broad ground for his definition, Bremner has been joined by Robert Payton, who has recently written the following: "In this text the word 'philanthropy' will be used in two ways: first as a comprehensive term that includes *voluntary giving, voluntary service, and voluntary association, primarily for the benefit of others;* and second as the prudent sister of charity, philanthropy and charity being interwined threads throughout most of the 3500 years of the philanthropic tradition in western civilization." Payton goes on to defend the concept by noting that "Until a better word is found, philanthropy will have to do. It is a protean word, like 'society' or 'religion.'" Moreover, he finds "two central ideas embraced by it in its present usage: *compassion and community.* . . . 'Compassion' . . . has a strong emotional quality to it; it is not thoughtless, but it is not calculating either. 'Community' has a more rational tone, more reflective; it can be emotional—with a vengeance—but it implies organization, plan, prudence, calculation."[6]

Charity, on the other hand, Payton contends, may be nearing

the end of its utility in modern thought. It is possible, Payton argues, that the concept of charity is today largely maintained by the various references to it in state and federal tax codes and that it may not survive the revision of these codes.

If philanthropy is to be defined so broadly as Bremner and Payton advise, then it follows that its "prudent sister," charity, will necessarily be a more limited concept. So Bremner advises in the introduction to his classic study, *American Philanthropy:* "[P]hilanthropy has covered a wider field than charity; the problems of the poor have not been philanthropy's only or even primary concern. The aim of philanthropy in its broadest sense is improvement in the quality of human life. Whatever motives animate individual philanthropists, the purpose of philanthropy itself is to promote the welfare, happiness, and culture of mankind."[7]

In his presentation to the authors' conference for the present volume, Bremner noted that philanthropy is a more "modern, twentieth-century" concept than charity. He asserted that it seems "bigger, more preventive, and more rational" than charity. And it also appears more acceptable to radicals, who have called for "change, not charity." To buttress his argument, Bremner noted that Christopher Jencks, in the Yale handbook on *The Nonprofit Sector,* has proposed using the term *charity* to apply only to giving that benefits the poor.[8]

Bremner's main definitional point, that both funding and advocacy should be included within the purview of philanthropy, has been challenged by other distinguished historians of the subject. In his definitive study of English philanthropy, David Owen flatly asserts: "This study has little to do with good works, personal service, or labors in the public interest, save as these were accompanied by substantial contributions of money from individuals and groups."[9]

More recently, philosopher William Frankena has limited the concept of *private philanthropy* to the acts of people of special means and efforts: "one cannot do *private* philanthropy in one's capacity as . . . an officer of a philanthropical organization, at least if one makes one's living by what one does as such an officer."[10]

Disagreement over the range of philanthropy's reach pervades not only scholarship but also practice. When the Institute of the National Society of Fund-Raising Executives sought to distinguish philanthropy from charity, it identified philanthropy in the broad sense given by Bremner but gave to charity the organizational connotation:

CHARITY A cause; a 501(c)(3) organization; an organization, institution, or advocacy group that seeks philanthropic support.

PHILANTHROPY The philosopy and practice of giving to nonprofit organizations through financial and other contributions; all voluntary giving, voluntary getting, voluntary service, and voluntary association and initiative.[11]

Differences in the breadth of application of the concept may suggest that philanthropy is one of those polysemic terms (one word with several meanings) that abound in the study of the third sector. Robert Payton extends the point when he notes that "The word philanthropy as presently used qualifies as what W. B. Gallie once called in a well-known essay an 'essentially contested concept.'"[12]

Not only is the word *philanthropy* used in many ways, but the implications involved in those uses lead in profoundly different directions. Consider Michael Gillespie's observation that "charitable institutions" may be seen as nondemocratic, elitist, unaccountable, and "absolutely counter to the fundamental premises of democratic liberalism." Gillespie continues: "It seems to me, however, that philanthropies claim to know something (and to try to impose something) that all liberals want to believe is impossible, namely, the good. Moreover, they want to see it brought to be. It seems to me, however, that it's precisely for this reason that we ought not to call the activities of philanthropic institutions too much into question, because. . . . they preserve one aspect of human character that has otherwise been relegated much too far into the background."[13]

The contesting of the meaning of the term, Gillespie is saying, ought to be resolved by attending less closely to its dark side, in recognition of the value of the activity's intentions and aspirations. A similar pragmatic development is found in one of the earliest uses of the term *philanthropy*, that by Sir Francis Bacon. Bruce Payne observes that Bacon reaches "back to Socrates, in fact, for a classical notion, and he has done so for a very interesting reason. . . . He needs a term of praise, and he reaches back to the Greeks because they have a notion of magnanimity. They have a notion of concern for the others, and while we often think of altruism, the Greeks didn't require the same kind of self-denial that it had seemed to require in a Christian moral vocabulary."[14]

The implication of these observations is that philanthropy, as a human action and in contradistinction to philanthropy as an organized activity, may be of sufficient value to transcend both the norms of democratic society and the traditions of Judeo-Christian culture. "Philanthropy I" may thus be seen as the human act of caring magnanimously for others and seeking to bring the good to fruition, while "Philanthropy II" becomes the more ambiguous organized process that sometimes tramples values of democracy and accountability or, alternatively, actively seeks to further these values. In either case, as Julian Wolpert has observed: "It's inherently appealing to move to a field that's not well defined. Philanthropy will continue to attract scholars because it is not well defined."[15]

What all this means for the study of philanthropy is to validate Payton's observation that the concept is "essentially contested." That is, it fits one set of views of the world as a progressive and valuable force, while it is seen from another perspective as retrograde, inegalitarian, and deceptive.

To those who employ an essentially liberal perspective, the crucial issue is whether and how altruism can persist in an age of narcissism. What seems notable from this perspective is the continuing willingness of some individuals, families, and firms to maintain their participation in a tradition of giving. To those who employ a radical structuralist perspective, on the other hand, the critical issue is the use of philanthropy to sustain privilege. Such scholars as Guy Alchon and Edward Berman have focused on the funding of a societal and value base designed to sustain structures of capitalist inequality. As Barry Karl has observed: "Foundations have been viewed as both conservative supports of a reactionary

Capitalism and as Trojan horses carrying left wing ideology into the center of the camp of American free enterprise."[16]

Clearly, what impresses Karl most about foundations is their persistence in the face of the alternative uses to which money might be put. And it is the declining rate at which new foundations are being formed that concerns Odendahl and Boris, in spite of the perception of America's wealthy that their charitable giving is essential to the maintenance of society. On the other hand, research into the history of twentieth-century philanthropy convinces Alchon of "the depth and extent of the technocratic and anti-democratic impulses animating to this day large areas of liberal capitalism's political culture."[17]

Philanthropy is a concept easily employed in a pejorative manner, and it often, if not always, focuses on a ridicule of charity. From a capitalistic perspective, philanthropy may give rise to the caricature of the do-gooder seeking to assist those who if truly worthy would be working to advance their own fortunes. The corresponding caricature from the left is that of the lady bountiful seeking to assuage guilt for her own fortune by ensuring that the poor do not revolt against the system that smiles on her and her family.

Among contemporary American thinkers, Brian O'Connell articulates most clearly the pragmatic and pluralistic appreciation of American philanthropy and its refutation of the sense that life is most centrally about self-advancement:

> It is unreasonable and even inappropriate to expect that all philanthropic organizations will be on the "cutting edge." While much of the good that philanthropy does is accomplished there, many funders find themselves encouraging organizations toward excellence, intervening where human misery is greatest, or nourishing the human spirit. . . .
> I believe that philanthropy helps us:
>
> - To Discover New Frontiers of Knowledge
> - To Support and Encourage Excellence
> - To Enable People to Exercise Their Potential
> - To Relieve Human Misery

- To Preserve and Enhance Democratic Government and Institutions
- To Make Communities a Better Place to Live
- To Nourish the Spirit
- To Create Tolerance, Understanding, and Peace Among People
- To Remember the Dead[18]

The image of philanthropy presented by O'Connell is an expansive one, which sees it as a key institutional process in building a civic, or public, sector in society. David Mathews has noted that the activities and organizations of this sector emerge, at least in part, from the traditions of the New England town meeting. These contemporary descendants of what I have called "idealistic" political theory allow for the advancement of a number of crucial political functions, as Mathews has argued:

- To provide the infrastructure of our political environment.
- To foster political socialization and develop public leadership.
- To improve the quality of public talk, to increase our problem-solving capacity, and to generate political will.
- To supply public power.
- To create the public itself.[19]

While voices like those of O'Connell and Mathews receive an attentive hearing from most Americans, the more widespread acceptance of democratic socialist conceptions in European thought means that the concept of philanthropy travels less well across the Atlantic. When assurance of a decent standard of living and a suitable quality of life becomes expected of government, little remains for charity, and the need for philanthropy is somewhat reduced, though not eliminated.

The American tendency to ignore arguments from the left cannot be accepted in a world in which such ideas are central to so many national experiences and ideologies. We will need to grapple with the contradictions involved in our view of philanthropy with the kind of determination Michael Gillespie has shown:

> In fact, philanthropies do not rely upon what individuals want, at any given moment, but upon what philanthropists think those people need. . . .
>
> Now what does this tell us about charitable institutions? It seems to me it tells us that they are nondemocratic. It tells us that they are elitist. It tells us that they run absolutely counter to the fundamental premises of democratic liberalism. It seems to me in this sense that all democrats and all liberals ought to be suspicious of philanthropic institutions. They're not accountable. . . .
>
> [Moreover] the recent and growing institutionalization of philanthropic activity bears all too great a resemblance to those institutions which liberalism confronted in the very beginning, and philanthropies will attract people into their bosoms who are no longer motivated by that simple impulse of altruism but simply, and all too often, by the impulse of power.[20]

Philanthropy may be held to critical view because it offers the guarantee of neither progress nor beneficence. As Michael Katz has brilliantly shown in his history *In the Shadow of the Poorhouse,* philanthropy can be misguided, ineffective, and deceptive in its application.[21] Where the advance of a society is concerned, no invisible hand guides the philanthropist. This form of activity, like so many others, may produce clarity *or* deception, hope *or* despair, progress *or* the persistence of injustice.

Philosopher Alan Gewirth observes that philanthropy is fair game for searching evaluation on three major grounds: its agents, its recipients, and its objects. The *agents* of philanthropy, philanthropists, may rightly be questioned as to their "right to use the wealth they possess": Are there others with a stronger right to possess or control that very same wealth? The *recipients* of philanthropy may rightly be questioned as to their justification in receiving its largesse: Do they present a genuine need worthy of philanthropic attention? The *object* of philanthropy may involve an overriding right to address more pressing needs than philanthropists may identify: Does the right to avoid starvation override the philanthropist's wish to endow an art museum?[22]

The contingencies involved in philanthropy have been evident throughout American history, as Robert Bremner suggests: "The dominant message of Americans concerned with philanthropy and welfare in the mid- and late-nineteenth century was the necessity for disciplining the charitable impulse so that good-will and benevolent intentions would be enlightened and directed by intelligence. The reformers' advice was not always consistent, was not always heeded, and, when followed, did not inevitably produce the promised results."[23]

We may be well advised to heed the wisdom of welfare theorist Roland Warren: "The idea of moving toward social and economic justice has great emotional appeal, but unfortunately the more specific we become, the greater the differences that arise both about the nature of a just society and about how to achieve it."[24]

Interactional Views of Philanthropy:
Exchange and Transaction

The deadlock that exists among the conventional paradigms of our social thought, particularly between conceptions of the right and left, challenges us to find a "third way" of defining philanthropy. One such approach, potentially able to transcend the divisions of prevailing paradigms, is that which sees philanthropy as essentially involving an exchange of values among people. Such a perspective is developed more fully by Susan A. Ostrander and Paul G. Schervish in Chapter Four. In this chapter, I shall simply point to its general form and identify it as a fruitful avenue for further definitional exploration.

The essence of the concept of exchange is that people meet to give and receive from each other. The theory of exchange is based upon the following basic assumptions: (1) individuals have a variety of needs, drives, and goals that they seek to attain; (2) some of these can best be achieved within the context of organizational participation; (3) organizations need some mechanism to influence the behavior of their activists.

In the case of philanthropy, exchange involves a set of transformations. Philanthropy involves a transfer of money, or other valuables that have a monetary value, from one set of hands to another. These valuables may be transferred wholly without expectation of return (in what Kenneth Boulding has identified as a pure "one-way" transfer of exchangeables), but they may also be traded for some mix of power, influence, and the commitment of values. At the least, most philanthropic contributions are traded, in part, for the return of a tax "write-off," which until recently allowed the wealthy giver to recover up to 70 percent of the contribution in the form of tax savings. Even at the lower rates that followed the 1986 tax law, a wealthy donor is able to "socialize" one-third of a charitable gift (often receiving it back in the form of a tax refund), while fellow citizens put up that one-third from their own tax payments.

Another form of exchange accompanies the unpaid service of members of boards of directors engaged in voluntary or philanthropic activity. As expectations for the productivity of board members have increased in recent years, there remains a strong belief that invitation to such service marks the personal and social success of an individual as well as her or his access to networks of wealthy and powerful people who are at least "good to know" as one advances one's own interests in economic society.

To be sure, the rewards of the philanthropist often far exceed the accompanying tax and status gains involved, consequential as those may be. Altruism survives as a powerful philanthropic motive, but it is mixed with the more directly individual gains already recounted.[25]

Schervish, Herman, and Rhenisch note that the problem of philanthropic influence is not a trivial one: "Through concerted philanthropic efforts, the wealthy, for good or for ill, for progressive or conservative ends, actually produce (rather than simply run or influence) the organizational world at the cutting edge of society." Philanthropy involves, they assert, an "intricate interplay between structure, culture, and practice."[26]

In a scholarly study to the point, Susan Ostrander explores the interaction between class and gender as the upper-class women she studied approached their philanthropic activities. One of her respondents, Mrs. Holt, "expressed the generally shared view that private money is somehow less constrained than public money: 'Private contributions are necessary in a democracy. It has a freer hand than public money.' At the heart of volunteerism and the role of private money in protecting the 'American Way' is the issue of private control, or private power." Ostrander continues: "These women are highly conscious of class. They have a genuine class analysis that they use to make sense out of their own lives, and they speak highly of the joys of their material standard of living and the freedom it gives them. They enjoy the pleasures of coming from well-known and well-respected families. And they appreciate the advantages of having direct and informal access to persons in positions of power who are their class, if not gender, equals."[27]

The concept of exchange appears in most conceptions of philanthropy, even if their developers seemingly highlight the "one-way" aspect of the donation. Consider Lord Beveridge's celebrated conception of the "philanthropic motive" as the "desire by one's personal action to make life happier for others." The giver gives, but the receiver is expected to live a happier life. Not a transaction as simple as buying a dozen eggs at the corner store—but a transaction nonetheless. Or see how Beveridge seeks to deal with the problem of misguided philanthropy: "Though the motives which lead to a charitable gift may in some cases be despicable, and in many cases are no better than a desire to exercise power though one is dead, this is not true generally."[28] A transaction between the dead and the surviving and not one to meet our approval—but again a transaction.

An exchange definition of philanthropy carries a number of advantages. It accommodates the perspectives of radicals, liberals, and conservatives alike in its assumption that people expect to receive when they give—whether the reward is a name on a building or an increased chance for a desired societal reform. Further, such a definition allows for the extension of philanthropy beyond the simple donation of funds to include the giving of any valued item, including time and personal energy. The complexity of the transactions involved also makes clear the necessity of a variety of intermediary organizations in the philanthropic enterprise—such as foundations, development officers, and fund-raising counsel. As we seek to define and elucidate philanthropy, we should at least be aware of the many expectations and interactions it involves. Tracking these expectations and interactions is a major contribution of the exchange perspective.

Toward a Definition of Philanthropy

A number of points central to the argument of this chapter may now be summarized:

1. Philanthropy *should* be seen as involving both individual acts of giving and organization to ensure the effect of that giving.
2. Philanthropy *may* be seen as involving the giving of both financial and human resources (time, volunteer work, and so on).
3. Philanthropy is *inescapably* a term with many shadings of meaning and implication; such is the nature of social analysis.
4. Philanthropy *does involve* a complex exchange of money, power, values, and expectations between the donor and the donee.
5. Charity (liberality to the poor) *remains* an important component of an adequate conception of philanthropy.
6. The pejorative implications of philanthropy *should* be accepted as real and seen as a challenge to improve rather than as an insult to be rebuffed.

Building on this reprise, it seems judicious, as Ostrander and Schervish show in Chapter Four, to view philanthropy as a concept appropriate to several levels of social analysis. That is, it is properly seen as pertaining to institutions (such as foundations), behavior (such as giving), and disposition (such as motivation).

It will no longer do to think of philanthropy as something characteristic only of a third (or voluntary or independent) sector, although there certainly exist important third-sector organizations properly identified as "philanthropic." The fact that philanthropy also involves giving and the motivations underlying giving means that it is also properly seen as a force that pervades all other sectors and institutions. Thus, as I have argued at greater length in *Mapping the Third Sector,*[29] philanthropy, like voluntarism, should be seen as a force capable of affecting the activity of such nonphilanthropic organizations as governments, households, and corporations.

This blurring of the sectors gives voluntarism an opening to permeate the other sectors, introducing them to the transforming powers of democratic control, concern with values, and the courage to create change. When the corporate executive calls upon the skilled volunteer to help develop structures for employee participation and control at the workplace, the powers of pervasive voluntarism will be seen. When the political leader calls upon the neighborhood associations to develop an agenda for legislative change that will then be supported, then the powers of pervasive voluntarism will be exercised. When the working mother calls upon the United Way to recognize that the future of her children depends upon the quality of after-school and emergency illness care, then the powers of pervasive voluntarism will become real.

If we look at philanthropy as a pervasive behavioral force in society, then we move beyond a simply sectoral, or institutional, view of its workings. We begin to see that not just third-sector organizations operate on the basis of "love of fellow beings": governments, households, and even corporations can have such an impact as well. We also begin to see that all organizations are philanthropic to a greater or lesser extent, whether they be foundations, governments, families, or corporations. The right question to ask, as Susan Ostrander has put it, may not be "What is philanthropy?" but rather "What is the philanthropic quality?" Philanthropy may have more meaning as an adjective than as a noun, Ostrander suggests.

Thus Nochem Winner regrets the emphasis placed in the literature on philanthropy on "notable and rich men." He argues that more attention should be paid to "communities and how they took care of one another, about the enormous contributions of immigrant traditions that inspired social responsibility in American life, about the utopian dreams of a host of prophets who sought to renovate American life."[30] And Robert Payton, as we have seen, similarly calls for the recognition of the centrality of "community" and "compassion" in our conception of philanthropy.

Arnaud Marts has noted: "If a history of the American people were ever written from a human, personal point of view, it would tell a new story. It would largely be given over to a study of how we have used our political freedom to found and maintain our great network of private agencies—instrumentalities of education, health, religion, culture, reform, character building, social welfare, and humanitarian aspiration. But our histories are written by students of politics, of government, of militarism, of economics, of commerce. Little is said about the generous efforts of private citizens to establish voluntary institutions for the service of their fellows."[31] If Marts were to add to his list of forgotten actions the human and caring responses of millions within our governments, families, and economic enterprises as well, the history of philanthropy would certainly become a predominant strand in the human experience.

It is now time to derive our own definition of philanthropy, ✶ asking that it accommodate the major points established in this chapter. The definition will be tripartite, with an overarching definition (noun), a definition as a pervasive force (adjective), and a more delimited institutional definition (also typically an adjective).

1. Philanthropy is, first, an intentional process of voluntary action, voluntary service, and voluntary giving aimed at advancing the public good. Here it is the disposition that is critical, the *intention* of the individual philanthropist and the individual recipient of the philanthropic donation to serve the good of humankind by a particular contribution of time, energy, or money.

Such action, service, and giving is "donative" in that it provides to a public purpose resources (time or money) that might have been used for private consumption or advantage. It is also donee linked in that it requires a beneficiary beyond the donor in order to complete the philanthropic transaction. Among the contributions provided by the donee to the philanthropic venture, therefore, is the linkage of philanthropy to the public good. Philanthropy may be led by supply, but it is validated on the demand side by the quality of the donee's response.[32]

2. Philanthropy is, second, those behaviors, in whatever context, that are directed toward the advancement of human service. This conception is typically viewed adjectivally, as in the phrases "philanthropic behaviors," "philanthropic actions," and "philanthropic quality." This aspect closely links philanthropy to the

building of democracy in the political, social, and even economic institutions of society.

In the context of secular American society, such behavior is often tinged with the self-interest of the donor: cause-related marketing aimed in part at increasing sales; conspicuous giving of facilities named for donors; public listing of donors by degree of contribution, with implied gains in social standing for the contributors; mandated "volunteerism" designed to inculcate values of service as well as skills for adult success among the young;[33] and in some cases, philanthropy as expiation for the commission of a public nuisance or even offense.[34] Modern philanthropy is in many ways an arena in which mixed motives prevail.

3. Philanthropy is, third, and more delimited than the first two definitions, that realm of institutional activity that is societally and governmentally entrusted as a nongovernmental organization to advance the public good. This usage is also typically adjectival, as in "philanthropic organization," "philanthropic association," "philanthropic sector," and "philanthropic foundation." Such philanthropic institutions play a central role in ensuring the coherence and efficacy of the matching process between private resources and unfulfilled needs that Ostrander and Schervish note is central to the philanthropic process.

Most succinctly, then, contemporary philanthropy may be seen as the *voluntary giving and receiving of time and money, aimed (however imperfectly) toward the needs of charity and the interests of all in a better quality of life.*

note

Notes

1. Hakim is quoted in Senators William S. Cohen and George J. Mitchill, *Men of Zeal: A Candid Inside Story of the Iran-Contra Hearings.* New York: Viking, 1988, p. 100. On Channel's admission, see Richard L. Berke, "Key Figure Admits Fraud Conspiracy on Contra Funds." *New York Times,* Apr. 30, 1987, p. 1.

2. *Oxford English Dictionary,* Vol. 7, 1933, p. 774.

3. *Webster's New Universal Unabridged Dictionary.* (2nd ed.) 1983, p. 1346.

4. F. Emerson Andrews, "Philanthropy in the United States: History and Structure." In John J. Corson and Harry V. Hodson (eds.), *Philanthropy in the 70s: An Anglo-American Discussion*. New York: Council on Foundations, 1973, p. 89. The Kekes reference is John Kekes, "Benevolence: A Minor Virtue." *Social Philosophy and Policy*. Spring 1987, *4*, 21–36.

5. Robert Bremner, *The Public Good: Philanthropy and Welfare in the Civil War Era*. New York: Knopf, 1983, pp. xii–xiii.

6. Robert L. Payton, *Major Challenges to Philanthropy*. Washington, D.C.: INDEPENDENT SECTOR, 1984, pp. 3, 23.

7. Robert Bremner, *American Philanthropy*. Chicago: University of Chicago Press, 1988, p. 3.

8. Bremner's comments were made at the authors' conference for this volume, Indiana University Center on Philanthropy, December 1987. The Jencks reference is to Christopher Jencks, "Who Gives to What?" In Walter W. Powell (ed.), *The Nonprofit Sector: A Research Handbook*. New Haven, Conn.: Yale University Press, 1987, pp. 321–339.

9. David Owen, *English Philanthropy 1660–1960*. Cambridge, Mass.: Harvard University Press, 1964; Merle Curti, "American Philanthropy and the National Character." *American Quarterly*, 1958, *10*.

10. William K. Frankena, "Beneficence/Benevolence." *Social Philosophy and Policy*, Spring 1987, *4*, 19.

11. National Society of Fund-Raising Executives Institute, *Glossary of Fund-Raising Terms*. Alexandria, Va.: National Society of Fund-Raising Executives Institute. The reference to 501(c)(3) pertains to the section of the United States tax code that defines a nonprofit, charitable organization.

12. Payton's observation is found in his afterword to *Philanthropy: Voluntary Action for the Public Good*. New York: ACE/Macmillan, 1988, pp. 266–273.

13. Michael Gillespie, comments reported in Center for the Study of Philanthropy and Voluntarism, *Setting the Research Agenda in Philanthropy and Voluntarism: A Discussion*. Durham, N.C.: Duke University, 1986. (Same source is referred to below as the Duke conference.)

14. Bruce Payne, comments at the Duke conference.

15. Julian Wolpert, comment at the Duke conference.

16. Barry D. Karl, "The Moral Basis of Capitalist Philanthropy." In *Working Papers for the Spring Research Forum: Philanthropy, Voluntary Action, and the Public Good.* Washington, D.C.: INDEPENDENT SECTOR, 1986, p. 109. For reference to Alchon and Berman, see Guy B. Alchon, *The Invisible Hand of Planning: Capitalism, Social Science and the State in the 1920s.* Princeton, N.J.: Princeton University Press, 1985; Edward H. Berman, *The Ideology of Philanthropy.* Albany: State University of New York Press, 1983.

17. Teresa Odendahl, Elizabeth T. Boris, and others, *America's Wealthy and the Future of Foundations.* New York: Foundation Center, 1987; Guy Alchon, "Foundations, Social Sciences, and the Origins of American Macroeconomic Planning." In *Working Papers for the Spring Research Forum: Philanthropy, Voluntary Action, and the Public Good.* Washington, D.C.: INDEPENDENT SECTOR, 1986, p. 81.

18. Brian O'Connell, *Philanthropy in Action.* New York: Foundation Center, 1987.

19. David Mathews, "Our Shared Life in All Its Forms." *Foundation News*, July/Aug. 1987, pp. 60–61. The reference to my work is Jon Van Til, *Mapping the Third Sector: Voluntarism in a Changing Social Economy.* New York: Foundation Center, 1988.

20. Gillespie, comment at the Duke conference.

21. Michael B. Katz, *In the Shadow of the Poorhouse: A Social History of Welfare in America.* New York: Basic Books, 1986.

22. Alan Gewirth, "Private Philanthropy and Positive Rights." *Social Philosophy and Policy*, Spring 1987, *4*, 56–57. See also in the same issue, Michael Hooker, "Moral Values and Private Philanthropy," for a lucid discussion of the responsibilities of the recipient of philanthropy.

23. Robert Bremner, *The Public Good: Philanthropy and Welfare in the Civil War Era.* New York: Knopf, 1983, p. xviii.

24. Roland Warren, "Toward Social and Economic Justice." In David G. Gil and Eva A. Gil (eds.), *Toward Social and Economic Justice.* Cambridge, Mass.: Schenkman, 1985, p. 253.

25. The question of the relative power of altruism and self-interest

in the philanthropic motive remains. Calvinist perspectives cloud this debate, raising the possibility that an individual may act as a pure altruist, even knowing that considerable personal returns (including eternal salvation) await those predestined to such generosity. As with a number of other theological and philosophical questions (consider the Berkeleyan question of whether philanthropy is real or imagined), I shall not delve further. For a review of the more secular aspects of the "mixed motives" issues, see Van Til, chap. 2.

26. Paul G. Schervish, Andrew Herman, and Lynn Rhenisch, "Toward a General Theory of the Philanthropic Activities of the Wealthy." In *Working Papers for the Spring Research Forum: Philanthropy, Voluntary Action, and the Public Good.* Washington, D.C.: INDEPENDENT SECTOR, 1986, pp. 226-277.
27. Susan Ostrander, *Women of the Upper Class.* Philadelphia: Temple University Press, 1984, pp. 132-133, 152. Another searching study of the self-interest of upper-income philanthropists is found in Teresa Odendahl, *Charity Begins at Home.* New York: Basic Books, 1990.
28. Lord Beveridge, *Voluntary Action: A Report on Methods of Social Advance.* New York: Macmillan, 1948, pp. 121, 199.
29. Van Til.
30. Nochem Winner, "Don't File the Filer Report." *Foundation News,* Mar./Apr. 1978, p. 6.
31. Arnaud Marts, *Philanthropy's Role in Civilization.* New York: Harper & Row, 1953.
32. Thich Nhat Hanh describes this process in the Buddhist tradition:

> Take a project. . . . which you consider important, as the subject of your contemplation. Examine the purpose of the work, the methods to be used, and the people involved. See that the work is to serve, to alleviate suffering, to respond to compassion, not to satisfy the desire for praise or recognition. See that the methods used encourage cooperation between humans. Don't consider the project as an act of charity.

Consider the people involved. Do you still see in terms
of ones who serve and ones who benefit? If you can
still see who are the ones serving and who are the ones
benefiting, your work is for the sake of yourself and
the workers, and not for the sake of service. The Praj-
naparamita Sutra says, "The Bodhisattva helps row
living beings to the other shore but in fact no living
beings are being helped to the other shore." Determine to work in the spirit of detached action.

Thich Nath Hanh, *The Mircle of Mindfulness: A Manual on
Meditation.* (Rev. ed.) Boston: Beacon Press, 1987, p. 96.

33.   An example of voluntarism imposed in the name of education
and socialization is found in the 1988 proposal of the late
Rutgers University President Edward Bloustein that all
Rutgers graduates engage in volunteer work as a condition of
graduation.

34.   An example here is the "alternative sentencing" of convicted
offenders to "voluntary" community service: if the choice is
between jail or such service, in what ways is the service "voluntary"? Or, consider the justification offered by one citizen
of Boulder, Colorado, for the building by a fellow citizen of
a controversially located mansion impinging on public park
land and the amenities of mountain views: "I don't like the
location of the Finoff house either, but I do like the Finoffs.
They have been great contributors to the cultural, educational, and business assets of this community. I enjoy having
them in our town and want them to feel welcome. . . . The
fact that we are able to enjoy the truly excellent Colorado
Music Festival is in no small way due to the efforts and contributions of people like the Finoffs, and I would like to publicly thank them" (Wallace Westfeldt, letter to the editor of the
Daily Camera, Boulder, Colorado, July 6, 1988).

Chapter 3

James W. Harvey
Kevin F. McCrohan

Changing Conditions for Fund Raising and Philanthropy

Philanthropic organizations face several new issues that challenge any "business-as-usual" attitude. Their ability to raise and allocate contributions is being reshaped by major social, economic, political, and competitive pressures, as well as by a transformed view of charity by its donor base. While some of these trends may enhance philanthropic resources, others threaten its current level of success. The uncertainties posed by a changing environment underscore the importance of philanthropic fund raisers to rethink their strategic planning. Emphasizing the urgency of adapting to change is INDEPENDENT SECTOR's call to double the level of giving in the next five years.

The goal of increasing the sector's capacity to serve society's needs comes at a time when several signs indicate that donor support may be waning. Although a record $104.37 billion was raised in 1988, separate reports from Yale University's Program on Non-Profit Organizations and INDEPENDENT SECTOR agree that the wealthy are less generous than previously thought.[1] Furthermore, volunteering is down among young single adults, while skepticism toward philanthropy is increasing. Another report, based on IRS data, indicates that upscale donors' rate of giving was lower in the mid-1980s than at the start of the decade.[2]

Concern over corporate support has also been expressed. A survey by the Council on Foundations found that chief executive officers expressed increased pessimism for future corporate giving.[3]

The survey also indicates that the next generation of company leaders are likely to be more tightfisted than the current group and are more intent on making sure that their donations advance the company's interests as well as those of the receiving philanthropy. Gifts to education should continue upward, but support of recreation, public policy, and the arts is expected to drop.

To achieve the new resource objectives and to manage the changing environment, philanthropic organizations would be wise to recognize that the base of giving, whether from individuals, foundations, bequests, or corporations, is undergoing fundamental change. For example, new tax laws, mergers and acquisitions, internationalization of American assets, concern for corruption and inefficiency, and new attitudes on the part of young adults and the wealthy are but a few of the forces that affect donor support today. Adding to these environmental pressures is concern that the giving programs of corporations that support philanthropy are in need of improved planning and more proactive thought.[4]

In this chapter, we review several of the major environmental issues and donor concerns that influence philanthropy and discuss how charities and their supporters are reacting to them. Central to this discussion is the presentation of a research-based screening model for supporters of philanthropy. The implications of its use by the recipient agency are also presented.

Philanthropy and Its Changing Environment

The environmental circumstances challenging managers of philanthropy represent threats and opportunities at a time when such managers are also confronted with a growing agenda of issues that require their attention. In effect, philanthropic organizations face a set of strategic decisions similar to those made by their corporate supporters. Philanthropic organizations that recognize these changes will be required to allocate resources among new recipient needs while at the same time addressing the warnings that may undercut their donor base.

This section presents the new risks to philanthropy that stem from changes in social, economic, and political conditions; a more dynamic competitive environment; and a declining level of donor support. Also discussed are some of the emerging issues that will call upon the resources of philanthropic organizations. The threats and the emerging issues are outlined in Tables 3.1 and 3.2, respectively.

Environmental Threats

Social Issues. Three social issues appear to be most significant for philanthropic organizations. First is evidence of declining support for philanthropy by the young, which is exacerbated by a propor-

Table 3.1. Current Environmental Threats to Philanthropy.

Social	Competition
Decreased giving on the part of the young; shrinking proportion of young givers	Increase in philanthropic organizations
Lower rates of giving from the rich	Inherent conflict of cause-related marketing
Growth of immigrant populations that do not share resident values toward philanthropy	Privatization of services
	Questionable fund-raising activities

Economic	Donor Support
Underemployment among traditional givers	Skepticism and lack of understanding of need for overhead
Reduction in real growth rates	Fragmented donor base
Internationalization of U.S. assets	Increased use of gifts-in-kind compared to funds
Corporate behavior: performance, mergers, and acquisitions	Decreased gifts of appreciated property
Importance of small business and difficulty of access	Inherent conflict in dual-agenda marketing
Gutting of middle management	

Political

Impact of tax reform on donation level
Reexamination of nonprofit laws
Establishment of standards for fund raising

Source: Adapted from James W. Harvey and Kevin F. McCrohan, "Strategic Issues for Charities and Philanthropies." *Long Range Planning*, 1988, *21* (6), 44–55.

Table 3.2. Emerging Issues Requiring Strategic Attention.

Social	Economic
Increasing elderly population	Underemployment
Increasing numbers of homeless	Technological invasions of worker
Increasing presence of families	privacy and job-related stress
among the homeless	
Feminization of poverty and pov-	Political
erty among children	
Continuing substance abuse	Need to react to vacuum in services
Supporting victims of domestic	as a result of government cuts in
violence	human services
AIDS contagion	
Increasing immigrant population	
requiring social services	

Source: Adapted from James W. Harvey and Kevin F. McCrohan, "Strategic Issues for Charities and Philanthropies." *Long Range Planning*, 1988, *21* (6), 44–55.

tional decline in this group in the population. The causes under-lying this effect are thought to be a combination of mistrust of existing institutions that address America's unmet social needs and a changed social outlook based on greed and social pressure for conspicuous consumption. Others see this decline of support as based on diminished real earning power compared to that of earlier generations.

Also of importance is the growing number of new immi-grants from non-European areas. Many of these groups, Hispanics and Asians in particular, are unaccustomed to supporting a "gener-alized" concept of charity, preferring instead to address family and community needs on an individual basis. Not unlike their youthful cohorts, such groups bring values that often are not supportive of America's approach to philanthropy. Understanding and working within the parameters of their unique values will test philan-thropy's ability to develop new offerings and approaches that ad-dress these differences.

The final threat is the evidence of decreased *rates* of giving on the part of the wealthy. Families earning less than $10,000 a year were found to give 2.8 percent of their incomes, while those earning more than $100,000 gave an average of 2.1 percent.[5] This decline in support of philanthropic organizations is due, in part, to shifting social values, lowered tax rates, declining purchasing power, and a changed Internal Revenue Code that now taxes the portion of gifts of appreciated property that exceeds the cost.[6]

Economic Issues. Presently, the U.S. economy is experiencing a number of economic changes that are having profound effects upon the ability of philanthropy to raise funds. Increased numbers of working poor, comparatively flat economic growth and purchasing power, internationalization of U.S. assets, corporate mergers and acquisitions, strains on small business, and the shrinking size of middle management are examples of the economic reasons for waning support of philanthropy. Furthermore, these trends increase the demand for social services. For example, double-income, middle-class families are finding the struggle to educate and provide care for their children more difficult than did their parents.

Additional strains on the ability to raise funds will result from the fragmentation of traditional corporate donor/philanthropy relationships that are associated with the current wave of mergers and acquisitions, as well as the internationalization of America's assets. In the former case, philanthropy faces the task of educating the new managers in the importance of their cause. In the latter case, fund raisers face the task of educating a foreign owner in the importance of the concept of generalized philanthropy by a third-party broker.

Donor support is also being affected by the growing importance of small business and the gutting of middle management, both of which involve "time and resource" barriers. Attempts to reach small businesses may not be cost-effective given their number, dispersion, ability to support philanthropic organizations, and lack of history of giving to philanthropy. Reductions in middle management also point to a resource squeeze on the part of this potential donor group.

Political Issues. As part of tax reform in 1986, Congress changed several rules that raise concerns as to the effect on individual giving behavior. As discussed more fully below, evidence of altered corporate support is already apparent because of this change in law.

Among other things, the law altered two key aspects of the treatment of charitable contributions by individuals. Prior to the passage of this bill, philanthropic groups argued strongly that certain proposed versions would have a major and even devastating effect on the independent sector.[7]

The language of the final legislation regarding charitable contributions states that individuals who do not itemize their deductions can no longer deduct amounts given to philanthropic organizations. The current legislation left unchanged past law that allows itemizers to deduct these donations, generally to a maximum of 50 percent of adjusted gross income. Another provision of the bill states that only the cost portion of appreciated property can be deducted, with the remainder being subject to taxation. The legislation also sets the deduction limit of nonappreciated items at 25 percent of their cost. In addition to more stringent verification in general, donated items valued in excess of $5,000 must be independently appraised.

Charities that rely heavily on donors who do not itemize may be hurt by these changes. However, the act also lowers tax rates for both individuals and business, thus potentially increasing disposable income and suggesting the possibility that larger gifts may be forthcoming to those charities whose following is motivated primarily by altruism. However, the overall evidence is that giving rates decline when tax rates decline because the value of the deduction is diminished. Of course, the immediate effect of the bill was to cause individuals to take advantage of the more beneficial laws prior to tax year 1986. The rush to contribute resulted in record giving from individuals and foundations.[8] Concern now surrounds the extent to which this larger-than-average amount of giving and the effects of tax reform might cut into subsequent years' contributions.

Finally, in light of the fund-raising and distribution activities of several tax-exempt organizations, pressure to reexamine current laws defining, guiding, and conferring tax-exempt status on fund-raisers is increasing. Calls from both within and without the third sector to adopt guidelines for standards setting in accounting, annual reports, and computation and disclosure of fund-raising expenses require more scrutiny of philanthropy's administration.

Competitive Issues. Today there are an estimated 850,000 nonprofit organizations, two-thirds of which developed after 1960. The more recently founded organizations bring to the marketplace innovative techniques for fund raising, resulting in unprecedented levels of competition. The number of organizations that use a single-cause orientation and "cause-related" marketing poses special problems for multiservice philanthropic organizations that may have greater difficulty communicating their mission to prospective donors.

Fraudulent activities, excessive fund-raising expenses, and diversion of funds to projects other than those for which the money was raised are a blight on the industry and add to donor skepticism. Privatization of human services by for-profit institutions poses a direct threat by serving the causes and clients once thought to be the sole domain of philanthropy.

Donor Support Issues. The importance of better understanding of the determinants of individual giving is demonstrated by America's historic dependence on individual contributions. Over the past fifteen years, an average of 83 percent of all philanthropic donations were given by individuals, while the remainder was donated by corporations, bequests, and foundations, which provided an average of 5, 7, and 5 percent, respectively. However, very little empirical evidence exists that addresses the determinants of philanthropic behavior.[9] Because American philanthropy is primarily supported by individual gifts, the necessity to better discern the underlying determinants of donation behavior is clear.

The 1985 Yankelovich survey of American giving[10] reported that the most important characteristics of the generous giver are all related to the donor's perceptions and values. The biggest factor predicting large donations by individuals is weekly attendance at religious services, while the other predictors are perceptions of their financial security, the availability of discretionary funds, and whether they volunteer time for philanthropy. Attention to religious commitment, feelings of financial stability, living within personal budgets, and encouragement of voluntarism are therefore key issues for philanthropy to support and track.

Skepticism and a lack of understanding of the methods and purposes of philanthropy and fund raising are resulting in lower donor support, particularly from young and wealthy individual givers. A greater threat, however, is the potential for these younger adults to continue their lack of support into the years when they will be looked to for the bulk of the national support of charity. There is evidence that the motivation for giving is based increasingly on enlightened self-interest rather than on "blind altruism." This accentuates the need to articulate the benefits donors receive for their money and time.

Specific evidence that younger adults and the wealthy are faltering in their support of charity is seen in the decreasing percentage of income given to philanthropy.[11] Diminished support by eighteen- to forty-nine-year-olds, a group representing the mainstay for philanthropic fund raising during the next decade, is especially worrisome to philanthropy and threatens long-term prospects for philanthropic organizations.

Although gifts from corporations, foundations, and bequests amount to only one-fifth the total given by individuals, these markets receive considerable attention from philanthropic organizations. Since individual corporate gifts are typically quite large, most charities target prospective and past corporate givers, and the loss of any of these large, single gifts is often devastating, especially to smaller organizations. For example, with the breakup of AT&T, one of the world's largest sources of philanthropic support was also divided. One of its programs, "American Orchestras on Tour," was cancelled, and as a result thirty U.S. symphony orchestras lost a total of $12 million.[12]

Until recently, corporate giving was increasing more rapidly than any other type, but was declining as a percentage of profits. However, in 1986 corporate giving *decreased* 2.24 percent. This decline has been attributed largely to the 3,000 to 4,000 mergers and acquisitions each year, economic slowdowns, and the gutting of middle management.[13]

Recently, the number of corporate gifts of property, equipment, and products has increased 200 percent. The most typical items donated include medical supplies, books, food, and computers. (In 1983, Electrolux donated 72,000 vacuum cleaners.) Such gifts frequently require considerable brokering to put them to best use. Increased giving of gifts-in-kind by corporate supporters diminishes the recipient's flexibility of use, increases costs of administration, and makes likely the need for a system of allocation to assign such gifts to where they can be best used.[14] Another change in the character of corporate giving is a change in giving agendas, which focuses on essentials such as clothing, food, and shelter, although commitment to issues of domestic violence, substance abuse, and the elderly remains strong.

One of the most significant changes in corporate approaches to charitable contributions is the use of the principle of enlightened self-interest, the same principle corporations use in their other economic determinations. "Dual-agenda" giving is the concept of requiring a fit between corporate objectives and the objectives of the philanthropic organizations they support.[15] This type of giving is based on a market-driven approach to company goals by generating support from a target customer base. Whether a cause is supported is determined by the alignment of corporate and customer needs.

The growth of such dual-agenda giving underscores the importance for philanthropic fund raisers to better understand their fit in the larger economic and social system. For example, Carter Hawley Hale Stores, Inc., uses enlightened self-interest to support the visual and performing arts. The purpose of this focus is to bring its name to the attention of upscale consumers who patronize the arts and who fit the profile of the Carter Hawley customer.[16] A similar idea has been adopted by Burger King, which contributes to programs that help students, teachers, and schools. Targeting its own employees by offering scholarships and lump-sum grants for academic performance has resulted in a 50 percent reduction in Burger King's turnover rate. Hallmark has shown analogous thinking by sponsoring fine arts and design programs in the hope of developing a supply of both employees and customers.[17]

Emerging Issues

Social Issues. The need for human services in America has been altered in terms of both magnitude and type. Perhaps the most predictable increases in the demands on our human care system are the result of greater longevity, a rapidly rising proportion of elderly, and the relative diminution in the number of younger workers who are needed to support the required increases in services. Current responses to this problem include increased taxes, declining benefits, elevated copayments, longer waiting times for services, and alternative delivery systems. For example, to contend with these broadened needs, home care is currently the fastest-growing setting for providing medical services for the elderly.

Challenges to philanthropy also stem from a new mix of social problems. The problems of the homeless, abandoned mothers, impoverished children, substance abuse, domestic violence, AIDS contagion, and new immigrant populations represent a set of issues never before faced in either the mix or the magnitude that currently exists.

Economic Issues. Underemployment is both a threat and an important issue that philanthropy will be called upon to address. For example, the working poor have increased the need for day-care services. Current estimates indicate that 25 percent of Americans have no health insurance. This inability to pay for services is having a significant effect on hospitals, many of which have already had to close their emergency facilities.

Political Issues. In his now famous reference to a "thousand points of light," President Bush lauded the voluntary actions of Americans. However, he also certainly implied that there will be a sharing of the federal responsibility for many of the issues noted above between the independent sector and the federal government. In fact, estimates show that government support of nonprofits fell an average of 20 percent during the period 1981–1984, while social service organizations lost 35 percent of their federal support.[18] This trend is predicted to continue at those rates. The resulting vacuum in human services has already placed additional demands on the resources of philanthropy.

Rethinking the Philanthropic Response

Key to a better understanding of the trends summarized above is to document them more fully and offer guidance to the strategic actions taken by both fund raisers and supporters of philanthropy.

The new environment has caused participants in philanthropy to rethink their positions, change their planning mechanisms, and develop several new tactical approaches.

Reliance on fund raising as a source of operating budgets is one of the unique aspects of nonprofit organizations, an aspect that adds greatly to their planning burdens. The typical nonprofit supports 25 percent of operating expenses from this source, but the level of dependence varies from nearly 100 percent for religious institutions to 10 to 20 percent for educational institutions. An average of 50 percent of nonprofits' operating budgets comes from their business activities and gains from endowments and trusts, while the remaining 25 percent is typically funded by various levels of government.[19]

One of the key tasks of strategic planning entails shifting resources out of markets with minimum potential into those that appear to be more fruitful. This approach thus offsets problems with known opportunities. If, for example, certain market segments show waning support, it may be possible to shift from those segments to others. Developing strategies that effectively address such shifts in market segments will surely test the managerial acumen of today's leaders of philanthropy.

One factor that further complicates the planning process for fund raisers is that the exchange process between clients and fund raisers is unique. While one constituency provides the gifts of money, material, and services, an altogether different group is the recipient, with the fund raiser acting as broker. This split between supplier and recipient markets produces additional burdens for fund raisers as they seek to assure donors that their gifts are efficiently distributed and serve a needy cause.

Needed: Improved Strategic Response

In response to these new pressures, philanthropic organizations are turning increasingly to strategic planning. Many are carrying out the central elements of strategic planning for the first time, initiating and reviewing mission statements, critically assessing competitive positioning, segmenting markets, evaluating diverse constituency perceptions of the philanthropic agenda in market exchange, auditing organizational capabilities, and scanning environmental trends. For example, Laura Landy, director of Initiatives for Not-for-Profit Entrepreneurship at New York University, indicates that "There aren't enough dollars to go around anymore, so managers of nonprofits are jumping feet first into segmentation, image-work, and consumer research."[20] For instance, with the help of Mobil, the New York–based Children of Alcoholics Foundation was able to develop a national outreach program that specializes in providing free written materials on the problems of alcoholism and its effects on children and on adults who were children of alcoholics. As a result of careful planning, several new programs have been developed to advance the foundation's mission, including a therapeutic program called Project Rainbow, where children aged six to eighteen years are encouraged to talk about their problems. The key to success appears to be a commitment to understand the various groups that sustain philanthropy and to develop new approaches that will solidify that support.[21]

New Methods for Reaching Markets

A 1987 *New York Times* article that summarized several innovations for reaching markets noted that special events and direct mail are increasingly being used because they can be planned with specific donor profiles in mind. In the past, the most effective solicitation method had been a person-to-person one. However, argued J. Richard Wilson, late president of the National Society of Fund-Raising Executives, new techniques to cope with a changing environment are inevitable. Augmenting direct mail with videotapes is one new technique that is increasing in popularity. "What they've done is marry a videotape and a brochure, and that can be very effective," says Henry Goldstein, president of Oram Group, Inc., a fund-raising management consulting company, adding that "where people try it, donations have increased." While organizations such as Sloan-Kettering Cancer Center plan to use the method, probably the most extensive current use of tapes is being made by Brown University, which mailed tapes to 6,000 alumni in a single year. Targeting 20 percent of the potentially most generous donors in each five-year reunion class, the university always follows up with a phone call or personal visit. As a result, giving to Brown's annual fund drive increased 24 percent in one year.[22]

To improve the likelihood that philanthropic organizations will reach their objectives, these new tactical approaches should reflect the underlying needs of the targeted group. Strategies to attract individuals between thirty-five and fifty years of age, for example, should be based on that age-group's unique concerns. Arthur White of New York-based Dan Yankelovich Group, Inc., states that younger donors "won't give more unless they know exactly where the money is going . . . [but they] give generously to . . . [groups that] give you a lot of information. You can't say to a young donor, 'Trust me to give away your money.' They want control, not assurances."[23]

New Methods for Generating Revenue

Also reviewed in the *New York Times* is MasterCard's current "Choose to Make a Difference" program, where the bankcard company agrees to donate 0.63 cents to a group of six charities each time the card is used, with a $2 million donation guaranteed. Through the use of these "affinity cards," the sponsoring bank promises to help charity each time a customer charges a purchase. "Typically, an affinity cardholder should produce between $8 to $12 per year to the affinity group," says George Hanold, president of Alliance Marketing, a company that sets up agreements between banks and groups. Furthermore, the bank generally gets a better membership response rate on cards offered through affinity plans. Organizations that have benefited from such programs include MedicAlert Foundation, March of Dimes, Child Welfare League, Sierra Club, and Boston University. The belief among beneficiary organizations is that funds raised are almost cost-free. On the negative side, George Hanold notes that because of growing competition, fund-raising "organizations are going to have to be more creative and more businesslike in approaching these programs."

Another recent fund-raising method is collecting change left over after travelers return from vacation. While not an entirely new idea, the program "Change for Good" carries the idea further. David Wood, special projects officer for the United States Committee for UNICEF, began a test program that resulted in gifts of $10,000 a month. Travelers watched a public service announcement explaining UNICEF'S immunization program before an in-flight movie on Virgin Atlantic Airways flights between London and the United States. An article detailing the UNICEF program was also included in the airline's magazine, along with an envelope for donations. Other airlines have expressed interest. "When one considers that there are 80 million international travelers, take whatever percentage you want who give a dollar, and you realize that UNICEF could be raising millions of dollars."

A different method of raising revenue that is receiving increasing attention is the sale of products and services, even if the resulting enterprises are not tax-exempt. For example, the American Red Cross is developing several projects designed to sell comprehensive health care products and services primarily to local industries. The idea is to generate funds by soliciting agreements to provide firms with health management, wellness, and counseling services on a contract basis, thus reducing their full-time staff and lowering fixed costs and therefore their break-even points. Adjunct to these programs will be the availability of competitively priced health care and diagnostic and emergency care products and literature.

Finally, another proposal is to secure the cooperation of the United States Postal Service to offer postage stamps that sell for a premium price. The spread between the face value and the cost of service would then be distributed to philanthropy. Although this technique is used in other countries, there appears little interest in the method domestically. Among the many unanswered questions concerning the stamp approach are donor response rates and criteria by which the contributions would be allocated to America's diverse philanthropic organizations.[24]

Caveats for Fund Raisers

Fund raisers should consider the pitfalls as well as the strengths of all revenue-generating techniques. For example, solicitations secured through credit card purchases or the foreign coin exchange approach may actually reduce overall giving because individuals may better remember that they have given than the size of the gift.

Having previously given may invoke resistance to subsequent solicitations. It is important to know the extent to which these fundraising techniques reach new givers, encourage those who would not ordinarily give, or raise overall annual contributions from the individual. For this reason, some fund raisers have engaged in tactics that are akin to cooperative advertising in that some credit card approaches offer the user the opportunity to designate one of several charities to receive the contribution. Of concern to philanthropy in such instances should be the extent to which individual agencies compete for such designation and the interrelatedness of their causes (health research, education, social service, arts, and so on) that may have a unique synergistic effect on gift giving across all agencies combined.

The use of videotape also requires careful consideration. It should only be thought of as a substitute for person-to-person contact in those situations where the amount of the expected gift or the probability of its receipt is rather low and where the cost-benefit ratio of a personal visit appears unrealistic. Other steps that are intermediate to the act of giving, such as specifying where to call for further information, should be integrated into these solicitation techniques. Finally, the development of revenue-generating products and services should be approached with great care. Relevant concerns include the extent to which they advance the philanthropy's cause, the acts of competitors, the effects on fund-raising effort results, and the propriety of taking business risks with donated funds.

Elevating Industry Professionalism

If philanthropy is to raise the level of industry professionalism, a commitment to executive development and management training is needed. William C. Phillips, vice-president and director of Alexandria, Virginia–based United Way of America's National Academy for Voluntarism, states, "In today's volatile environment, we support the trend of 'back to basics.' Rather than stressing the narrow 'skill-building' approach, we now emphasize a generic approach in our training that includes courses in planning, control, marketing, research, communications, and supervisory tasks. With training based at this broad level, our people are in a better position to develop strategy the way it should be—initiated by those closest to the customer." A review in *Fortune* addresses the issue of professionalism as a key concern to both managers and donors, noting that "as they straighten out finances and hack at overhead, they spring more money for program."[25]

Strategic Planning to Address New Demands from Donors

Concern for overhead is one of several responses philanthropic leaders have made to the recognition of a more enlightened donor base. John D. Rockefeller III once observed that "Giving is entered into in just the same careful way as investing" because "donors want to know something about the return on their money." According to marketing professor and industry consultant Alan Andreasen, the strategic response appropriate to this type of need is for fund raisers to view themselves as investment advisers and adopt an informational, portfolio approach to their client donors. By supporting an array of agencies and services that maximize their investment return, philanthropic organizations support the view that the business of charity is, in part, helping people give wisely.[26] From the philanthropic organization's perspective, this portfolio approach is also important in order to self-subsidize deficit-producing activities that represent the core mission.[27] Part of this new enlightened donor trend is the insistence that nonprofit organizations be well managed and have sound prospects for survival. Evidence of the need for this insistence is underscored by the report that fund-raising costs of selected charities vary considerably, ranging from 2 to 38 percent of funds raised, and that groups with prestigious-sounding names and seemingly important causes have pleaded guilty to mail fraud.[28] To combat such problems, states are increasingly taking action against questionable fund-raising activities. For example, the Commonwealth of Virginia has recently banned some fund raisers, while state regulations require professional solicitors to provide the state with more complete records, including lists of contributors and bank account numbers.[29] The evidence is mounting that fund raisers are responding to donor concerns that their charities be well managed.[30]

Although the Supreme Court has ruled that high fund-raising costs cannot automatically be considered a sign of fraud, Larry Campbell, California's registrar of charitable trusts, argues that in the absence of accounting standards, charities are under considerable pressure to engage in "creative accounting" that "renders the financial reports meaningless." In response to this lack of standards, the American Institute of Certified Public Accountants is continuing to develop a set of guidelines, any departure from which "would have to be justified."[31]

The Investment Test

Two major concerns of prospective donors are the *purpose* served by funds raised and the *temporal efficiency* by which the funds can be raised. These two considerations combine the prospective donor's portfolio with management concerns to form an "investment test." The extent to which a philanthropy "passes" this test can mean a great deal to its fund-raising efforts.

The *purpose* issue is referred to by Jerry C. Welsh as "giving vision of a solution." Having a clear purpose gives prospective donors easily understood information about the use of their contributions and has a considerable positive effect on donor behavior, particularly among younger adults, as well as being of key value to corporations.[32] The issue of *temporal efficiency*, the proportion of funds raised that actually supports needed services within a reasonable time horizon, also appears to be of considerable importance to donors and industry analysts. The standard that no less than 60 percent of funds raised should be earmarked for services that support the charity's cause after a development time of five years is primarily advocated by the National Charities Information Bureau (NCIB) but also receives wide industry support.[33]

The Cost of Fund Raising

An important aspect of the "investment test" approach is the efficiency with which a nonprofit raises and disburses funds for its cause. While no reliable statistics exist regarding average fund-raising costs, insights into the range are provided by several sources.

The NCIB standard is that fund-raising costs should not exceed 30 percent of contributions. In the February 1987 *Wise Giving Guide,* published by NCIB, approximately 50 percent of the 400 charities reviewed failed to receive NCIB's overall approval because of a failure to meet various standards, a lack of information about the agency, or an agency review that was not yet complete.

Philanthropic organizations that have yet to build an established following, especially those that rely primarily on direct mail, have particular difficulty in meeting NCIB standards for fund-raising expenses. The Council of Better Business Bureaus (CBBB) states that fund-raising expenses that exceed 35 percent are excessive and calls for improved standards, including the publication of an annual report. Further, the CBBB standards propose that no less than 50 to 60 percent of raised funds go to support programs. Further compounding the problem is the lack of standards in determining fund-raising costs.[34] Using an average of 75 percent of funds raised to support services translates into an estimated $25 billion of the funds raised in 1987–88 never reaching those whom philanthropy serves.

An important consideration for philanthropy is whether knowledge of fund-raising efficiency is considered by prospective donors and what, if any, effect this has on gift giving. The possibility of this relationship raises three specific questions for fund raisers. First, in terms of maintaining and expanding donor support, what incentives, if any, are there for philanthropy to lower fund-raising costs? Second, if such incentives are found, should fund-raising efficiency be viewed as part of the case building; that is, is it part of the philanthropic "product" as viewed by prospective donors? Should this part of the product be emphasized in the fund raiser's program of communication, or would campaign success be less than optimal? Last, what is the specific relationship, if any, between fund-raising efficiency and donor support? Is there a "threshold effect" where a certain level of efficiency is absolutely crucial to obtain donor support? Is there a "penalty" for failing to communicate level of efficiency? Can information concerning the relationship between efficiency and donation serve as an obtainable fund-raising goal?

The overall challenge to philanthropy raised by the issue of fund-raising efficiency is underscored when one considers the possibility that "excessive" costs may in fact deter people from giving. Put another way, there is ample anecdotal evidence that donors want to know that their hard-earned contributions support needed services, not fund-raising efforts. They want a good return on their investment.[35]

A Screening Model for Supporters of Philanthropy

To explore the effect of fund-raising efficiency on donor support, Harvey and McCrohan[36] used a nationwide sample to confirm that perceived efficiency did, in fact, lead to higher levels of giving. Furthermore, this relationship held after being controlled for income, previous volunteering behavior, and attitude toward the fund raiser, other variables generally accepted as predictors of level of giving. With minor exceptions, there was a steady increase in the level of donations as the donor's belief in the level of fund-raising efficiency (as measured by the percentage of donations reaching the needy) increased. An important threshold level of efficiency was identified as operating at and above the 60 percent range. This suggests that charitable organizations can attain significantly higher levels of giving with minor increases in fund-raising efficiency and that lower levels have a serious negative effect on donor support. The first large increase in giving, in relation to fund-raising costs, was found as perceived efficiency increased to the 61 to 70 percent level. This finding not only supports the 60 percent convention noted as an adequate relationship between fund-raising costs and the amount distributed to the needy, but it also emphasizes the point that donor support below the 60 percent convention is significantly lower.

New Perspectives for Contributors

The need for corporations to improve their planning processes in support of charity is the focus of a report by INDEPENDENT SECTOR. As a result of its findings, a ten-point "standards of excellence" guide was developed on the basis of the characteristics found to be associated with programs of corporate giving considered by

INDEPENDENT SECTOR to be the most effective. These standards are (1) budgeting, including publicly announced long-range goals; (2) well-developed objectives for a program of giving; (3) clearly defined priorities for giving that include consideration of the needs that are geographically proximate and in proportion to employee work sites, not just corporate headquarters; (4) at least a 20 percent budget "holdout" for flexible funding; (5) involvement of both top management and rank-and-file employees in the budgeting process; (6) easily available and clear application procedures and guidelines, along with efficient processing of requests; (7) a "proactive" approach to giving based on an understanding of the needs within the stated funding framework; (8) funding keyed to earnings, usually 1.5 to 2 percent of pretax profit; (9) distinction between cash contributions and other types, such as volunteering or gifts of inventory or other company assets, so that one is not substituted for the other; and (10) the program being treated as "any other business function in the corporation."[37]

Shell Oil is a noteworthy example of attempts to professionalize the contribution function by identifying "several social-performance planning areas within its strategic management plan and assign[ing] vice presidents to each of these areas. These officers are responsible for goal setting."[38]

Fund-raising efficiency is also of importance for the supporters' side of the giving partnership. On the basis of the belief that any unwise expenditure in the long run is bad for society, those that control or influence giving have a particular responsibility to ensure that individual and corporate funds are not squandered, even if the waste may occur in the administration of an outside agency— the recipient philanthropy.

A Portfolio Approach to Philanthropic Support

In general, managers would be well advised to reward charities with demonstrated fund-raising efficiency. The examples of Carter Hawley Hale's support of the visual and performing arts, Gannett Foundation's helping communities work together to assess human service needs, United Technologies' promotion of schools that produce engineers, Burger King's contributions to programs that help students, and Hallmark's sponsoring of fine arts and design programs show dual-agenda giving in action. A different, less-focused view of the role a company can play in philanthropy is offered by Bear Stearns, investment bankers. This organization has an established philosophy of encouraging individual contributions of managing partners by requiring them to give a percentage of their salary and bonus.

Fund-raising efficiency, however, should not always be an overriding consideration since there is a temporal component to the proportion of raised funds that support services. Just as any new product faces start-up costs and is consequently a cash drain, the same is true of charities. One way of viewing charities in this time and efficiency relationship is to borrow from the Boston Consulting Group's product portfolio concept. Figure 3.1 indicates how charities can be evaluated by positioning them on a diagram that compares the level of efficiency (defined as the percentage of each dollar that reaches the needy) above and below 60 percent with the length of time the charity has been in operation, more or less than five years, which is the developmental horizon advocated by the NCIB. The matrix can provide the framework for a portfolio approach to decision making and consequently aid in the professionalization of corporate giving.[39]

The Corporate Giving Agenda

Increasingly, corporate giving is being seen not solely as philanthropy but rather as an established part of doing business, being present in the community, and acting in the corporation's own self-interest. An additional benefit of corporate giving, regardless of the efficiency level of the philanthropy supported, is that perceptions of corporate social responsibility are higher for firms with greater levels of giving, even for those that had earlier violated the antitrust statutes.[40] This finding supports the notion that corporate giving provides a halo effect that can overcome prior transgressions.

To improve their decisions for supporting philanthropy, corporate givers should consider using the matrix presented in Figure 3.1 to direct the flow of contributions regardless of the firm's perspective on giving. Whether a firm views giving as an altruistic

Figure 3.1. Philanthropic Portfolio Matrix.

| | | | EFFICIENCY | |
			High Over 60%	Low Under 60%
y	u			
o	a n			
u 5 n d		Emerging	Potential
n d e		Performers	Performers
A g	r			
G				
E				
o	o			
l	v 5		Proven	Institutionalized
d	e		Performers	Nonperformers
	r			

Emerging Performers. The "stars" of charities. They are not only efficient but have achieved their efficiency in a relatively short period of time.

Proven Performers. The mature, successful, efficient, mainline charities. The "cash cows" of the BCG matrix.

Potential Performers. The classic "question marks." They have not achieved the requisite level of efficiency. However, they are new and are in the process of investing money to build up their donor base.

Institutionalized Nonperformers. The "dogs" of the philanthropic market-place. Although they have been in operation for an extended period of time, they have failed to generate support from the public, to control their management costs, or both.

Source: Adapted from James W. Harvey and Kevin F. McCrohan, "Strategic Issues for Charities and Philanthropies." *Long Range Planning,* 1988, *21* (6), 44–55.

or a self-serving endeavor, it may want to allocate funds according to both views. Altruistic giving would be appropriate for any charity in any quadrant but the institutionalized nonperformer group. Self-serving giving would be better focused in the potential performer quadrant. This is suggested because the firm and possibly society benefit as the charity develops its donor base and becomes successful. In the event that this does not happen, the firm itself has at least benefited by focusing on a charity that supports causes consistent with company goals or that will familiarize a relevant customer group with its name.

Conclusion

This chapter has explored the value of philanthropy's developing strategies that emphasize fund-raising efficiency and service as well as the benefit of donors' adopting temporal efficiency and enlightened self-interest as criteria in their charitable decision making. The examples and evidence presented in this chapter point to several key issues for philanthropic fund raisers. The clearest implication is the importance to philanthropy of instituting an ongoing commitment to environmental scanning and strategic planning. Failure to monitor the increasingly changing context of fund raising will test the survival skills of even the largest and most sophisticated of today's philanthropic organizations. Beyond this broad admonition, however, fund raisers should address several specific issues.

The evidence summarized here suggests that philanthropic organizations will likely face a decline in support if they do not address the dual issues of temporal fund-raising efficiency and enlightened self-interest. Other issues that must be faced include the skepticism of younger adults and diminished rates of giving among the wealthy. Developing means to enhance giving by young adults and the wealthy is an important challenge to philanthropy. The era of the uninformed, altruistic donor is waning, replaced by the era of a better-educated and demanding contributor.

A new approach to giving is also an issue when one is developing strategies to solicit the support of corporate givers. As already noted, businesses are becoming more selective in their giving, and dual-agenda giving, supporting those charities that provide some synergy with organizational mission, is increasingly being used. Furthermore, there appears to be considerable reason for corporate givers to use a portfolio approach to their choices, supporting those charities that meet the temporal fund-raising efficiency test and avoiding support for institutionalized non-performers.

Notes

1. P. Farhi, "Contributions to Charities Set Record in '87." Washington Post, June 23, 1988, p. C1; "Wealthy People Give

Less Generously Than Once Thought, Survey Finds." *Chronicle of Higher Education,* Oct. 6, 1988, p. A37; S. Rich, "Few Rich Are Exceptionally Charitable, Study Says." *Washington Post,* Sept. 21, 1987, p. A12.

2. B. Edmondson, "Who Gives to Charity?" *American Demographics,* Nov. 1986, p. 45.

3. M. Cox, "Corporate Living Is Flat, and Future Looks Bleaker." *Wall Street Journal,* Oct. 17, 1988, p. B1.

4. C. Beyer, "Issue Alert: Corporate Giving." *Public Relations Journal,* Apr. 1986, *42,* 12–13.

5. "Wealthy People Give Less"; Edmondson.

6. A. Swardson, "Charities over Tax Reform Barrel." *Wall Street Journal,* Jan. 30, 1985.

7. R. A. Beck, "Hard Times for Charities." *Community,* Jan. 1985, p. 2.

8. American Association of Fund-Raising Counsel, *Giving USA.* New York: American Association of Fund-Raising Counsel, 1988.

9. V. A. Hodgkinson, "Positioning Ourselves as a Sector: Research and Public Policy." *Journal of Voluntary Action Research,* Apr.-Sept. 1985, *14,* 17–24.

10. Yankelovich, Skelly and White, Inc., *The Charitable Behavior of Americans, Management Survey.* Washington, D.C.: INDEPENDENT SECTOR, 1986.

11. Edmondson.

12. P. Maher, "What Corporations Get by Giving." *Business Marketing,* Dec. 1984, p. 80.

13. L. Asinof, "Corporate Charity Peaks as Companies Rethink Their Giving." *Wall Street Journal,* Apr. 30, 1987, p. E1.

14. N. L. Ross, "Giving Products Instead of Money." *Washington Post,* July 27, 1987, Washington Business, p. 1.

15. A. Pifer, "Philanthropy, Voluntarism, and Changing Times." *Journal of the American Academy of Arts and Sciences,* Winter 1987, *116,* 119–131; T. S. Mescon and D. J. Tilson, "Corporate Philanthropy: A Strategic Approach to the Bottom Line." *California Management Review,* Winter 1987, *29,* 49–61; R. E. Wokutch and B. A. Spencer, "Corporate Saints and Sinners: The Effects of Philanthropic and Illegal Activity on

Organizational Performance." *California Management Review*, Winter 1987, *29*, 72; P. R. Varadarajan and A. Menon, "Cause-Related Marketing: A Coalignment of Marketing Strategy and Corporate Philanthropy." *Journal of Marketing*, 1988, *52*, 58–74.

16. W. Wall, "Helping Hands: Corporations Are Effecting Changes in the Ways They Make Gifts to Charitable Agencies." *Wall Street Journal*, June 21, 1984; J. Kornbluth, "Ace of Hearts." *New York*, Oct. 13, 1986, p. 76; Asinof.

17. A. Hunt, "Strategic Philanthropy." *Across the Board*, July/Aug. 1986, *23*, 23–30.

18. P. Kotler and A. R. Andreasen, *Strategic Marketing for Nonprofit Organizations.* Englewood Cliffs, N.J.: Prentice-Hall, 1987, chap. 1.

19. B.L.R. Smith and N. Rosenbaum, *The Fiscal Capacity of the Voluntary Sector.* Washington, D.C.: Brookings Institution, 1981.

20. Wall; F. Howe, "What You Need to Know About Fund-Raising." *Harvard Business Review*, Mar.–Apr. 1985, *18*, 22; Edmondson.

21. Hunt.

22. D. Cole, "What's New in Fund Raising?" *New York Times*, Nov. 29, 1987, p. 17.

23. Edmondson.

24. Cole, p. 17.

25. G. Kinkead, "America's Best-Run Charities." *Fortune*, Nov. 9, 1987, pp. 144–150ff.

26. A. Andreasen, "A Marketing Challenge for United Way." *Community*, Sept. 1985, p. 14.

27. A. Andreasen and R. P. Nielson, "Deep Pockets for Doing Good." *Time*, June 16, 1986, p. 51.

28. W. Bogdanich, "It's Hard to Tell Good Charities from the Bad." *Wall Street Journal*, Jan. 25, 1985; "Feeling Charitable? Find Out Where the Money Goes." *Business Week*, Nov. 17, 1986, p. 212.

29. B. Carton, "Va. Probes Indian Groups Records." *Washington Post*, Aug. 2, 1987, p. B1.

30. Kinkead.

31. B. Carton, "Worth of Charities Is Hard to Assess." *Washington Post,* Aug. 2, 1987, p. B8.
32. Edmondson.
33. "Feeling Charitable?"
34. M. J. Gross, Jr., "A New Study of the Cost of Fund-Raising in New York." *Philanthropy Monthly,* Apr. 1976; S. J. Smallwood, "Finding the Costs of Fund-Raising." *Trusts and Estates,* 1979, *118,* 36–37; "Better Business Bureau's Standards for Charitable Solicitations Released." *Fund-Raising Management,* May 1982, *14,* 42; J. M. Greenfield, Determining Your Fund-Raising Costs." *National Society of Fund-Raising Executives Journal,* Spring 1984, p. 20.
35. S. Rose-Ackerman, "Charitable Giving and 'Excessive' Fund-Raising." *Quarterly Journal of Economics,* May 1982, p. 195; D. Johnston, "The Challenge of Charity Activists." *Los Angeles Times,* Jan. 23, 1985, pt. V.
36. J. W. Harvey and K. F. McCrohan, "Fundraising Costs—Societal Implications for Philanthropies and Their Supporters." *Business and Society,* Spring 1988, pp. 15–22.
37. Beyer.
38. Mescon and Tilson.
39. Mescon and Tilson.
40. Wokutch and Spencer.

PART TWO

Philanthropy in Society

Chapter 4   *Susan A. Ostrander*
                                        Paul G. Schervish

Giving and Getting: Philanthropy as a Social Relation

≋≋≋≋≋≋≋≋≋≋≋≋≋≋

In the decade since the Filer Commission Report, a growing body of research and theory has sought to clarify the nature of philanthropy, the institutional boundaries of the nonprofit sector, and the giving behavior of individuals and organizations. Most of this research conceptualizes and studies the philanthropic world as a world of donors. This work, including some done by the present authors, has focused on explanations of why and how and under what circumstances people give voluntarily of their money and time.

This research is important and should continue. It is also important to recognize that an exclusive focus on donors runs the risk of obscuring issues that are of concern to recipients and therefore to philanthropy as a whole. The common language of giver and receiver used to characterize philanthropy suggests a one-way relationship in which valued goods and services move only in one direction, a point of view we challenge here. A donor focus also ignores the ways in which recipients actively take part in defining what goes on in the world of philanthropy, ways in which recipients are agents in creating philanthropic institutions and relations.

Note: The authors are listed in alphabetical order. Paul Schervish would like to gratefully acknowledge Andrew Herman, who helped develop a number of the ideas concerning the theoretical nature of philanthropy and the strategies of philanthropy carried out by donors.

Attention tends to be diverted from the social needs that recipients have and that donors seek to address, and from what gifts actually accomplish from the perspective of those who receive them. Strategies that recipients and their advocates use to obtain support are generally left unexplored and unspecified.

Of greatest concern to us here is that the relatively exclusive focus on donors obscures the most fundamental sociological fact about philanthropy; namely, that philanthropy is a social relation of giving and getting between donors and recipients. The major aim of this chapter is to conceptualize and explore philanthropy in this way. This relational understanding of philanthropy elevates the position and priority of the recipient. It brings the recipient into theory, research, and practice in the field. Conceptualizing philanthropy as a social relation has the potential, we believe, for contributing to the making of a better match between the resources and needs of donors and the resources and needs of recipients. It can therefore help to improve philanthropic practice by developing a philanthropy that is more responsive to social need.

We begin this chapter by explaining what we mean by this understanding of philanthropy as social relation. We differentiate philanthropy from two other kinds of social relations, commercial transactions and electoral politics. Next we lay out an array of strategies that the two major parties in the relation—donors and recipients—use to gain the attention and favorable response of the other. Each of the strategies is defined by the relative power with which donors and recipients approach each other, that is, the extent to which each party takes into account the needs and interests of the other. Strategies as we conceive them are composites of three dimensions: complex goals, strategic rationales, and practices. Finally, we consider briefly some implications of our conceptualization of philanthropy and the strategies for philanthropic practices.

Throughout the chapter, we speak of the social relation that is philanthropy as an interaction between what appears to be only two actors: donors and recipients. We recognize, however, that a whole set of actors exist between and within these two sides of the social relation and that mediate the interaction. On the donor side, the relation to recipients is mediated by organizations such as foundations and funding exchanges and by individual office and field staff members who represent such organizations. On the recipient side, the relation to donors is mediated by grant-seeking organizations (including universities, hospitals, museums, churches, and social service agencies) that provide services to clients and consumers and by advocacy groups that work politically for social change. Other organizations and individuals combine donor-side and recipient-side roles, such as the United Way and the Black United Fund, which both raise and disperse funds. Thus, while we speak here of donors and recipients, we in fact mean to include the chain of donor-side and recipient-side agents that represent and carry out the wishes, concerns, and interests of the two ultimate actors at either end of the chain of interaction.

In the following discussion, we speak of recipients most frequently, although not exclusively, as organizations that provide services for clients and consumers or that advocate for social change. In contrast, we tend to speak of donors as individuals who give money to support such organizations. This approach makes sense since over 80 percent of donors are individuals, where virtually all legally recognized tax-exempt recipients of these contributions are organizations.

The strategies we develop here to conceptualize the orientations and actions of recipients and donors in the social relation that is philanthropy emerged from three sources: our own research on philanthropic donors and recipient organizations, the literature on philanthropy and fund raising, and our conversations with other scholars and activists in the world of philanthropy. Donor strategies presented here were developed from the research of Schervish and Herman on wealth and philanthropy.[1] Recipient strategies were developed from what is known about donors and from the trade literature on fund raising[2] as well as indirectly from Ostrander's field work in voluntary social service agencies.[3] A major task for future research is to specify which strategies and under which conditions these are most likely to result in a match between the resources and needs of donors and the resources and needs of recipients.

Philanthropy as a Distinctive Social Relation

Philanthropy, in our way of thinking, is not distinct because of its location in a clearly defined or bounded institutional sector or realm. Philanthropy as we conceive it here is not limited to a "third" or voluntary or nonprofit sector.[4] Our point is that philanthropy is a particular type of social relation that may occur in government and corporate settings, and it most certainly occurs in families and neighborhoods. The other kinds of social relations we look at here—commercial transactions and electoral politics— also are not defined or limited by a particular institutional realm. Commercial transactions occur not only in the economic market- place but throughout social life wherever goods and services are exchanged for monetary compensation. Electoral politics is not lim- ited to government organizations or the institution of the state but represents a mode of exercising power and decision making wher- ever votes are taken to establish positions, determine officeholders, and decide policy directions. In the same way, our notion of phi- lanthropy as social relation is more extensive than the notion of philanthropy as institution or organization.

Like other social relations, that between donor-side and recipient-side actors contains identifiable patterns of interaction. Like other social relations, it is a transaction in which both parties get and give as a condition for establishing and maintaining the relation. At the same time, in this and many other social exchanges, the relation between the two parties is not an equal one. For a number of reasons a power difference between donor and recipient emerges from the current character of philanthropy as a social re- lation. The general tendency is for donors to occupy positions that give them substantially more active choice than recipients about how to define the philanthropic transaction and how to take part in it. Recipients also can and do make choices that affect what happens to themselves and to donors and shape the way philan- thropy is organized.

This relative inequality between donors and recipients and the disparity in the extent of active choice available to each party derive from the larger societal context in which philanthropy oc- curs. We conceptualize this context by drawing on social theory about human agency and societal structure.[5] Social structure both creates and is created by human action and choice in an iterative process. Once created, social structure defines the terms and bound- aries of choice, presenting both obstacles and possibilities for action. Donors and recipients, then, are both constrained and facilitated by the structure of philanthropy in what they do and how they think. At the same time, both donors and recipients participate as agents in reinforcing or changing this structure of philanthropy—the structure that then in turn forms the context for their own thinking and acting in the philanthropic world.

Commercial Transactions, Electoral Politics, and Philanthropy

If it is not an institutional or legal boundary that separates philanthropic relations from commerce and politics, then what is it? What distinguishes philanthropy as a particular kind of social relation? The most important distinction we make between philanthropy and commercial and electoral relations revolves around the *media of communication* through which needs are put forth in each case. Each type of relation differs in how a request or demand is made and in how such demand elicits a response. Commercial appeals or demands are made in terms of dollars, while electoral appeals or demands are made in terms of votes. Philanthropic appeals are made in normative or moral or value terms.

In commercial transactions, consumer demands or needs generate a response from suppliers of resources largely to the extent that demands are expressed through dollars. Needs are communicated to suppliers or producers through what economists call "effective demand," that is, demand backed up by and made efficacious by the power of monetary votes or dollars. It is not just the existence of needs or demands that is important in getting a response, but also the fact that these needs can mobilize or generate a response that produces what is demanded. Similarly in electoral politics, needs or interests get attended to largely to the extent that they can be expressed as votes—what one might call another kind of effective demand.

The important question here is just what makes commercial and electoral demands effective in eliciting responses? It is, we believe, that commercial and electoral demands are regulating and "coercive." That is, they are presented through quantifiable media upon which suppliers depend for their very existence in material terms. Elected officials must have votes. Commercial suppliers must have consumer dollars. The demands of voters and consumer dollars cannot in the long run be ignored. In philanthropy the demands are not compelling in the same way.

In philanthropic relations, the media for communicating recipient needs or demands are neither votes nor dollars but rather words and images that are put together in such a way as to make a normative or moral appeal for support. In philanthropy, demand is made efficacious by inviting the supplier or producer to attend primarily to the needs expressed themselves rather than to the medium through which they are expressed. Philanthropy thus recognizes or responds to what can be called "affective" rather than "effective" demand.[6] By this we mean that philanthropy is mobilized and governed by a moral or normative currency that ultimately appeals to the nonmaterial or "affective" aspects of the giver's consciousness rather than to a particular material interest.

This approach to philanthropy should not be interpreted as meaning that demands or needs expressed by institutions or organizations presently defined as "charitable" or philanthropic do in fact always operate according to the moral or normative currency that we see as the defining characteristic of philanthropy defined in these relational terms. Indeed, it is one of our points that the nonprofit sector is no more exclusively the realm of philanthropic relations than the for-profit sector is exclusively the realm of commercial relations or government is the exclusive realm of electoral relations. For instance, nonprofit hospitals may in fact be characterized largely by commercial relations just as for-profit hospitals may in fact respond philanthropically, as we have defined the term, when they mobilize some services around patient need rather than ability to pay. Put simply, when appeals or demands are not expressed primarily in normative or moral terms, they are not philanthropic in the sense we mean that term here, regardless of the social setting from which they come.

The Tendency of Philanthropy to Be Donor-Led

The major consequence for the way that philanthropy works as a social relation arises from its governance more by moral than by material or electoral claims. Because normative appeals do not carry the same kinds of rewards or sanctions as money or votes, philanthropy (unlike commercial transactions or electoral politics) tends to be driven more by the supply of philanthropic resources than by the demand for them based in recipient needs. Because philanthropic appeals are normative or morally based, they tend therefore to be "weaker" and less compelling than when the currency is votes or money. This means that attention to recipient needs may not always remain prominent or determinant in the minds of those providing donor resources or in the minds of those who seek funding on behalf of ultimate beneficiaries.

Commercial and electoral relations retain at least some semblance of consumer and voter sovereignty. That is, they tend to be demand-led in the sense of being responsive in some degree to consumer needs and voter interests. Suppliers or producers in commercial and electoral relations are constrained at least to some extent by the countervailing power of consumers to buy other products from other producers and by voters to cast their ballots for other candidates.

Philanthropic donors—by which we mean suppliers or producers of monetary resources essential for philanthropy—are not similarly constrained by the countervailing power of recipients and their representatives. This is because philanthropy tends to be supply- or donor-led. That is, recipients enjoy little or no ability to ensure or "discipline" the response of donors. Appeals in the form of words and images arranged in a normative display cannot be accumulated as can dollars or votes. As a result, philanthropic donors who supply the resources essential to meeting recipients' needs are not threatened by the withdrawal of the media for expressing the need. The consequences of philanthropy being supply-led are profound for both donors and recipients. We characterize two such major consequences by the terms *donor ascendancy* and *recipient influence*.

Donor Ascendancy and Recipient Influence

Because normative appeals offer little, if any, immediate extrinsic reward or sanction to a potential donor, any single appeal can be refused without any direct negative material consequence. It is, of course, true that donors are not exempt from pressures to give money to "charitable" causes as a part of their climb to success in the corporate world or as a result of belonging to certain social networks.[7] Still, for the most part, the obligation to give money is essentially based on moral grounds—because it is the right and good and sincere gesture to be made—without direct material censure or reward. Normative claims impose this obligation only to the extent that donors recognize and heed them. So recipient groups find themselves dependent on donors not only for funds. Ironically, they depend as well on donors for the very recognition of the legitimacy of the appeals by which recipients make claims on donors in the first place.

The structural tendency in philanthropic relations is, therefore, to grant more power to the donor than to the recipient. As we noted earlier, donors occupy positions that afford them substantially more choice or agency about how they define the social relation that is philanthropy and about how they act and think in it. The concept of agency thus explains more about how the philanthropic world looks and works from the vantage point of the donor. The concept of social structure explains more about the vantage point of the recipient. One of our aims here is to specify the social relation between donor and recipient in such a way as to provide practical guidelines toward empowering recipient groups and the beneficiaries they represent. We want to increase the influence, bargaining power, and choices of strategies available to recipients in their relation with donors and potential donors. Simply defining philanthropy as a social relation in which there is some kind of reciprocal exchange is itself a first step in this direction. As we said earlier, it brings recipients more prominently into the relation.

Given our discussion of philanthropy as donor-led, it is now clearer why and how recipients exercise less choice, power, and influence than donors. Recipients are dependent on donors for their organizational existence and for the well-being of their clients, consumers, and employees. The imperative of finding a donor leads recipients to search actively and continuously, to "prospect" as it is sometimes put in the fund-raising literature. This is done at considerable effort and expense. Small recipient organizations and those whose activities are controversial are at a distinct disadvantage in mounting the fund-raising or "development" efforts. While it is true that some donors choose to search actively for recipients, donors do not have to carry on this kind of activity as a condition of their existence. They can choose among the requests that come to them from grant-seeking recipients. Indeed, one of the problems of being a well-known donor is that one is constantly receiving requests for contributions and having to decide which of them to grant.

Although donors certainly cannot be said to depend on recipients for their actual and material existence, it could be said that donors depend on recipients for the moral and normative and perhaps social meaning of their existence. Recipients have their own influence and their own set of resources to give to donors. In recipient appeals to potential donors, the moral currency that is used is not without value and command. As will be seen in our discussion of philanthropic strategies, donors respond to a whole array of nonmaterial incentives, ranging from making a sincere effort to meet social needs to fulfilling a moral duty, obtaining psychic satisfaction, achieving social and personal legitimation, gaining status in the community, or achieving a social agenda.

Although philanthropy as currently constituted tends toward donor ascendancy, in actual practice the balance of power does not always remain firmly established on the side of the donor. Whenever recipients or their advocates introduce and enforce normative claims or incentives that affect donors, the balance of power begins to shift toward recipients. It is, then, not always the case that philanthropy is governed by the supply of donor resources though this does not refute the structural tendencies we have noted here. Framing the issue in this way does call for a specification of the conditions under which the structural tendencies get modified so that recipients have more influence. The strategies we next consider differ in the extent to which they contain possible directions for creating and strengthening such conditions. As we will show, it is not simply a matter of the degree to which recipients and their needs are taken into account by donors. It is also a matter of the qualitatively different ways in which this comes about.

Strategies in Philanthropy: Modes of Interaction
Between Donors and Recipients

By focusing on philanthropic strategies of donors and recipients, we are able to characterize philanthropy in a different way than by types of donor motivations, the size of gifts, or the cause or purpose for which gifts are dedicated. While these matters are certainly important, none really helps us to understand how donors and recipients actively participate in philanthropy. By conceptualizing strategies of philanthropy as modes of consciousness and modes of engagement, we highlight the different ways that people on the donor and recipient sides of the relation come to think about and carry out philanthropy.

The strategies as we conceive them are a composite of three dimensions: a complex goal, a strategic rationale or consciousness, and a strategic practice or mode of engagement. These dimensions can perhaps be best understood as answers to a series of questions. What is the multiple set of goals or ends that each party seeks to accomplish or bring about through participation in the relation? How does each think about or understand the way in which the relationship between them is or ought to be constituted in order to accomplish these ends? How is this presented or communicated to the other so as to gain access and attention? What kinds of claims and appeals are made, and how exactly are they expressed? What does each party actually do? What specific practices are engaged in and how are they carried out?

The strategies, as we have developed them, differ in regard to the quality of the social relation between donor and recipient. We discuss this difference in terms of (1) the kind of involvement, contact, and communication between the two parties or sides; (2) the kind of specific knowledge each has about the other; and (3) the relative priority given by the two parties to what donors want in comparison to what recipients need. An important focus here, as we have said, is one particular aspect of the social relation of philanthropy, namely, the media of expression or communication between donor and recipient. These strategies are not mutually exclusive or exhaustive. A particular donor or recipient probably participates in more than one at a time, and the strategies we list are by no means

complete. Given our earlier discussion about the donor-led character of philanthropy and the power of the donor, we present donor-
side strategies first because we see them as framing an important
context within which recipients must think and act.

Donor-Side Philanthropic Strategies. In previous research, Schervish and Herman[8] identified sixteen qualitatively different strategies or "logics" of philanthropy that are carried out by donors,
distinguishing them according to differences in goals, modes of
consciousness, and modes of practice. Here we discuss nine of those
strategies, locating them within three broad approaches by which
donors understand and carry out their relation to recipients. The
three general donor-side approaches we will consider here are the
personal-engagement, mediated-engagement, and donor-oriented
strategies (Table 4.1).

Personal-Engagement Strategies. In the personal-engagement approach, donors attend immediately and directly to the needs of recipients and, as the name implies, are in personal, physical contact
with them. We describe three specific types of personal-engagement
philanthropy, each of which shares a common set of goals. Individuals who carry out personal-engagement philanthropy are attempting to do more than fulfill their personal aspirations and support
a beneficial outcome for recipients. Those who pursue the various
types of personal-engagement philanthropy also seek to know and
be known by the ultimate beneficiaries of their support and in some
cases to allow beneficiaries to actually enforce attention to their
needs. The way such donors think about their relationship to recipients reflects a concern to learn as much as possible about the recipients and their specific needs. Accordingly, the distinctive
practice that characterizes personal-engagement forms of philanthropy revolves around efforts to be in personal contact with recipients, to learn their appeals, and to ensure that these appeals become
binding on them.

A number of diverse types of philanthropy fall under this
general category of personal-engagement philanthropy. The extreme instance of the direct personal matching of donor resources
to recipient needs is *consumption philanthropy.* In this approach

Table 4.1. Donor-Side Strategies.

Personal-Engagement Strategies: direct personal contact and exchange of information between donors and beneficiaries, with priority given to recipient needs

  1. *Consumption*: donor is also beneficiary of gift
  2. *Therapeutic/empowering*: donors seek simultaneously to enhance their own sense of self-empowerment and to give over some active organizational control to beneficiaries
  3. *Adoptive*: donors attend personally to recipient needs in an ongoing and multifaceted relationship

Mediated-Engagement Strategies: contact between donors and recipients mediated by organizations or other individuals though knowledge and concern for recipient needs may be high

  1. *Contributory*: donor gives to a cause with no direct contact with recipient
  2. *Brokering*: donors solicit other key donors in their own network
  3. *Catalytic*: organizers donate time to mobilize large number of other donors in a mass appeal

Donor-Oriented Strategies: donors governed and mobilized by their own circumstances rather than by those of recipients

  1. *Exchange*: giving propelled by mutual obligation within a network of donors
  2. *Derivative*: giving based on obligations associated with job expectations or family responsibilities
  3. *Noblesse oblige*: philanthropy grows out of decision to designate part of family money for social involvement

---

donors contribute to causes or organizations from which these donors directly benefit. The match is so complete simply because the donor and beneficiary are the same. Consumption philanthropy, it turns out, is the largest single category of philanthropy because it includes contributions to churches, schools, cultural institutions, and professional organizations, from which givers and their families directly benefit.

Even though the other two forms of personal-engagement philanthropy are much less prominent, they are important to describe because they indicate possible directions for the future development of philanthropy. One such approach is what we call *therapeutic* or *empowerment* philanthropy as it takes form in various funding organizations such as the Vanguard Foundation and the Funding Exchange. The term *therapeutic* is coupled with the term *empowerment* to emphasize how the practice of philanthropy is viewed and concretely organized by donors to come to grips simultaneously with their own need to become personally empowered in regard to their wealth and their desire to empower others. The feelings of donors who pursue this approach that their own needs have been denied or obscured in their lives of wealth lead them to be particularly sensitive to the experience of powerlessness among those at the opposite end of the economic spectrum. The upshot is the creation of an organizational structure with two unique aspects. First, in regard to donors there is a requirement that they contribute relatively equal amounts so that no one donor is overly able to influence decisions. Also, there is the more or less informal expectation that donors will meet among themselves to discuss how they can grow in their self-understanding as socially responsible wealthy individuals. Second, in regard to recipients, such donors constitute boards of directors composed of nondonors, representatives of recipient groups, and beneficiaries. They also establish organizational bylaws that ensure the articulation and enforcement of recipient claims by limiting or even eliminating giver control over funding decisions.

A third form of personal-engagement philanthropy is called *adoptive* philanthropy. In adoptive philanthropy, donors become personally involved in the lives of the beneficiaries they seek to help. This is typified by Eugene Lang's and others' efforts in the I Have a Dream program. In addition to devoting funds to a cause, the goal is for donors to involve themselves directly in the lives of inner-city students in an effort to motivate and guide them toward a college education. Working in and supporting the Boys Club and Girls Club and in Big Sister and Big Brother programs are obvious examples. Others include efforts by suburban churches to assist inner-city churches, corporations that commit themselves to develop a particular neighborhood or assist particular schools, individuals who assist particular artists or scholars as does the MacArthur family, and a respondent in the Study on Wealth and Philanthropy who supports a writer's retreat for women. Many other examples could be enumerated, but the point is, again, that personal attention to particular needs of the beneficiaries is foremost in the donor's mind, in part because the recipient is physically in the donor's social world.

Although substantially different in how they come to recognize and heed the moral claims of recipients, adoptive, therapeutic/empowerment, and consumption donors all have in common the highest regard for the needs of the recipients. In fact, by being so directly in contact with the ultimate beneficiaries and not just with their advocates, such donors often go so far as to give over legal governance at least in part to these beneficiaries, their advocates, or third-party professionals such as social workers and academics.

Mediated-Engagement Strategies. A second level and type of attention to recipient issues is represented by a variety of strategies in which contacts with the recipients are indirect or mediated by organizations or individuals who serve as advocates on behalf of recipients. In general terms, the composite goal is to contribute to important concerns while, at the same time, remaining somewhat insulated from having to expend time in contact with ultimate beneficiaries. If the strategy of personal engagement is like retail relations in the commercial sphere, mediated engagement is like wholesale relations. The strategic consciousness revolves around discerning how much and to what one should contribute while the practice tends to be limited to making such contributions and getting others to do so as well.

The most common form of such mediated engagement is termed *contributory* philanthropy. This approach, second only to consumption philanthropy in the amount of giving, is the form most likely to occur in all income groups and is the most familiar popular image of philanthropy. The contributory strategy revolves quite simply around obtaining and mobilizing financial resources on behalf of a cause. The term *contributory* is used to emphasize the fact that philanthropic involvement is primarily in the form of monetary contributions rather than in time or skills. In addition, there is virtually no direct contact between the donor and the ultimate beneficiary. Rather, the moral appeal to which donors respond is formulated and presented by a grant-seeking or advocacy organization. This, of course, is the most common mode of fund raising by such groups as OXFAM America, CARE, the NAACP, universities, hospitals, symphony orchestras, peace groups, and numerous other traditional and progressive organizations devoted to raising funds for important causes and needy recipients. It is important to note that the contributory strategy often reflects a very high level of commitment and devotion by contributors to fulfilling the needs of the ultimate beneficiaries and, indeed, to the beneficiaries themselves. But the relation to them remains indirect and impersonal, mediated by various intermediary organizations and individuals.

A second form of mediated interaction occurs in *brokering* philanthropy. Here organizational officers, board members, or other interested parties devote their efforts to fund raising by seeking contributions from major donors. Once again, a high degree of affective commitment may motivate brokering donors as they demonstrate by spending time and effort to solicit contributions from others. We usually see this strategy exercised by wealthy individuals who turn to their social and business associates to raise funds for a cause. But such brokering is not limited to efforts by the rich to solicit contributions from their peers. The nonwealthy also pursue the brokering strategy by seeking pledges from friends and associates for each mile traversed in the various "walks" and "runs" on behalf of efforts to relieve hunger and cure AIDS, to name just two.

A less widespread but equally visible form of mediated engagement is *catalytic* philanthropy. If the vast majority of participants in the mass-involvement types of philanthropy like Boston's Walk for Hunger are engaging in brokering philanthropy, many of those organizing and directing such efforts are engaging in catalytic philanthropy. Like brokering philanthropy, the major goal is broadening the base for fund raising on behalf of a cherished cause but, again, without requiring any direct involvement with beneficiaries by those giving time and money. In contrast to brokering philanthropy, however, the catalytic strategy—as its name implies—is directed toward mobilizing not a small number of personally known peers but a large number of unknown contributors. Accordingly, catalytic philanthropy is often led by media stars, sports figures, and other celebrities. They lend their names, notoriety, and personal efforts to raise money by eliciting an affective engagement of a broad popular base. What the sociologist Robert Merton discovered more than forty years ago in his study of Kate

Smith's dramatic success in getting Americans to invest in war bonds is directly relevant here. The public's perception of personal sacrifice and dedication by celebrities on behalf of a cause induces more contributions than what would be generated by a verbal appeal alone. Even when the central figures who lead such catalytic projects are not publicly known at the inception of a mass-participation drive, they often become so over time. For instance, those of us who live in Boston have witnessed how the dramatic success of the Walk for Hunger coincided with the rise to prominence of its inspirational founder and organizer, Dan Daley.

In contrast to the strategy of personal engagement, then, the strategy of mediated engagement does not entail a direct knowledge of or contact with the final beneficiaries of the philanthropic efforts—although the strategy does not preclude it. The major advantage of this strategy is its relatively efficient fund-raising process—one that appeals to donors because it leaves them relatively unencumbered in that they can retain whatever degree of social distance from the recipients they desire. The most serious disadvantage is that in the absence of a systematic direct contact between donors and recipients, it is possible for extraphilanthropic personal and organizational goals to become substituted for the moral claims of beneficiaries. Donors continue to respond to direct normative appeals in this strategy. However, there is the possibility of substantial slippage between how such normative appeals are recognized and responded to when mediated by advocacy groups and how they might be recognized and responded to if donors were placed in personal contact with those in need.

Donor-Oriented Strategies. A third general strategy encompasses a number of philanthropic approaches that tend to be governed almost exclusively by donor-side rather than recipient-side considerations. The major characteristic of what we call a donor-oriented giving strategy is that it is primarily attentive not to recipient needs but to donor interests and obligations. It is not the pull of engagement with recipients but the push of obligation that governs this strategy. The complex goal or teleology of donor-based philanthropy, then, revolves around fulfilling a set of obligations derived from family, business, or social relationships. Dedication to specific causes remains a goal of philanthropy, but it is not key to what mobilizes philanthropy in the first place. The strategic consciousness centers around learning and recognizing the expectations of one's position in relation to peers rather than in relation to those outside one's personal circle. The major practice is moving back and forth between responding to the expectations derived from one's social position and getting others in one's social purview to do the same.

Concretely, one prominent form of donor-based giving is *exchange* philanthropy. In this strategy, individuals give to a cause at the request of an associate in anticipation that in the future they will be able to call upon that associate to contribute to their cause. Individuals participate in a network of friends and associates each of whom feels free to call upon the other to support a favored project. Again, it is not that the beneficiaries disappear completely from the picture; it is just that the needs of beneficiaries are not what motivates philanthropy in the sense of setting it in motion. In contrast to the affective dedication surrounding personal-engagement and even mediated-engagement philanthropy, exchange philanthropy is matter of fact and dispassionate in tone. Whatever urgency emerges results not from what individual donors deem important but from the need to fulfill a social obligation that reproduces the bonds in a social network of friends and associates.

In a similar vein is *derivative* philanthropy, in which philanthropy is once again starkly supply-led in the sense that giving of money and time is derived from the everyday expectations of employment or social status. Schervish and Herman[9] found that this gets played out most commonly in two arenas. The first is at the workplace. A number of respondents indicated that they expect their senior staff to be engaged in some form of philanthropic activity or community involvement as a condition for working in their firm. Other respondents, especially attorneys, indicated that they were on the receiving end of such imposed obligation, again in the form of service within the broader community and not simply in the performance of pro bono legal work. The second arena wherein derivative philanthropy is relatively prominent is in volunteer networks of women of the upper class. Here the traditional family and social roles accorded wealthy women become expressed in the realm of philanthropy as the expectation that they devote substantial amounts of time to various volunteer activities, ranging from the simplest clerical tasks to the most arduous of managerial responsibilities. Although younger generations of women eschew the imposition of such roles and many who carry them out are deeply critical of their status, the point is that this is a form of philanthropy that is clearly supply-led. The engagement of donors occurs in response to the mobilization of normative expectations in their own world rather than the mobilization of moral claims in the world of others.

A final form of donor-initiated mobilization is *noblesse oblige* philanthropy. This term is used in a nonpejorative sense to emphasize that for many the inherited practice of philanthropy is derived from the expectation that community involvement is a traditional family obligation. What connects this strategy to inherited wealth is not an attitude of condescending parentalism but the fact that those pursuing this strategy inherit along with their wealth a set of expectations about how they are to use their wealth. Money is conceived as divided into three categories: an untouchable principal or capital, an amount for daily consumption, and an amount for philanthropic endeavors. Once again it is the nature of socialization and an understanding of money derived from a particular status—here, membership in an established family line—that induce philanthropic activity, rather than the pull of moral obligation. Recipient needs may come into play in determining the specific causes to which such individuals devote their time and money, but the fact of involvement is determined from another quarter, namely, a preexistent duty to allocate a certain part of one's time and money to philanthropic endeavors.

As we will also see in the case of the recipient-side strategies, the donor-side strategies can be understood as differing in regard to the kind of relationship that exists and is carried out between donors and recipients. The three specific approaches summarized under the rubric of donor-oriented giving exemplify that pole of the relationship most expressive of the underlying tendency of philanthropy as it is now organized to be supply- or donor-led. Exchange, derivative, and noblesse oblige philanthropy all center around efforts by donors to fulfill obligations derived from relations with those in their social circle rather than from relations with recipients. In the strategies grouped together as mediated-engagement philanthropy, there is a shift in psychological attention toward the needs of beneficiaries and a shift in practice toward heeding and responding to the world of beneficiaries even though personal contact with recipients does not occur. The most direct communication and contact between donors and recipients takes place, as we have said, in the personal-engagement strategies such as consumption, adoption, and therapeutic/empowerment philanthropy. Compared to donor-oriented approaches, especially, personal-engagement strategies shift the direction of concern to the ultimate beneficiaries of philanthropy. It is not just that donors come to heed the needs of recipients in a more direct and responsive manner that distinguishes approaches to philanthropy that bring donors and recipients into personal contact. It is also that a set of conditions are set in motion that have the potential for transforming the very way donors and recipients think about and interact with each other, both individually and as social groups.

Recipient-Side Philanthropic Strategies

We have developed three strategies that recipient organizations can use to gain the attention and favorable response of donors and potential donors. They are needs-based, opportunity-based, and agenda-based strategies (Table 4.2).

Needs-Based Strategy. The foremost goal of the needs-based strategy is to put forth as straightforwardly and in as unmediated a fashion as possible the preeminence of beneficiaries' needs. The central concern always remains the depth and scope of the needs and interests of the people—potential clients, consumers, beneficiaries—for whom or with whom the philanthropic project is being proposed and carried out. The two major ways that beneficiaries' needs may be directly and forthrightly communicated to donors are, first, for a grant-seeking organization to serve as a broker between donors and beneficiaries and, second, for beneficiaries to frame and express their needs directly to donors on their own. In some cases, the two approaches are joined, as when beneficiaries become an integral

Table 4.2. Recipient-Side Strategies.

Needs-Based Strategy: needs of beneficiaries are presented forthrightly to donors as the sole basis for mobilizing contributions; these needs may be presented either by the beneficiaries themselves or by recipient organizations or groups on their behalf

- Recipient frames need as inherently worthy of attention
- Recipient poses relationship to donor as a collaboration around a shared responsibility
- Recipient appeals revolve around efforts to communicate information about beneficiaries and their need

Opportunity-Based Strategy: needs of beneficiaries are recast and expressed as donor opportunities representing social or political benefit for the donor beyond simply responding to the needs themselves

- Recipients' appeals are formulated to persuade donors that responding to the needs of beneficiaries simultaneously provides donors with valued rewards
- Recipients may present the proposed project or program as an opportunity for the donors to make an innovative or distinctive contribution to the community, to enhance their own status or influence, to make a good investment, or to enter a prominent donor network
- Recipients may offer donors reduced costs or special access to programs or activities of recipient organizations

Agenda-Based Strategy: needs of beneficiaries are submerged and even compromised as recipients offer donors the chance to fulfill interests arising from events or circumstances in the donors' personal, family, or professional life

- Recipients cultivate personal relationships with current and prospective donors by focusing on what donors want or need as the condition or incentive for making a gift
- Recipients remain alert to new and emerging donor agendas as old agendas are fulfilled or fade in importance
- Recipients often maintain and update detailed prospecting files on individual donors

part of the group actively seeking funds. This is the case, for example, with a battered-women's shelter whose staff and board members seeking the grant include women who have been or might be in the future residents of the shelter.

Given such a strong focus on the needs and interests of the beneficiaries, beneficiaries are more likely to be involved directly in this strategy than in the opportunity- or agenda-based strategy. Indeed this involvement is itself often one of the goals of the needs-based strategy. If beneficiaries are not involved directly (as is perhaps most often the case), grant seekers still press clearly, forcefully, and sometimes dramatically the import of their need. This is the case, for example, with the appeals made by Mother Teresa. In addition to convincing donors of the import of the need itself and involving ultimate beneficiaries in the philanthropic process, those pursuing the needs-based strategy often seek to educate the community as a whole in an effort to press the needs in a broader arena.

The strategic consciousness or rationale expressed in a needs-based strategy focuses on a relationship between donor and recipient of a shared sense of responsibility and obligation to the community and its needs. Donors are not held in special esteem in this view. Rather, they are often seen as collaborators in a relationship of mutual respect and cooperation. Recipients take it as a given that donors wish to contribute and be involved in projects that seek to address community needs, and that if given the chance to do so, they will come forward and give what they can. Recipient groups are not hesitant in their zeal for seeking funds, and the relationship is conceived as being less hierarchical than is typically the case. The intrinsic rewards for donor contributions are highly valued both by the recipients and by the donors to whom this kind of appeal is attractive. These rewards include the intrinsic worth of being part of a community with connections to others and the inherent satisfaction of doing with and for others.

Recipient-side practices consistent with a needs-based strategy are targeted toward donors who are likely to be responsive to a direct and immediate appeal. Possible specific fund-raising tactics might include mailings to lists of donors who have given to similar programs. Mailings would likely include substantial amounts of concrete, explicit information about the need or interest being addressed. Testimony from potential or actual beneficiaries might be included. Telephoning from known lists and door-to-door campaigning, especially in areas most affected, are other tactics consistent with this strategy. Public speaking engagements, ads in the public media, and opportunities for donors to meet with potential or current beneficiaries could be arranged.

From the point of view of recipient-side organizations, the needs-based strategy has a number of advantages. It allows these recipient groups and the beneficiaries with whom and for whom they work to define the issues or needs that are important and the projects most appropriate and feasible to address them. Because the needs-based strategy focuses the appeal to donors around these points, it is the most recipient centered.

Opportunity-Based Strategy. In the recipient-side strategy we call the opportunity-based strategy, the mode of gaining access to the donor and a favorable response shifts toward the donor. While the importance of the needs addressed and the value of the project designed to address them are not ignored in this or any other strategy, here recipient needs are mediated through and expressed as donor opportunities. The goal of the transaction is to persuade the donor of the value of this opportunity. It is a strategy that requires that the recipient have more specific knowledge about the donor and what the donor might want and value than is the case with a needs-based strategy.

The strategic consciousness or rationale on the part of the recipient in the opportunity-based strategy conceives of the relationship with the donor as one in which the recipient who is seeking the grant must pose some reward—perhaps social or political or even indirectly material—that will induce the donor to make a gift. Giving is not seen as its own reward here, and so the recipients feel indebted to and beholden to the donor. This is less likely to occur in the needs-based strategy, where recipients do not feel compelled to provide something extrinsic in return for a gift.

The basis for asking donor support here is what recipients have to offer to donors beyond the satisfaction of giving itself. Recipients can offer donors the opportunity to be seen as innovators in the community, to make their mark by funding a project posed as a new and exciting solution or an innovative response to a need or interest. Appeals may be expressed so as to persuade donors to give to a program that is professionally managed, fiscally responsible, and efficiently organized—in other words, a good investment. The recipient group may offer, explicitly or implicitly, the donor the chance to be brought into the organization in a decision-making position as a member of the board. This may be presented in such a way as to imply that the donor's position at his or her place of business may be enhanced by such voluntary activity, thus contributing to the donor's economic and social well-being. Becoming a donor may be presented by recipient groups that are seeking a gift as the opportunity to become part of a community network of other donors of high status, thus also enhancing one's own social position and opportunity to have a voice in community affairs. To facilitate such networks and to provide entertainment as well as raise funds, recipient groups that use the opportunity-based strategy may organize events that provide donors a chance to see friends and be seen, to combine pleasure with social conscience. While some donors may view this kind of appeal as an onerous social obligation, to others it is an indispensable part of their social and business lives. The onus is on the recipient group that is seeking the gift to discover what will appeal to which donors and to carry out that particular form of appeal.

The practices used to express the opportunity-based strategy seem likely to include a strong visual packaging of the program as innovative and exciting, as an entrepreneurial opportunity for the donor. A selling package that emphasizes financial reports and evaluations of the program and its organization might be used. Donors with high name recognition and social status or "star" status may be used to appeal to other potential donors. The recipient organization may offer donors free or reduced-cost services, such as discounted subscriptions to symphonies, museums, and theaters, or implicit promises to university donors that members of their family will have an edge in admission. In these instances, the donor also becomes a user, as in the earlier discussion of consumption philanthropy.

In the opportunity-based strategy, groups that are seeking grants must still argue the importance of the need persuasively, but this and the capacity of the proposed project to meet the need are not seen as sufficient to get the gift. In addition, this strategy requires that the recipient group obtain information about potential donors that anticipates what they might want as the basis for an appeal. It requires that recipients learn relevant fund-raising techniques that focus not just on their needs but on the interests of the donors.

Agenda-Based Strategy. The third and final recipient-side strategy for seeking funds we will describe here is the most donor centered of the three. An agenda-based strategy is organized around and mediated through tactics that pose for donors a chance to carry out some preestablished agenda of their own or to fulfill some interest arising from an event in their family, professional, or business life. Recipients approach fund raising by locating specific donors who have some agenda and by persuading them—often indirectly and with discretion—that the agenda can be met in the course of giving to a certain project or organization. This strategy requires that the recipient have detailed and personal knowledge of the donor. It is a strategy that requires an investment on the part of recipient groups that can be made only by the largest, most affluent, and most professionally staffed grant-seeking organizations.

The claims that recipient groups that use this strategy make on donors include some event in the donor's life, such as a recent inheritance, change in marital status or parental status, graduation from college, geographical move, or illness or death of a family member. Files that catalogue this kind of information are kept on current and potential donors. Critical events in business or professional life include a recent promotion, surge in company profits, new position on a board of directors, a geographical move of corporate headquarters, or the need to counter some adverse publicity as a result of a boycott, union strike, industrial accident, or pollution alert.

The specific practices that accompany an agenda-based strategy for grant seeking are articulated in the fund-raising literature on what is called "prospecting" and in advertisements for costly workshops where recipient groups learn the techniques appropriate to this strategy. Expensive reference manuals with names, addresses, and other personal information about wealthy donors are printed and frequently updated. The fund-raising literature that emphasizes this approach advises recipient groups to do "investigative work" on potential donors and to keep elaborate and detailed "prospecting files" on individuals who may be persuaded to give.[10] Information from personal conversations between donors and the staff or volunteers of the grant-seeking organizations and from a wide range of other sources such as newspaper clippings are to be included in these files. Annual reports of the donor's business are collected along with any other information that can be found about the donor's company. Medical records, credit records, family counseling files, and academic records are referred to in one source as "hot potatoes" that should be used with discretion and a sensitivity to the need for confidentiality. Grant seekers are cautioned by one fund-raising manual that though "It may take a long time to establish a real working relationship with the keepers of these records," the rewards will be worth the effort and the grant seeker should stay with it. [11]

The agenda-based strategy seems problematic from the point of view of many recipient groups and, in at least some instances, the donor as well. The outlay of resources on the part of the recipient is very high, and some ethical questions seem troublesome. The use of donors' medical and counseling records does not seem to us justifiable no matter how effective they might be in getting a gift. The need of clients and consumers seems to almost disappear in the agenda-based strategy, and the usefulness of the project in meeting that need is at best seen as secondary. The strategy seems most suited to a donor base of a small number of large donors, given the investment that must be made in order to get the gift. The donor may be personally very involved in the recipient organization if convinced that a personal agenda can be played out and a donor need met. The basis for the donor's involvement, however, may or may not be consistent with what recipients and beneficiaries want or need. Once the donor has fulfilled his or her need, interest in making further gifts to the recipient organization may end. Donors with their own agenda may also expect—or be seen by recipients as expecting—formal and public recognition of their efforts, such as naming opportunities and ceremonies of appreciation that are highly publicized.

The three recipient-side strategies we have outlined here differ according to the kind of involvement between donor and recipient, knowledge about the other, and the relative priority given to donor or recipient interests. Involvement of the various parties and contact among them over time seem highest in the needs-based strategy, where donors, beneficiaries, and recipient groups are all very invested in addressing the need or concern in a collaborative

manner. Since the needs-based strategy is centered around beneficiary needs, recipient groups and donors are required to know only
of each other's mutual interest and concern as a condition for the
gift and for the relationship between them.

In the opportunity-based strategy, the degree of involvement
or contact of the various parties with one another is less than in the
needs-based strategy. They are required to have enough contact with
one another for the recipient to receive the gift and for the donor
to fulfill the desired opportunity obtainable through the gift. Recipients would seem to require somewhat more detailed information about donors than is the case in the needs-based strategy. Since
the opportunity-based strategy is more donor centered than the
needs-based strategy, the recipient organization has to know what
opportunities will appeal to which potential donors, and donors
have to know what opportunities are being offered beyond the
chance to respond to and participate in some community project or
program.

The agenda-based strategy requires recipients to accrue perhaps the most intensive knowledge of a personal nature about donors. The appeal for a gift is mediated through a personal, private
agenda of the donor's that the recipient discovers through detailed
investigation. Since this strategy is almost exclusively donor centered, recipients must have detailed information about the donors
in order to ascertain their agenda.

Implications for the Practice of Philanthropy

As we have discussed, philanthropy typically is mobilized and governed more by availability of donor resources than by the existence
of recipient needs. The implications of what we have had to say here
about reconceptualizing philanthropy as a social relation between
donor and recipient and about developing and applying philanthropic strategies that represent the interests and concerns of donors
and recipients flow from this tension that is generated by a supply-
led or donor-led process. As a counterbalance to the structural tendency of philanthropy to be supply-led—and therefore for donors
to have more power in the relation than recipients—conditions need
to be specified under which recipients can and do have influence in

the philanthropic relation. As we have said, it is our belief that this counterbalance—that bringing recipients in—will improve the quality and performance of philanthropy for donors and recipients.

One principle in particular seems to derive from the arguments we have made here: donors have needs to be fulfilled as well as resources to grant, and recipients have resources to give as well as needs to be met. In other words, *donors and recipients both give and get in the social relation that is philanthropy.* In consumption philanthropy, where donors and recipients are one and the same, we see that recipient needs are the most heeded. We think it is not accidental that such consumption philanthropy turns out to be the largest form of philanthropy in terms of size of contributions. What can be learned from this is not that consumptive philanthropy itself should be extended but rather that contributions are mobilized most strongly when donors see their interests and concerns to be the same as those of recipients or closely identified with them. This is counter to the more traditional view of philanthropic relation in which givers and receivers are socially distant and hierarchically arranged.

In each of the strategies we have laid out here, donors and recipients can be seen both as wanting something from each other and as having something to give that the other values. If recipients could be clearer about this, it would counter their tendency to go "hat in hand" to potential donors. It seems to us that recipients could use the needs-based strategy more often than our review of the fund-raising literature would suggest they do, or at least are advised by that literature to do. A fundamental assumption made over and over in this literature is that donors will not give to a project simply because it is presented as an effective way to address an important community need or interest. The desire on the part of a donor to be a part of a community effort, the satisfaction of being an active participant in creating one's own community and being connected to others in a collaborative project, the enlightened self-interest on the part of donors who recognize that they might benefit directly or indirectly from some philanthropic project—these are not seen as sufficient to motivate donors to give. In *Proven Tips and Secrets for Winning Grant $$,* for example, grant seekers are advised that while they "must present a clear picture of why [their] program is necessary" and they must "solicit community involvement in the grantsmanship process," the most important factor is the ability to "tailor each proposal to the individual requirements of funders."[12] Grant seekers are urged to keep the donors' wants constantly in mind and to "appeal to them often" in the proposal.[13] Even more bluntly, *Grantsmanship: Money and How to Get It* advises, "Tailor the letter [of inquiry] to the [funding] organization's opportunity, not the applicant's need."[14]

This kind of advice, repeated frequently and, as the above quotations illustrate, in very similar language, seems to advocate the use of what we have conceptualized here as the opportunity-based and agenda-based recipient-side strategies of grant seeking. Although these strategies may be effective in one sense, they are the most donor centered, and they require the largest investment and effort on the part of recipients. The agenda-based strategy in particular requires that recipient groups have a substantial amount of information about donors in order to find out what donors want and how they as recipients might satisfy those wants as a condition of "winning" the gift. The fund-raising techniques that are applied, again, especially in the agenda-based approach, often require the counsel of "experts" who constitute a whole new industry that can be called the fund-raising business. Clients and consumers, along with the needs and interests they carry, are the least visible in these strategies and the appeals and practices that derive from them.

The needs-based strategy that we have conceptualized here places the concerns and interests of the grant-seeking organization and the clients and consumers it serves at the center. It is less costly to carry out. It empowers recipients because they are the ones who define the need and the program, ideally in collaboration and in dialogue with clients and consumers and with donors. The depth and scope of the need and the interest in all parties in addressing that need with an effective program are seen as sufficient to win the gift. Donors are envisioned as members of the community who have resources that they are willing to contribute in return for the satisfaction of community involvement and participation. While individual donors may indeed use their philanthropic activities to create opportunities for themselves or to carry out their own personal or professional agendas, these are not the focus of the grant-seeking organization's appeals. They are seen as individual matters not at the center of the social relation that is philanthropy.

Our call for a recipient movement toward the needs-based strategy corresponds to a parallel call for a donor movement away from donor-oriented strategies and toward mediated-engagement, especially personal-engagement, philanthropy. From the point of view of donor strategies, the implication is to encourage increased donor engagement—both personal and psychological—in the needs and interests of recipients. Such engagement may well lead to increased monetary contributions by donors, but this is not the only or even the most important consequence. Engagement between donors and recipients has the potential for transforming the practice of philanthropy in a more profound way. The projects funded may become more in line with what people need and less with what they can get funded. As the hierarchical and nonreciprocal distinction between donor and recipient becomes replaced with more collaborative approaches, philanthropy has the potential of becoming more innovative and creative, not only in regard to types of social projects that it initiates but in regard to the interactive quality of social relations that it exemplifies.[15] A philanthropic practice that emphasizes a personal-engagement strategy for donors and a needs-based strategy for recipients would be organized around the values of reciprocity, cooperation, mutual respect, accountability, and commitment.

By conceptualizing philanthropy as a social relation rather than as an institution, sector, or organization, we have attempted to locate in a positive way the distinctive attribute of philanthropy. What constitutes philanthropy is not the legal tax status of an organization or the deductibility of a contribution. Rather, it is an interaction between donors and recipients that revolves around an effort to match what donors have to give to recipients with what recipients have to give to donors. Much of this matching tends to be talked about as donors giving concrete resources to recipients and recipients giving nonmaterial or intrinsic rewards to donors. This is true enough for much of the current practice of philanthropy. However, our definition of philanthropy as a social relation and how it gets carried out in the more mutual donor and recipient strategies indicates that there is more to it than this. When philanthropy is practiced at its best, donors are given material opportunities—and not just psychic rewards—through their relation to recipients. In turn, recipients are given various kinds of nonmaterial resources—in addition to material support—such as respect, empowerment, and esteem when philanthropy is recognized and carried out as a reciprocal social relation.

In this chapter we have taken the first step toward conceptualizing philanthropy as a reciprocal relation and toward laying out a range of strategies that donors and recipients use in that relation to orient and guide their behavior. It is the task of future research to specify the conditions and circumstances that increase the use of the strategies that are most open to bringing recipients into philanthropy as mutual partners.

Notes

1. Andrew Herman and Paul G. Schervish, "Varieties of Philanthropic Practice Among the Wealthy." Paper presented at Annual Spring Research Forum of INDEPENDENT SECTOR, New York, Mar. 19-20, 1987; Paul G. Schervish and Andrew Herman, *Final Report: The Study on Wealth and Philanthropy.* Submitted to the T. B. Murphy Foundation Charitable Trust, Boston College, 1988.

2. See, for example, *Fundraising Review,* Feb. 1982 through Dec. 1987; Jerald Panas, *Mega-Gifts: Who Gives Them, Who Gets Them.* Chicago: Pluribus Press, 1984; Michael Seltzer, *Securing Your Organization's Future.* New York: Foundation Center, 1987.

3. Susan A. Ostrander, "Voluntary Social Service Agencies in the United States." *Social Services Review,* Sept. 1985, *59,* 435-454; "Elite Domination in Private Social Service Agencies: How It Happens and How It Is Challenged." In Thomas R. Dye and G. William Domhoff (eds.), *Power Elites and Organizations.* Newbury Park, Calif.: Sage, 1987; "Private Social Services: Obstacles to the Welfare State?" *Nonprofit and Voluntary Sector Quarterly* (formerly *Journal of Voluntary Action Research*), 1989, *1.*

4. Peter Dobkin Hall, "Abandoning the Rhetoric of Indepen-

dence: Reflections on the Nonprofit Sector in the Post-Liberal Era"; Susan A. Ostrander, "Introduction" and "Toward Implications for Research, Theory, and Policy on Nonprofits and Voluntarism"; and Jon Van Til, "The Three Sectors: Voluntarism in a Changing Political Economy." In Susan A. Ostrander, Stuart Langton, and Jon Van Til (eds.), *Shifting the Debate: Public/Private Sector Relations in the Modern Welfare State.* New Brunswick, N.J.: Transaction Books, 1987. See also Paul G. Schervish, "Bringing Recipients Back In: Philanthropy as a Social Relation." Paper presented at INDEPENDENT SECTOR Academic Retreat, Indianapolis, June 7–8, 1988; and Jon Van Til, *Mapping the Third Sector.* New York: Foundation Center, 1988.

5. Anthony Giddens, *The Constitution of Society.* Cambridge, Mass.: Polity Press, 1985; Paul G. Schervish, Andrew Herman, and Lynn Rhenisch, "Towards a General Theory of the Philanthropic Activities of the Wealthy." Paper presented at Annual Spring Research Forum of INDEPENDENT SECTOR, New York, Mar. 13–14, 1986.

6. Schervish and Herman.

7. Joseph Galaskiewicz, *Gifts, Givers, and Getters: Business Philanthropy in an Urban Setting.* New York: Academic Press, 1986; Susan A. Ostrander, *Women of the Upper Class.* Philadelphia: Temple University Press, 1984; Michael Useem, *The Inner Circle.* New York: Oxford University Press, 1984.

8. Schervish and Herman.

9. Schervish and Herman.

10. James K. Hickey and Elizabeth Kochoo, *Prospecting: Searching Out the Philanthropic Dollar.* (2nd ed.) Washington, D.C.: Taft Corporation, 1984; Jeanne B. Jenkins and Marilyn Lucas, *How to Find Philanthropic Prospects.* Ambler, Pa.: Fundraising Institute, 1986.

11. Jenkins and Lucas, p. 16.

12. Education Funding Research Council, *Proven Tips and Secrets for Winning Grant $$.* Arlington, Va.: Government Information Services, 1987, p. 36.

13. Education Funding Research Council, p. 46.

14. Marquis Academic Media, *Grantsmanship: Money and How to Get It.* (2nd ed.) Chicago: Marquis Academic Media, 1987.
15. Susan A. Ostrander, "Why Philanthropy Neglects Poverty: Some Thoughts from History and Theory." In Virginia A. Hodgkinson, Richard Lyman, and Associates, *The Future of the Nonprofit Sector: Challenges, Changes, and Policy Considerations.* San Francisco: Jossey-Bass, 1989.

Chapter 5   *James R. Wood*
                                    James G. Hougland, Jr.

The Role of Religion
in Philanthropy

Ninety-five percent of Americans say that they believe in God, 70 percent belong to a church, and 40 percent report that they attend church or synagogue every week or almost every week.[1] Clearly, religion is an important element of American culture. This chapter argues that much religious activity *is* philanthropy and that religion also affects much everyday philanthropic activity that is not under the auspices of religion. Then, from a social science perspective, the chapter looks at the cutting-edge issues that are affecting the relationship between religion and philanthropy and discusses some of their implications for practitioners who seek gifts of time and money for their organizations, both religious and secular.

Religion's Impact on Philanthropy

Religion as Philanthropy. Not everyone readily perceives religion as philanthropic. Recently, an economist, upon learning that almost 89 percent of philanthropic giving in America is by individuals and only about 11 percent by foundations and corporations, scoffed: "Well, yes, but that counts people giving to churches!" It does indeed. In 1986 almost 47 percent of philanthropic giving was to religious institutions and causes.[2] If we define philanthropy as "active effort to promote human welfare," some may want to argue that not all giving of time and money to religious institutions is

99

philanthropic. But even if we subtract the time and money directed at teaching doctrine or providing worship, the contributions of religious institutions in the areas of health, education, emergency relief, and other forms of human welfare are impressive.

A study of fifty-eight Indianapolis congregations found that all but one of them supported at least one ecumenical community action project; in addition, most provided food and clothing for needy families, forty-six of the fifty-eight contributed to racial justice programs, thirty-five contributed to social service centers, sixteen provided tutors for inner-city schools, and several were centers for Meals on Wheels.[3] All of these congregations also contributed to denominations that carried out worldwide emergency relief.

We often underrate the importance of religious organizations in maintaining facilities that are used by the wider community. In one year, an Indianapolis church allowed sixty community organizations to use its building for a total of almost 3,000 hours—more than six times the number of hours that the building was in use for church activities. The church stated: "In opening our church doors and sharing our physical property with 'non-members' and 'non-church organizations,' we seek to symbolize the opening of our lives as Christians to all [people] and groups regardless of their needs, backgrounds, creedal positions, or economic status."[4]

This church provides a dramatic example. A recent national study of more than 600 Presbyterian congregations reports that 86 percent allow community groups or programs to use their buildings.[5]

These are but a few of the numerous ways that giving time and money to religious organizations supports active efforts to promote human welfare.

Religion's Impact on "Nonreligious" Philanthropy. Religious organizations mobilize people for philanthropic activities not under the auspices of religion. In a recent study of a sample of 800 individuals, representing adults in the state of Indiana, telephone interviews determined the kinds of philanthropic activities in which they were involved and how they got involved. The study found that church participation is an important influence on both volunteering time in the community and giving money for community agencies. The greater their church participation, the more hours per week people spend helping others and the more money they give to nonchurch charities such as United Way, youth organizations, and a variety of health-related groups.

In some respects the influence of the church and the influence of certain other organizations are quite similar. However, data show that the impact of churches on the amount of helping in a community is greater than that of any other single type of organization because considerably more people are active in churches. For example, according to an Indiana report, the number who were active in churches was more than twice the number who were active in youth and school service organizations and more than three times the number who were active in civic clubs. When respondents described organizations that recruited them into philanthropic activities, churches were the organizations most often mentioned—more than twice as often as the next most mentioned type of organization, youth organizations. In fact, churches were mentioned by 25 percent of those who volunteered their time to help others. [6]

How Religion Influences Philanthropy. Religion influences philanthropy both in and outside the churches partly through fostering philanthropic values. But values do not automatically produce actions. The most impressive evidence that values alone are not enough to explain philanthropic action is Gunnar Myrdal's classic study of the racial problem in the United States. [7] Myrdal found convincing evidence of Americans' belief in the "ideals of the essential dignity of the individual, of the basic equality of all [people], and of certain inalienable rights to freedom, justice, and fair opportunity." [8] All Americans "with a part of themselves" believe in these values. According to Myrdal, the American dilemma is that, though we truly cherish these values, we often do not live by them. We give verbal allegiance to them but in our day-to-day lives we operate from another set of values that are more selfish. For example, Myrdal observed that we say we believe in equality, but we do not want blacks as our foremen, as members of our clubs, or as neighbors.

Milton Rokeach has developed Myrdal's point in a useful way, showing that it is not just our controversial values that we neglect in our daily lives. We all have selfless values in our repertoire of values, but they tend to be organized in a hierarchy with the more selfish values at the top of our consciousness as we go through a typical day.[9]

Religious rituals and sermons can raise and sustain our consciousness of our selfless values. One important way in which they do this is through a language of moral discourse that allows people to think and talk about their actions in selfless terms. Robert Bellah and his coauthors in *Habits of the Heart* found in the people they studied a need for "a moral language that will transcend their radical individualism."[10] However, they studied an atypical segment of the population. The majority of Americans learn just such a language in their churches and synagogues, and many of them use that language in interpreting their actions and the actions of others around them.

Yet raising our consciousness of our selfless values and teaching us a language of values to sustain that consciousness are not enough to ensure philanthropic activities. There has to be another step. *We must be plugged into social arrangements where group expectations press us toward specific actions.*

One of the primary ways that Americans get plugged into such social structures is through their churches and synagogues. For example, one study found that frequency of church attendance increases donation of funds to relief organizations, provision of relief goods for victims of disasters, and the performance of disaster relief services for victims. The study concludes that a primary way in which churches mobilize members to participate in helping others "is through the provision of organizational means for such activity."[11]

The findings of the Indiana study support this explanation. When people who said that the church encouraged them to help others were asked *how* the church encouraged them, most said that in their churches they received information about who needed help and how to help them. A third of them said that they received this information in face-to-face communications, such as in sermons or in the context of a worship service or Bible class. Also, about 14 percent said that a church leader (for example, the minister or a committee chairperson) asked them to volunteer their time to help others in the community.

Left on our own, we will spend a quiet evening with the

family, catch up on our work, or get some needed exercise or diversion from the problems that occupy us during the workday. All of these are respectable pursuits. Despite strongly held philanthropic values, it is easy to persuade ourselves not to get involved with helping others. It is mainly when we are plugged into small groups, projects, committees, or organizations that we get up from our easy chairs and go out to lead a scout troop, serve meals at a community center, raise money for United Way, or make plans for a new mental health center.

Religious organizations have an important impact on philanthropy because they effectively plug us into structures of action that at the same time raise our consciousness of our selfless values, press us to implement those values, *and* provide us with opportunities to do so.

The Cutting-Edge Issues in Religion and Philanthropy

Alternatives to Religious Influence on Philanthropy. Some scholars believe that traditional American religion is losing its impact on American society. If so, one of the most pressing questions that faces scholars and practitioners of philanthropy is What can take the place of religion in providing motivation and structures of opportunity for philanthropy?

Studies of past and present social movements—such as the movements against slavery and for women's suffrage; or the civil rights, antiwar, welfare rights, and women's movements—may be helpful in approaching this question. Though religion provided motivation for many people in these movements, many others were motivated by other values and interests. Perhaps these values and interests could motivate philanthropic activities in the coming era, which may be marked by a dramatic decline in participation in traditional religion.

More problematic than the secularization of the motivation for philanthropy is the issue of providing the structure for philanthropic activities. Diverse voluntary associations do provide such structures in some measure, though no category of such associations approaches the scope of opportunities currently provided by religious organizations. Perhaps such associations can expand their philanthropic activities if church-provided opportunities decline.

"Umbrella groups" that coordinate the activities of hundreds of associations of various categories might provide the communication chains, social networks, and other opportunity structures that would take up the slack if religious organizations decline. INDEPENDENT SECTOR's current program Daring Goals for a Caring Society may provide the prototype for such activities. That ambitious program seeks to enlist "all voluntary organizations, government at all levels, foundations, and the business community, as well as . . . men, women, and youth from all parts of the country and all segments of society" in a program that will "double charitable giving and increase volunteer activity 50 percent by 1991."[12]

Another approach to this issue is to encourage the sorts of changes in government and in government's cooperation with the third sector of society that have come about as the result of social movements. The structures for affirmative action compliance are examples. Other examples are provided by the War on Poverty programs that took the initiative to search out the needy and find ways to help them. The vast structure of government can be enlisted and transformed so that the demise of religion's huge structural support for philanthropy would be less important.

Given the wealth and power of business corporations and Americans' propensity to promote human welfare through the private sector, corporations will have to play a major role in the expansion of philanthropy (and in making up for any decline of support from religion). There appears to be growth in the systematic involvement of businesses in recruiting and supporting volunteers for a variety of philanthropic activities in the community. For example, a recent report stated that the Honeywell Retiree Volunteer Project, which links volunteers and agencies, has 850 retired people who spend a day or two a week in a total of 230 community agencies.[13] A recent Canadian survey found that almost 70 percent of more than 900 employer respondents "reported adopting a supportive approach to employees engaging in volunteer work. . . . Sixty-one per cent of respondents allow the use of such facilities as rooms, grounds, vehicles, photocopying, word-processing, or computing. Permitting the employee to take time off work or to adjust the work schedule to the demands of voluntary work is also a frequent practice. Fifty-eight percent of organizations offering encouragement or support said that they allow time off work for voluntary activity; most of these allow some of this time off with pay."[14]

Kathleen L. Leonard estimates that more than 500 U.S. corporations have volunteer programs. Moreover, a number of cities now have citywide corporate volunteer councils (CVCs) in which several corporations coordinate their volunteer programs. These programs include "involving employees in assessment of community needs, providing a clearing house for matching employees' skills with volunteer openings in nonprofit agencies, referring staff to volunteer placement councils, sponsorship of group projects such as telethons, walk-a-thons, community clean-up drives, loaning of staff and executives for short- and long-term assignments with educational institutions and community organizations, in-house training of disadvantaged youth by corporate employees, and community involvement grants to organizations in which employees already volunteer their time."[15]

Yet although businesses are increasingly interested in volunteer programs, most have not fully institutionalized them. "Of 350 companies who recently submitted descriptions of their volunteer programs, only 14 percent have any written policy to authorize these programs. The fate of many corporate volunteer efforts, and indeed, of several CVCs, still depends on the personal commitment of the individual staff member assigned to the responsibility rather than on the job description and long-term policy."[16]

Corporations may be better sources of increased giving of money than of increased giving of time. Corporations have long been considered potential sources of funds for charitable activities. For some time, the Internal Revenue Code has allowed corporate tax deductions for gifts to charity. From 1960 through the early 1980s, corporations' contributions represented about 1 percent of their net income before taxes,[17] and some tendencies for increased giving have existed since then.[18] In some communities, corporate officials' expectations about each other have encouraged very generous programs of giving.[19] It is therefore possible that corporations will be in a position to compensate for any reduction in religious-based giving.

For several reasons, however, it is unlikely that corporate giving will represent the equivalent of religious giving. First, the *amount* of corporate giving tends to vary with earnings and profitability. For this reason, an economic recession could have a serious impact on the level of corporate giving.

Second, *motivations* for corporate giving differ from those for individual and religious giving, and these motivations may have an impact on the level and type of giving. McElroy and Siegfried's interviews with corporate executives suggest two major motivations. First, corporate giving is perceived as conducive to long-term profits because it allows not-for-profit organizations to provide critical services. For example, the availability of medical, educational, and cultural opportunities is helpful in convincing potential employees to accept employment in a community and also relieves firms of the necessity of providing such services on their own. However, contributions that are perceived as enhancing profitability may be limited because (1) many potential recipients of such contributions will not be perceived as being related to profitability, and (2) since benefits can seldom be confined to donors, corporate executives will find it tempting to minimize their own contributions in the hope that others will provide the needed support.[20]

Public image enhancement provides a second motivation for corporate donations. Though contributions are not viewed as a substitute for advertising, they are seen as useful for enhancing a tendency for the corporation's name to be perceived in positive terms. This motivation may lead to a high level of giving, but it is unlikely to lead to an even distribution of contributions because corporations interested in public relations are likely to restrict their contributions to high-profile but noncontroversial organizations. Corporation executives may be delighted to support a United Way or symphony orchestra campaign; however, welfare rights organizations or fledgling theater groups are likely to have to find their support from other sources.

The *distribution* of contributions is a third problematic aspect of corporate philanthropy. McElroy and Siegfried summarize the pattern of corporate donations as follows: "The bulk of the contributions (45 percent) is given to health and welfare organizations, most of which are United Way gifts. Education receives almost one-fourth, and both arts and culture and civic organizations receive most of the remainder."[21] It is clear that organizations promoting structural change must look elsewhere for support.

Finally, the tendency toward *mergers and corporate growth* may affect the pattern of contributions in profound ways. McElroy and Siegfried found that larger organizations (1) give proportionately less to health and welfare organizations, probably because United Way contributions are regarded as a fixed obligation and therefore do not respond fully to changes in firm size; (2) give proportionately more to educational organizations, probably because of their higher proportion of educated managers and professionals; (3) develop corporate policies prohibiting gifts to certain types of organizations (particularly religious organizations); and (4) are more likely than smaller firms to contribute to national organizations, thereby reducing the opportunity for local and regional organizations to benefit from their gifts.

Corporations with multiple sites contribute more dollars per employee to organizations in their headquarters city than in the cities where other operations are located. This means that the establishment of manufacturing operations away from corporate headquarters will not necessarily represent a windfall for nonprofit organizations in the area of the plant, though impacts will increase with the number of employees.[22] Mergers, however, may lead to both a reduction in the company's employees in the former headquarters city and a decreased ration of contributions per employee.[23]

Corporate gifts are an important part of philanthropy in the United States, but even if tax laws were adjusted to encourage increased corporate giving, for corporations to compensate fully for decreases in contributions from other segments of society (whether religion, the government, or foundations) would require changed corporate motivation. Moreover, because of limited numbers of staff members in charge of decisions about corporate philanthropy, it currently seems unlikely that many corporations will ever be on the "cutting edge" of philanthropic activity. In addition, as Securities and Exchange Commissioner Bevis Longstreth has noted, there is cause for concern about the lack of accountability of corporate managers who "dispense other people's money as they see fit."[24] In his view, "It is essentially a governmental function to decide what public interest goals we, as a society, ought to be pursuing and then to fund the pursuit with government dollars. If we do not like the policies that the government has set up for us, we should change the government rather than try to get the corporate structure retooled to perform what is essentially a governmental function."[25]

While Longstreth would presumably have similar concerns about the lack of accountability of religious leaders, his logic suggests that systems of nongovernmental philanthropy are best served by a variety of types of donors. A system in which religious donations were replaced by corporate donations would lose diversity while increasing the influence of a particular segment of society.

Any dramatic decrease in traditional religion would have a tremendous impact on philanthropy. Whether that impact would be devastating depends upon whether other organizations and institutions in the third sector, government, or business could take up the slack. There appears to be great potential in these organizations for facilitating philanthropy. But, as noted above, there are some special problems. Philanthropic values would be especially precarious in business organizations, where the basic values are economic. Even though there are some strong arguments for business to encourage philanthropic activities out of their own enlightened self-interest, these programs would probably be the first to go during an economic crunch. Moreover, businesses and, to some extent, government agencies are also far more likely to encourage programs that pursue noncontroversial goals. Yet it may well be that the distinctive contribution to American society by those aspects of traditional religion most expected to decline—the liberal mainline denominations—has been their ability not only to address controversial issues and champion unpopular causes but to draw large numbers of people and great amounts of resources into these activities.

Elsewhere, Wood has described some of the conditions that allow some churches more than others to champion controversial causes. A number of these conditions can be summarized as conditions that insulate decision makers from pressures to remain uninvolved. Perhaps there are also conditions under which certain corporate and government leaders are insulated in a similar way.

For example, corporations that do not sell a product directly to consumers may be less sensitive to their public image and hence more likely to champion unpopular causes.

The Decline of the Mainline Denominations. We have argued that the decline of the mainline denominations would make an important difference to philanthropic activities, and we have sought to evaluate possible alternative sources of the motivation and recruitment of such activity. However, whether the mainstream denominations, especially the liberal ones, will decline in their influence on American society is highly debatable. There is good evidence that the decline in membership of the liberal denominations is due more to demographic than to theological or social concerns issues. Moreover, increasing education in the United States appears to favor the major denominations over the more fundamentalist ones. And remember that, though the fundamentalists have captured the media's eye, the major denominations are still influential in the centers of power. One reason for this influence may be the religious composition of Congress. In recent years, while the media were playing up the political role of Jerry Falwell, the Congress rarely took actions favorable to his positions. This is partly because the Congress is made up of people in mainline polity and traditions. Though Falwell's following (despite his claims) is overwhelmingly independent Baptist, the Congress is made up predominantly of members of the mainline churches that have supported more liberal policies. Only 11 percent of U.S. senators identify themselves as Baptists, of which undoubtedly some of these are of the more liberal American Baptist churches. Nineteen percent are Roman Catholic, and 47 percent are members of the most liberal mainline religious bodies (United Church of Christ, 3 percent; Presbyterian, 8; Methodist, 15; and Episcopal, 21). The situation in the House is similar. There, only 8 percent are Baptist. Twenty-seven percent are Roman Catholic, 6 percent are Jewish, and 35 percent are of the most liberal mainline religious bodies. In general, then, it appears premature to speak of the decline of the influence of mainline denominations.

Evangelicalism's Impact on Philanthropy. Much thinking about the relationship between religion and philanthropy has focused on

religious participation in mainline denominations that are connected to a variety of other organizations and have reached an
accommodation with the larger society. The 1970s and 1980s, however, saw the growth of a number of religious organizations that
take a critical or separatist stance toward many of the ideas and
practices of the larger society. It is important to see whether the
continuing growth of religious organizations on the evangelical-
fundamentalist right will change the relationship between religion
and philanthropy.[26]

Evangelicals tend to concentrate on individuated and expe-
riential paths toward salvation. Social action occurs in the limited
sense that proselytization among members of the larger society is
encouraged, but efforts to change the structural characteristics of
society do not fall within the normal behavior of evangelicals when
they are acting in terms of their religious identification. Although
Hunter has identified some tendencies toward accommodation and
civility among religious conservatives, he notes that the self-
definition of religious fundamentalists has traditionally emphasized a reaction against modernity.[27] Evangelical involvement in the
larger society has increased over time, but Hunter interprets it in
terms of efforts to prove the superiority of evangelicalism. This
analysis (developed by a scholar with sympathies for evangelicalism) raises questions about the likelihood that involvement in evan-
gelical/fundamentalist churches promotes widespread involvement
in the larger society.

Empirical analysis by Hunter suggests that there is little promotion of civic involvement or concern among evangelicals. Evangelicals are less likely than those with any other religious identification
to list community involvement or political involvement as important
"Christian priorities."[28] Moreover, a content analysis of books written
for evangelical readers reveals considerable emphasis on self-develop-
ment but little attention to the disadvantaged.[29]

Hammond[30] has attempted to disentangle the influences of
evangelical identification and socioeconomic status on civic involvement. Without controlling for other variables, evangelical
identification is negatively associated with civic involvement, but
the relationship disappears when income is controlled. While evangelicalism in itself does not lead to a withdrawal from the world,

it appears to do nothing to promote increased involvement in other activities. Following Marsden,[31] Hammond suggests that such findings occur because of an absence of systematic political thought within the evangelical movement. While he recognizes that evangelicalism represents a socially significant "cry of alarm" in response to the declining legitimacy of many social institutions, he doubts its ability to reverse historic currents. Heinz, too, has stressed the evangelicals' tendencies toward premillennial pessimism and countermythology. He notes that their strong emphasis on the family as a symbol of endangered values has led them to oppose such programs as centers for battered women and abused children. As a result, any social involvement inspired by evangelical Christianity is likely to be limited on the basis of ideological concerns.[32]

Events during the 1970s and 1980s have led Wuthnow and Liebman to develop different views of the social implications of evangelicalism. Research conducted prior to the mid-1970s inevitably concluded that conservative religiosity and sociopolitical involvement were negatively related,[33] but political involvement by evangelicals has increased markedly since the early 1970s. As a result, Wuthnow cautions against interpreting religion in terms of "static clusters of beliefs organized around simple tenets." Because "religious systems are dynamic configurations of symbolism and ritual,"[34] areas of social action that once were considered irrelevant to evangelicals may be redefined as highly important. Poll results (summarized by Wuthnow) suggest that this occurred in the area of voting behavior beginning in the mid-1970s, and it may well occur for other areas of social activism as "the symbolic boundaries between religion, morality, and politics" are rearranged in the future.[35] As these changes occur, traditional evangelical responses to social change (which at one time were confined to separatism and confrontation)[36] are being replaced by involvement in such areas as electoral politics. This change has been interpreted in terms of increased upward mobility on the part of the evangelicals themselves[37] and increased "accommodation to the cultural plurality of modernity."[38]

Conservative religion has always had a number of different strains,[39] and the responses of the various groups to social change have been quite different. In addition, an individual's membership

112 Critical Issues in American Philanthropy

in a religious organization may be only one of several affiliations. As a result, the formal positions of the organization on any given issue may be poor predictors of the attitudes and behavior of the individual member. It is not surprising, then, that evangelical affiliation is associated with a plurality of views.[40]

Politics and philanthropy are different areas, but it is likely that the diversity of political attitudes will be mirrored by diversity in philanthropic activity. Simple statements about the relationship between participation on the religious right and philanthropic activity may be inappropriate for many individuals, both because of diversity within the religious right and because of the existence of nonreligious influences on the philanthropic behavior of many people. Evidence on increased voting and political behavior among evangelicals shows that significant numbers of evangelicals can be mobilized to participate in meaningful ways. In the absence of such mobilization, however, the evidence (summarized by Hunter and Hammond, among others) suggests that evangelical participation generally fails to encourage broader civic participation. Despite the dynamic quality of religious beliefs and their relationships to social action, the impact on social action of religious movements that traditionally have defined themselves in terms of opposition to secular trends is likely to be limited.

The Politicization of Religion. Though involvement in politics may cost religious organizations some support and could eventually jeopardize their tax-exempt status, the politicization of religion may increase its effectiveness in implementing philanthropic values. To the extent that church members have thought that religion and politics should not be mixed, it has been difficult to channel their energies into some of the most effective means of changing community policies and structures. All the media hype on the political involvement of fundamentalist church people may make it easier to mobilize religious people to address the structural barriers in our society that stand in the way of the implementation of philanthropic values. In general, local churches have been more inclined toward food pantries and soup kitchens than toward challenging local employment practices and welfare policies. And they have been more inclined to tutor underprivileged children than to support the fair housing policies and zoning regulations that would give those children easier access to the best education. Maybe politicization will eventuate in more politically astute action on behalf of philanthropic values.

But this will not be the case if religious leaders take an anti-intellectual approach to issues that inhibits thinking about them in structural terms. The debates over creationism serve to highlight this important issue affecting religion's influence on philanthropy. A number of fundamentalist religious groups reject many of the canons of modern education. Not only findings of the physical and biological sciences related to evolution are challenged, but also many of the fundamental findings of the social and behavioral sciences are branded as "secular humanism" and strongly opposed. This is not a new issue, but this kind of anti-intellectualism is becoming more institutionalized because of the proliferation of private religious academies for elementary and secondary education and the colleges and universities under the sponsorship of the televangelists.

Tamney and Johnson[41] have argued that the Falwell mentality will fade away as education in the United States increases. But that would not be true if people were increasingly educated under the auspices of the fundamentalists.

Ethical Implications of Religious Fund Raising. Speaking in 1986, Gordon Macdonald of the InterVarsity Christian Fellowship warned of a coming backlash against manipulative techniques used to raise funds for religious causes. Manipulative techniques, he said, generate "cynicism and hardness, and indicate a misuse of trust."[42]

Reason for concern about techniques used by religious organizations clearly existed before 1986. Concerns included misleading communications, questionable tactics to collect names of prospective donors, and a lack of fiscal accountability.

In 1980, a Lexington, Kentucky, resident who had ordered a free gift from the Rex Humbard ministry received a letter signed by Rex Humbard with the following paragraphs:

> Last week I knelt at the prayer altar to pray for every member in the Prayer Key Family book.

And I wanted to pray for you . . . but your name was
not there.

I wanted to pray for God to bless you in a very special
way, *to meet every one of your financial needs* and to com-
fort every heart as only He can.

I can actually feel these prayers being answered.
Homes are put back together . . . bodies are healed . . . and
discouraged hearts are comforted.

When you give, you receive. When you give as a
Prayer Key Family member, you receive the blessings of our
program every week in your home. And then by giving, you
are also putting your faith in action. *So you can trust God
for your needs to be met.*

I want you to receive all of these blessings of the
Prayer Key Family.[43] [emphasis added]

Humbard's letter promises such tangible premiums as two
prayer keys and a monthly letter. It also states unambiguously that
monthly contributions are expected. However, it appears appropriate to ask whether Humbard is promising some benefits that are
beyond his personal power to deliver.

The fact that these solicitations were mailed to people who
requested a free gift may also raise questions as to whether names
are being collected under false pretense. Humbard is not alone in
this practice. The Christian Broadcasting Network regularly solicits
contributions from viewers who phone its "prayer counseling ministry" for advice.[44]

Accountability has been a problem of particular concern for
some time. Since the early 1970s, the national Council of Better
Business Bureaus has tried without success to obtain reports on the
finances and activities of the Oral Roberts Evangelistic Association.
The only acknowledgment of its efforts was received in 1983, when
a lawyer wrote: "It is regrettable that the Association cannot fit itself
into the standards as set forth by the Bureau, but the operations of
the Association are so unique that this does not seem feasible."[45]
Other organizations have responded by saying, "We are accountable
only to God." A Better Business Bureau official has replied that

such a stance prevents donors from knowing where their money goes or how it is spent in religious fund-raising organizations.[46]

The editor of *Fund Raising Management* reacted as follows: "It is true they are accountable to God—but they are also accountable to their donors. For they are stewards of other people's property. The burden of accountability falls heaviest on religious fund raisers, not only from the nature of their calling, but from the fact that of the $90 billion donated to charities in the United States, almost half goes to religious causes."[47]

Despite ethical questions regarding fund-raising techniques and accountability, the economic impacts of religion continued to grow throughout the 1980s. In 1986 Jerry Falwell's organization, with 2,000 employees and an annual payroll of $32 million, was one of the largest employers in Lynchburg, Virginia. Falwell's $100 million annual budget exceeded the city's by $35 million. Not too surprisingly, when Falwell objected to his organization's tax status and threatened to move, the Lynchburg City Council voted (5–2) to eliminate back taxes and to ask the state legislature for tax exemption on Falwell's properties.[48]

The stakes were therefore very high when serious accusations of unethical conduct on the part of some prominent televangelists began to surface in 1987. The first controversy, involving fund-raising *techniques*, was sparked by Oral Roberts's contention that he would be "called home" unless he raised $8 million by the end of March. This tactic was widely criticized by other evangelists. Jimmy Swaggart, for example, labeled it "spiritual extortion" that placed God "in the same category as a terrorist or a kidnapper."[49] Though less strongly worded, the response from fund-raising executives was equally critical. Kenneth Albrecht, president of the National Charities Information Bureaus, said that Roberts's technique "exerts undue pressure on his supporters and followers" and concluded that Roberts's tactics are "bad for him, his cause, fund raising and philanthropy."[50]

The controversy over Roberts was soon overshadowed by allegations regarding the *use* of funds within PTL, as well as the sexual behavior of Jim Bakker and associates. As those who had complained about the lack of accountability of many religious groups might have predicted, PTL had used significant portions of donors' dollars for large salaries and opulent living quarters for Jim and Tammy Bakker. The PTL controversy continued as questions were raised about Jerry Falwell's motives in becoming Bakker's temporary replacement. During this period (and continuing into 1988), PTL's fund-raising appeals dropped all pretense that donations would be used for any purpose other than organizational survival. Although less publicized, Robert Schuller (of "Hour of Power") was also the subject of allegations in 1987. He was accused of misleading communication to donors and criticized for excessive hiring of relatives.[51]

In addition to the controversy about PTL, 1988 was marked by revelations that Jimmy Swaggart, one of the most vocal critics of Oral Roberts and Jim Bakker, had been involved in liaisons with a prostitute. Though ethical questions about the collection and use of donations were not involved in the allegations, it became clear that Swaggart would defy disciplinary action from his denomination partly because his absence from the pulpit (and the airwaves) would jeopardize the continuing flow of contributions to his organization.

Fund raisers for religious and many other kinds of organizations had reason for concern with the events of 1987 and 1988. These well-publicized episodes had the potential for raising serious questions on the part of possible donors about the tactics used by fund raisers and the possibility that funds would be used for individual enrichment or organizational maintenance rather than the goals emphasized in fund-raising appeals. By May 12, 1987, the Christian Broadcasting Network, which had not been accused of financial irregularities, reported that it had lost $12 million in revenue. In March 1987 (before allegations had been made about him), Robert Schuller's "Hour of Power" collected $2,753,212—about $900,000 less than in the preceding March.[52]

The scandals also introduced possibilities for tighter regulation and closer scrutiny. For example, in early 1988, the Internal Revenue Service implemented a new act of Congress (the "Pickle" law) with a regulation requiring nonprofit organizations to provide at their offices, to anyone requesting it, a copy of IRS Form 990, which provides detailed information on an organization's finances and the salaries of its top officials. According to *Christianity Today,*

"Some observers credit the new regulation to post-PTL ministry-reform efforts."[53] On a more positive note, the scandals also set the stage for more effective self-regulation. The Evangelical Council for Financial Accountability added 100 new members—about a 30 percent increase—in 1987. Their president stated that the PTL affair "spurred our growth like nothing else."[54] In addition, the board of National Religious Broadcasters approved a code of ethics that would require disclosure of all sources of income and all expenditures.[55] Apparently, increasing numbers of religious broadcasters believe that they stand to gain by codes of ethics enforced by professional associations.

Raising Funds Through Marketing. While many of the controversies of the late 1980s centered on religion, trends in religious fund raising largely mirrored those occurring in the society as a whole. During the 1980s, several events and trends combined to raise the apprehensions of fund raisers. Fund-raising executive Daniel Hansler observed that fund raisers were forced to become "better marketers" during the 1980s because of (1) the tax reform act, which reformed the financial incentive for some charitable contributions; (2) increasing numbers of nonprofits competing for funds; and (3) a new "baby boomer" generation, which while not necessarily less altruistic than its predecessors, was less responsive to traditional appeals. Hansler asserts that fund raisers must adapt to this environment by becoming more responsive to "the needs and hot buttons of the various donor markets,"[56] as well as by becoming more accountable for the results produced by their organization. In his view, worthy causes alone are inadequate to attract the attention and loyalty of potential donors.

Hansler's view was hardly revolutionary by the time he had expressed it. Several years earlier, Nelson Rosenbaum, president of the Center for Responsive Governance, had sparked some controversy by saying that nonprofits must become more businesslike and face a "survival of the fittest" scenario.[57] In the meantime, such events as the Statue of Liberty restoration had shown that the line between business and philanthropy could become very thin. In the Statue of Liberty case, American Express Travel Related Services agreed for one fiscal quarter to contribute one cent to the statue's restoration fund every time its card was used—record profits were posted for that quarter.[58]

Within this climate, telemarketing, the use of premiums, and similar techniques all received increased emphasis among religious and nonreligious fund raisers alike. Interestingly, both Jimmy Swaggart Ministries[59] and the 700 Club[60] were presented by *Fund Raising Management* as exemplary in their use of such techniques. As two fund raisers noted: "The distinction between *not-for*-profit and *for*-profit is growing less and less clear as the non-profit sector mimics the organization, management, and outlook of the private sector."[61]

Many viewed these trends as healthy because of their presumed association with accountability and efficiency. Others, however, have expressed the fear that the priorities of organizations and their leaders might become distorted in the process. In response to an apparent fear that religious fund raisers would begin emulating the life-styles of corporate executives, Bruce Wilkinson (president of Walk Thru the Bible Ministries) told delegates to the Development Association for Christian Institutes, "Your life-style should reflect your calling. Fancy cars and $6,000 rings are out of place."[62] Interestingly, the editor of *Christian Century* has argued that PTL's problems should be considered a corporate rather than a religious story. Describing televangelists as "entrepreneurs who have manipulated modern technology into a collection of financial fiefdoms," he says that enterprises "will finally be judged according to their adherence to the biblical tradition, the tradition of the church's life and practice, and the results realized in the lives of their supporters."[63]

Organization theorist Philip Selznick has argued that organizations should avoid "institutional surrender," the adoption of expedient steps that violate their missions.[64] Wall's argument would suggest that this is precisely what happened to some televangelists. As he notes, however, the PTL experience parallels that of many organizations outside the realm of religion.

As has already been seen, marketing emphases on the part of religious organizations may have driven some to cross the line between ethical and unethical practices, but this, too, is a reflection of broader societal trends. For example, several organizations that claim to protect and expand Social Security and Medicare benefits have been accused of sending out misleading mailings that lead potential donors to believe that they have received official government notices.[65]

When such practices are discovered, they likely erode trust and increase pressure for tighter regulation of nonprofits in general. The misleading mailings are likely to cause more stringent postal regulations.[66] This parallels the role of PTL's experiences in leading to tougher IRS regulations for all nonprofits.

While most popular attention has been focused on nonprofits that appear to be engaging in unethical behavior, some observers have expressed concern that a market-driven approach may be damaging even for those nonprofits that maintain formal standards of ethics and accountability. Gurin has expressed the fear that commercialization threatens an organization's integrity in the sense that it may lose its ability to keep its larger objectives in sight.[67] Baker and Murray[68] argue that representatives of nonprofits may become so involved in the details of management that they lose their ability to perceive or to articulate "the mission and high ideals" represented by their organization. In addition, they fear that a business-like orientation will affect contributors who will begin making contributions for their private advantage rather than altruism: "If we ask people to invest, they will invest where the yield is highest; if we ask them to give, they will give where the need is greatest."[69]

Religion's Potential for Transforming the Climate of Giving. According to some observers, a tendency to view giving as an investment (noted above as a matter of concern) is nothing new in the United States. Robert Reich has stated that "charitable" programs increasingly involve a redistribution of resources among the comfortable. When resources are transferred to the less comfortable (for example, the poor), it is assumed that they will be handled irresponsibly. As a result, degrading and damaging standards of accountability are imposed even as the proportion of resources devoted to such groups contracts.[70]

One procedure that has been proposed for reducing the perception of "us" versus "them" involves focusing benevolence on the community level or making similar use of intermediate groups. Benevolence within such settings has the potential for enhancing the realization of interdependence between suppliers and recipients of aid. Unfortunately, Reich notes, communities and groups are often so homogenous or stratified in terms of their inhabitants or participants that they are inappropriate settings for a genuine redistribution of benefits. "The idea of community as neighborhood offered a way of enjoying the sentiment of benevolence without the burden of acting on it. Since responsibility ended at the borders of one's neighborhood, and most Americans could rest assured that their neighbors were not in dire straits, the apparent requirements of charity could be exhausted at small cost. If the inhabitants of another neighborhood needed help, they should look to one another; let them solve their own problems, and we'll solve our own. The poor, meanwhile, clustered in their own, isolated neighborhoods."[71]

The dilemma posed by Reich's analysis is how to draw on feelings of community without encouraging people to think of the community only in terms of those who share their socioeconomic characteristics. Religion, which is never explicitly discussed by Reich, may, under some circumstances, provide such encouragement. Traditionally, religions have focused attentions and loyalties on small communities of believers and their deities. As Bryan Wilson notes, however, the "great religions" have involved efforts to broaden the scope of thinking to include much larger populations.[72] While the success of such efforts has been limited, religion in some versions may play a role in efforts to draw on the strength of group processes without creating the belief that those beyond the small group's boundaries are less worthy.

In other versions, of course, religion may exacerbate tendencies to view the world in terms of "us" versus "them." This is particularly true for those groups that interpret social problems in terms of the individual shortcomings of those who have not been converted to the right way of life.[73] When such conceptualizations are accepted by privileged sectors of society, it is unlikely that systems of social benevolence will enhance the dignity of the recipients of aid. Ironically, however, the consequences of such belief systems may be very different if they are held by the less privileged members of society. Unity achieved on the basis of exclusionist religious beliefs may lead to the group solidarity necessary for less privileged groups to survive in a repressive society. Within recent American history, the black church may serve as the best-known example of an institution that has often been the focus for movements leading to empowerment, but this is not a new phenomenon. Writing of radical religious movements during seventeenth-century England, Christopher Hill has noted: "The theory of justification by faith helped men to live because of the inner hope it gave. It is a *relatively* democratic theory: the elect form a spiritual aristocracy, which bears no relation to the worldly aristocracy of birth. The theory gave a select group of the underprivileged third estate sufficient courage, conviction and sense of unity with each other to be able to force their way towards religious and political freedom by means of a tightly disciplined organization."[74]

Reich argues that "altruism" should be replaced by "solidarity."[75] While his emphasis is on the solidarity of society as a whole, solidarity within less privileged groups can be an important step toward their meaningful participation in the larger society. Because of its symbolic and organizational resources, religion can enhance the development of such solidarity.

Considerable publicity during the 1980s focused on violations of ethical standards by leaders of several religious organizations. Ultimately, however, the ethical implications of religion for public and private philanthropy may be broader than the scandals of the 1980s would suggest. Without dismissing the possibility that religion will simply fade into irrelevancy, we also note that it could either promote reflection among the privileged about the ethical implications of systems of benevolence or allow recipients of aid to develop the solidarity to survive ethically questionable systems of assistance.

Cultural Drifts Detrimental to Philanthropy. Cultural drifts are those gradual changes in society that add up to major changes in values and life-styles. Consumerism, "spectatorism," and changes in women's rights and roles are examples of far-reaching drifts that affect people's perceptions of the discretionary time and money they have to give to philanthropic causes.

In the early decades of the twentieth century, the American economy became increasingly dependent on the production and consumption of consumer goods. Advertising began to encourage a growing ethic of consumerism. According to Freedman and D'Emilio, this ethic "also fostered an acceptance of pleasure, self-gratification, and personal satisfaction."[76] The developing consumer culture was a powerful force undermining "the old middle-class values of hard work and self-denial and fostered a new ethic of determined hedonism."[77]

From watching American television or observing any of the other manifestations of Madison Avenue's understanding of what motivates Americans, one could easily become depressed about the future of either religion or philanthropy. The challenge is real precisely because each person does have selfish values as well as selfless ones. However, though far more advertising money is spent on trying to induce people to act from selfishness than is spent trying to bring out our selfless values, churches and voluntary associations provide social network anchors for selfless values that are far more effective than advertising.

Television viewing commands a large proportion of Americans' discretionary time. The average American now watches more than thirty hours of television per week.[78] The vast majority of viewing hours are of programs that can be classified as entertainment. Moreover, Robinson has demonstrated that people who spend more time watching TV spend less time participating in organizations.[79] One study presents evidence that TV viewing uses the largest proportion of Americans' free time—31 percent, compared to 27 percent for socializing and conversation, 14 percent for other mass media use, and 5 percent for religion and organizations.[80] Since there is good evidence that the average American spends less than an hour a week helping other people in the community, it appears that time spent watching entertainment TV is currently twenty-five to thirty times that spent in helping others in the community. We can take heart, however, in Robinson's finding that TV is the first daily activity people would sacrifice if something more important came along.

The changes in women's roles that have directed more and more women into full-time careers outside the home have an important impact on churches' ability to deliver volunteers to community agencies. These changes include increasing numbers of families for whom a woman is the breadwinner, and an economic situation that for most families requires two incomes to achieve the standard of living most Americans have come to expect. The increased desire and opportunity for women to have paid careers, together with a strong feminist reaction against volunteer work as a symbol of the exploitation of women, also inhibit churches' ability to provide volunteers.

According to Kaminer: "Today the career volunteer looks and often says she feels like a dinosaur. Over one half of all the women and over one half of all the wives in this country work for money. Women head over nine million of America's families and comprise 43 percent of the paid labor force. Economic hardships and the emergence of a popular feminist movement have made paid work a cultural norm even for married women, for the first time, and made equal pay and equal employment opportunities for all women matters of rights as well as necessity."[81]

However, looking primarily at middle- and upper-class women, on whom the feminist movement had most effect, Kaminer concludes that these women are coming back to a positive view of volunteerism, though as a supplement rather than as a substitute for paid careers. "Even a prestigious, highly paid job is rarely worth more than what it buys, rarely what we would choose to do if all our time were our own. Volunteering still has something to offer a professional woman—the freedom to choose her own work, to pursue a cause or a passion, or simply to relax in a job she can shape and control, to experiment and enjoy herself. Volunteering is a chance to do her own work instead of someone else's, and it can serve her well as she takes her place in the 'real' world of men and money. Women who combine paid work and volunteering have always known that the two are not incompatible but complementary. There is no inherent conflict between paid work and volunteering, no need to abandon one to embrace the other."[82]

Implications for Practitioners in Philanthropic Organizations

Leadership. Whether materialistic values will increasingly displace selfless values within Americans' value repertoires depends in large part on the nature and quality of leadership in the churches and other voluntary associations that command so much of the attention, time, and energy of the American people. Wood has argued that value-based leadership so often found in churches can apply as well to a whole range of voluntary organizations, probably including all philanthropic organizations.[83] For example, just as church leaders appeal to biblical values to pull their members into actions that help others, civil rights organizations can appeal to the First Amendment, the Bill of Rights, and concepts within the Declaration of Independence. Leaders can help members look beyond themselves to others whether it is to create jobs in the present or to preserve the environment for future generations. This type of leadership has implications for member socialization as well as for the way appeals to members are cast. The more strongly members hold the organization's values, the more responsive they will be to a value-based appeal.

But leaders have to do more than raise consciousnesses of selfless values; they have to design organizational structures so that members are plugged into groups and committees that provide information and opportunities to act out those values, both in giving money and in giving time. INDEPENDENT SECTORS's Daring Goals for a Caring Society is an ambitious attempt to do this on a national scale. Almost every local community, in addition to religious organizations, already has a number of youth-oriented, civic, fraternal, and cultural organizations that, given proper leadership, can play the role of plugging individuals into the community's efforts to promote human welfare.

Offering Appropriate Incentives. Knoke and Wood[84] have shown that an organization's incentive systems are important to the development of member commitment. Value-based leadership offers normative or purposive incentives. There may be other incentives appropriate to carrying out the objectives of philanthropic organizations. For example, the fun and fellowship often associated with fund-raising activities or volunteer projects may be an important motivator and are entirely appropriate so long as they are in good taste. However, it is important to note that a study by Knoke[85] demonstrates that the offering of material incentives for participation in purposive organizations may recruit members who are not committed to realizing the purposes of the organization. Such members can be a particular problem when controversies over policies arise. Moreover, if Kaminer is right, the growing cadre of working women, especially the professionals, are more likely to be induced by the offer of meaningful volunteer activities that accomplish important societal purposes.

Building Legitimacy in the Community. The organization's reputation in the community is dependent on raising the general public's consciousness of its values and demonstrating that the organization indeed pursues those values. Just as televangelists' base of support erodes rapidly if they are found diverting funds for selfish purposes, philanthropic organizations will lose community support if they use funds inconsistently with their appeals. Legitimacy in the community is enhanced by stress on accountability, including the release each year of an audited financial statement that fully discloses the sources of funds, how they were spent, and the proportion of each dollar that goes directly to further the announced cause. Belonging to appropriate accrediting groups with codes of ethics or subscribing to the standards of such groups (for example, the National Charities Information Bureau) will also enhance legitimacy.

Board Development. Obviously, the professional or top volunteer leaders of philanthropic organizations cannot carry out their leadership tasks alone. Fortunately, there is an encouraging trend to give more attention to the selection, recruitment, training, and motivation of governing boards. Board members who, upon recruitment, are challenged to devote considerable time and money to the cause and who are promised the training and access to information that allow them to participate effectively become an essential part of the organization's leadership.

Addressing Controversial Issues. The accomplishment of each of the above objectives is more problematic when the philanthropic organization takes on controversial causes. Current examples of such causes include civil rights, abortion (either an anti-abortion or a pro-choice position), and support for Israel or for the Palestinians.

In addition to leadership strategies that stress values, it may be helpful for the organization to associate itself with a coalition of larger organizations that support the controversial cause (as mainline denominations have associated themselves with the National Council of Churches). At least some of the negative public response might then be diverted to the coalition. In any event, the organization would not stand alone in the face of controversy. Where policies are controversial among the members themselves, national church bodies have effectively employed revenue-sharing strategies that allow the local groups some control over the particular forms of action in their own communities.

In the long run, organizations, both religious and secular, may contribute most to philanthropy when they create those conditions in which people can debate important issues face-to-face with others with whom they have formed common bonds. Several organization studies have shown that some religious congregations do an especially good job of providing such a forum.[86] Other organizations can learn from religious ones that a strong attachment to universalistic values provides a basis for constructive resolution of the differences that inevitably arise when a group seeks actively to promote human welfare.

Notes

1.   "God and the American People: 95% Today Are 'Believers.'" *Emerging Trends,* June 1985, 7, 1; "4 in 10 Adults Attended Church in Typical Week of 1987." *Emerging Trends,* Jan. 1988, *10,* 1.
2.   AAFRC Trust for Philanthropy, *Giving USA.* New York: AAFRC Trust for Philanthropy, 1987.
3.   James R. Wood, *Leadership in Voluntary Organizations.* New Brunswick, N.J.: Rutgers University Press, 1981.
4.   Wood.
5.   Presbyterian Church (USA), *The Presbyterian Congregation Profile Study, Report Number One.* Louisville, Ky.: Research Unit, Presbyterian Church (USA), n.d.
6.   James R. Wood and Elton Jackson, "Religion and Public-

Spirited Behavior in Indiana: A Research Report." Unpublished report to Lilly Endowment, 1987.

7. Gunnar Myrdal and others, *An American Dilemma: The Negro Problem and Modern Democracy*. New York: Harper & Row, 1963.

8. Arnold Rose, *The Negro in America*. Boston: Beacon Press, 1948, p. 2. This book is Rose's condensation of the much larger book *The American Dilemma* by Myrdal.

9. Milton Rokeach, *The Nature of Human Values*. New York: Free Press, 1973.

10. Robert N. Bellah, Richard Madsen, William M. Sullivan, Ann Swidler, and Steven M. Tipton, *Habits of the Heart*. New York: Harper & Row, 1986, p. 10.

11. L. D. Nelson and Russell Dynes, "The Impact of Devotionalism and Attendance on Ordinary and Emergency Helping Behavior." *Journal for the Scientific Study of Religion*, March 1976, *15*, 47-59.

12. The program is described in a brochure, *Daring Goals for a Caring Society—A Blueprint for Substantial Growth in Giving and Volunteering in America*. Washington, D.C.: INDEPENDENT SECTOR, 1986. The blueprint described draws heavily on churches; still, the net effect of the program could be to better equip society to carry on philanthropic activities with the churches playing a less prominent role than they now play.

13. Honeywell report.

14. Kenneth D. Hart, "Emerging Patterns of Volunteerism." *Canadian Business Review*, Spring 1987, p. 15.

15. Kathleen L. Leonard, "Corporate Volunteers Cooperate in New York City." *Public Relations Quarterly*, Fall 1984, *29*, 11-17.

16. Leonard.

17. Katherine Maddox McElroy and John J. Siegfried, "The Effects of Firm Size and Mergers on Corporate Philanthropy." In Betty Bock, J. Harvey Goldschmid, Ira M. Millstein, and F. M. Sherer (eds.), *The Impact of the Modern Corporation*. New York: Columbia University Press, 1984, pp. 99-138.

18. Lawrence A. Wien, "Commentary." In Bock, Goldschmid, Millstein, and Sherer, pp. 141–147.

19. Joseph Galaskiewicz, *Social Organization of an Urban Grants Economy: A Study of Business Philanthropy and Nonprofit Organizations.* Orlando, Fla.: Academic Press, 1985.

20. McElroy and Siegfried, p. 106.

21. McElroy and Siegfried, p. 123.

22. McElroy and Siegfried, pp. 124–125.

23. However, McElroy and Siegfried found that the situation was more complicated than this (based on managers' estimates of the impact of 115 mergers on contributions in the cities that had been headquarters before the acquisition). "Forty-one percent were reported to have increased contributions in the former headquarters city, 21 percent were thought to have reduced contributions, and 38 percent reported no impact of the acquisition on contributions. Somewhat surprisingly, acquisitions were reported to *increase* contributions in a metropolitan area losing corporate headquarters at a two-to-one rate. The reason is that most mergers involve a large firm with a substantial, systematic contributions program that acquires a smaller firm with a small, unstructured contributions history. . . . Although a larger firm may have a smaller contributions to profit ratio than the smaller acquired firm, this fraction times a much larger total contributions budget than the smaller firm's may generate a larger absolute amount of contributions for the former headquarters city" (p. 126).

24. Bevis Longstreth, "Commentary." In Bock, Goldschmid, Millstein, and Sherer.

25. Longstreth, p. 151.

26. James Davison Hunter, *American Evangelicalism: Conservative Religion and the Quandary of Modernity.* New Brunswick, N.J.: Rutgers University Press, 1983. Hunter has said that contemporary evangelicals are characterized by their adherence to (1) the belief that the Bible is the inerrant Word of God, (2) the belief in the divinity of Christ, and (3) the belief in the efficacy of Christ's life, death, and physical resurrection for the salvation of the human soul.

27. Hunter, p. 41.

28. Hunter, p. 68.

29. Hunter, p. 98.

30. Phillip E. Hammond, "Another Great Awakening?" In Robert C. Liebman and Robert Wuthnow (eds.), *The New Christian Right.* New York: Aldine, 1983, pp. 207–223.

31. George M. Marsden, *Fundamentalism and American Culture: The Shaping of the Twentieth Century Evangelicalism, 1870–1925.* New York: Oxford University Press, 1980.

32. Donald Heinz, "The Struggle to Define America." In Liebman and Wuthnow, pp. 133–148.

33. J. Alan Winter, "Political Activism Among the Clergy: Sources of a Deviant Role." *Review of Religious Research,* Spring 1973, *14,* 178–186.

34. Robert Wuthnow, "The Political Rebirth of American Evangelicals." In Liebman and Wuthnow, pp. 167–185.

35. Wuthnow, p. 184.

36. Robert C. Liebman, "The Making of the New Christian Right." In Liebman and Wuthnow, pp. 227–238.

37. Richard Quebedeaux, *The Worldly Evangelicals.* New York: Harper & Row, 1978.

38. Hunter, pp. 7–9.

39. Hunter, pp. 7–9.

40. Stuart Rothenberg and Frank Newport, *The Evangelical Voter: Religion and Politics in America.* Washington, D.C.: The Institute for Government and Politics of the Free Congress Research and Education Foundation, 1984. Rothenberg and Newport, for example, have noted the following results from their 1983 nationwide survey: "A majority [of evangelicals] support voluntary school prayer in the public schools and tuition tax credits, but they also support the Equal Rights Amendment and the dissemination of birth control information in the public schools. Slight pluralities favor both increased defense spending and the nuclear freeze, but there are high levels of opposition to both. This ideological hodgepodge holds true even for the more religious or fundamentalist subsamples" (pp. 149–150).

41. Joseph Tamney and Stephen Johnson, "The Moral Majority

in Middletown." *Journal for the Scientific Study of Religion,* June 1983, *22,* 145–157.

42. "Avoid Manipulative Techniques in Fund Raising." Special conference report in *Fund Raising Management,* May 1986, *17,* 70–71.

43. Private communication.

44. "Striking the Right Balance Between Mission and Premiums." *Fund Raising Management,* Feb. 1985, *15,* 26–36.

45. "Swaggart Criticizes Oral Roberts' Life-Extension Plea as 'Spiritual Extortion.'" *Fund Raising Management,* Mar. 1987, *18,* 11–12.

46. "Swaggart Criticizes," p. 12.

47. William Olcott, "Fund Raisers Are Accountable." *Fund Raising Management,* Mar. 1987, *18,* 5.

48. "Will Falwell Move from Lynchburg, Virginia?" *Fund Raising Management,* Nov. 1986, *17,* 12–14.

49. "Swaggart Criticizes," p. 11.

50. "Swaggart Criticizes," p. 12.

51. "Problems for Schuller." *Christian Century,* Sept. 30, 1987, *104,* 818.

52. "Scandals Take Toll." *Christian Century,* July 1–8, 1987, *104,* 585.

53. "More Scrutiny for Nonprofits." *Christianity Today,* Mar. 4, 1988, *32,* 48.

54. "The Televangelist Fiasco: Top '87 Religion Story." *Christian Century,* Dec. 23–30, 1987, *104,* 1163–1165.

55. "Ethics Code for NRB." *Christian Century,* Oct. 7, 1987, *104,* 849.

56. Daniel F. Hansler, "Must Non-Profits Be Market-Driven?" *Fund Raising Management,* Dec. 1984, *17,* 78–79.

57. Nelson Rosenbaum, "Non-Profits Urged to Try Business Approach." *Fund Raising Management,* Aug. 1982, *13,* 47.

58. Daniel Philip Baker and John J. Murray, "The Business of Philanthropy: Have We Gone Too Far?" *Fund Raising Management,* Jan. 1986, *16,* 68–72.

59. "Testing Telemarketing Reveals Donor Efficiencies." *Fund Raising Management,* Nov. 1984, *15,* 50–63.

60. "Striking the Right Balance Between Mission and Premiums." *Fund Raising Management*, Feb. 1985, *15*, 26–36.

61. Baker and Murray, p. 68.

62. "'DACI' Meeting Accents Donors, Telemarketing, Finances." *Fund Raising Management*, Aug. 1986, *17*, 66.

63. James M. Wall, "The Fall of the House of Bakker." *Christian Century*, Apr. 8, 1987, *104*, 323–324.

64. Philip Selznick, *Leadership in Administration*. New York: Harper & Row, 1957.

65. Michael B. Scanlon, "Congress, Senior Citizens and Misleading Direct Mail." *Fund Raising Management*, Jan. 1986, *18*, 31–36.

66. Scanlon.

67. Maurice G. Gurin, "Is Marketing Dangerous for Fund Raising?" *Fund Raising Management*, Jan. 1987, *17*, 72–76.

68. Baker and Murray.

69. Baker and Murray, p. 72.

70. Robert B. Reich, *Tales of a New America*. New York: Times Books, 1987.

71. Reich, p. 171.

72. Bryan Wilson, *Religion in Sociological Perspective*. New York: Oxford University Press, 1982.

73. Meredith B. McGuire, *Religion: The Social Context*. Belmont, Calif.: Wadsworth, 1981.

74. Christopher Hill, *The World Turned Upside Down*. Harmondsworth, Middlesex, England: Penguin Books, 1975.

75. Reich, p. 287.

76. John D'Emilio and Estelle B. Freedman, *Intimate Matters*. New York: Harper & Row, 1988.

77. Barbara Ehrenreich, "Intimate Matters." *New York Times Book Review*, Apr. 24, 1988, p. 7:33.

78. Mark S. Hoffman (ed.), *The World Almanac and Book of Facts: 1988*. New York: Pharos Books, 1988, p. 361.

79. John P. Robinson, *How Americans Use Time*. New York: Praeger, 1977.

80. Cobbett S. Steinberg, *Viewing Habits and Attitudes*. New York: Facts on File, 1980.

81. Wendy Kaminer, *Women Volunteering*. New York: Anchor Press, 1984, p. 2.
82. Kaminer, p. 216.
83. Wood.
84. David Knoke and James R. Wood, *Organized for Action*. New Brunswick, N.J.: Rutgers University Press, 1981.
85. David Knoke, "Organizational Incentives." *American Sociological Review*, June 1988, *53*, 311–329.
86. James R. Wood, "Leaders, Values and Societal Change." In James R. Andrews, *Public Speaking*. New York: Macmillan, 1987, pp. 271–280.

Chapter 6   *Justin Fink*

Philanthropy
and the Community

~~~~~~~~~~~~~~~~~~~~~~~~~~~~~~~~~~~~

Despite our abiding faith in America's promise of equal opportunity and upward mobility through individual initiative, many people in both urban and rural America still are not making it. During
the same period of the 1980s in which the Dow topped 2,700, estimates of homeless people living on New York City streets were as
high as 35,000, and some forty new soup kitchens had appeared in
Philadelphia. In the 1980s, Harrington's "other America" became
Wilson's "permanent underclass."[1] Only those who were leading
the most affluently insular lives could dispute the assertion that the
proportion of those among us who were living in poverty had increased. Also increasingly difficult to maintain was the faith that
the needs of the poor and the civil rights of the elderly, women,
minorities, and the disabled would ultimately be addressed through
the magic of the marketplace in an era of governmental laissez-faire.

At the same time, our two other mechanisms for social provision and reform, government and private philanthropy, were con-
founded by transition and uncertainty. Not only had public
funding for human services declined overall, but research showed

Note: Quotations not otherwise cited in this chapter are drawn from a five-
year study by the author. Names have been fictionalized. The author also
gratefully acknowledges the contributions to this chapter of Calvin
McCants, executive director of the Institute for Nonprofit Management
Training, and Howard University, Washington, D.C.

a clear decline in public dollars targeted to the indigent in favor of services provided to the middle class.[2]

As for philanthropy, the news was both good and not so encouraging. *Giving USA*, the annual chronicle of charitable activity, estimated a remarkable $104 billion in donations during 1988.[3] However, while individual giving was up, other evidence charted a leveling of corporate giving[4] and contributions to religion,[5] as well as a serious concern about the rate of foundation formation.[6] Most discouraging perhaps were the reports of the Conference Board[7] showing philanthropic giving to health and human services having dropped for more than a decade in terms of total share, and coming back only modestly in 1988.[8] Finally, a study by the Council on Foundations reported future corporate CEOs as being "less committed to philanthropy."[9] Seemingly, these trends imperil our ability to make up for a loss of public dollars for charitable work through private giving.

The first responses to acute or emergent social needs have often come from forces at the community level closest to those needs. Local networks and community-based organizations (CBOs)—as opposed to large public or private institutions—have repeatedly provided the seedbed for new forms of social provision as well as an impetus for social reform. For small and large communities, and often society as a whole, grass-roots voluntary action tends to function as a civic early warning system by calling attention to problems and providing some degree of initial intervention.

Yet if it can be said that the cutting edge of responsiveness to social problems is still found close to home, how sanguine can we be about the efficacy of that tradition in an increasingly complex social environment? In the present chapter we turn attention to some of the flashpoints in relations between those newly forming groups who seek philanthropic support and those who have it to give. The big concern here is *the ability of those at the lower end of the "nonprofit market" to make an effective case for support and to access the resources of those at the high end who can afford to be generous.* The aim is to underscore some of the factors that constrain philanthropy's ability to help support a community's responses to acute social needs and problems and to nurture social justice through local voluntary action. This larger issue revolves around several key questions:

1. What ideological forces are working to condition the success of emerging community nonprofits whose mission is focused on underserved or disenfranchised constituencies?
2. What developments in community organization life are affecting the ability of emerging and smaller groups to compete for support? For instance, what are the implications of increasing professionalization and organizational and technical complexity for grass-roots efforts on behalf of groups such as low-income and minority communities, women, the elderly, and the disabled?
3. What are some of the barriers that voluntary organizations at the grass roots face as they seek philanthropic support? And given an ever more crowded field of voluntary action, shifting social values, and inevitable limits to the growth of philanthropy, what are the prospects for inclusiveness and fairness in the distribution of philanthropic resources?

Philanthropy and voluntarism are vague and often fuzzy concepts that need to be clarified. While individual donors, corporate contributors, and foundation officers, United Way donors and leaders, and religious benefactors of public service do not comprise a monolithic or unitary phenomenon, they can be seen to comprise the donative side of philanthropy. Leaders of voluntary organizations, community activists, and advocates for a plethora of causes, programs, and services might be said to be their less patient, supplicant counterparts. In keeping with the focus of the present volume, we are looking, then, at emerging, often small organizations, mainly at the community level, that are engaged in voluntary association, service, and giving for the public good but whose constituencies represent traditionally disadvantaged or disenfranchised groups and causes.

Finally, today neither the fate of community-based groups nor the vicissitudes of philanthropy can realistically be discussed apart from trends in public funding. In light of the historical impact of governmental funding on voluntary service activity at the community level, we will give some attention to public support as we examine the evolution, status, and prospects of community-based organizations. The first section will attempt to clarify some of the ideological issues that remain very much a part of the contemporary debate. A second section looks at some of the changes community-based organizations have undergone. Succeeding pages examine challenges small nonprofits face as they attempt to address changing community needs, along with current trends that may ultimately serve to condition the fate of voluntary service at the grass-roots level.

The Ideological Context: Philanthropists and Activists Face Persistent Ambiguities—Together

In earlier times, social action on behalf of the indigent and the mentally ill, the abolition of slavery and the achievement of civil rights, and attempts to bring about reforms in child welfare and education were all rooted in local voluntary action. For newcomers to American society, mutual aid societies and fraternal organizations served as a means for survival, assimilation, and the retention of cultural identity and ties.

Throughout the 1980s that tradition of local voluntary action continued to be manifest in such actions as the attempts of community-based organizations to improve deteriorating urban neighborhoods and the environment, and the early response of churches and volunteer community groups to the needs of the homeless and the victims of AIDS. At the beginning of the decade it was estimated that, throughout the United States, thousands of community-based organizations and civic groups were tax-exempt and countless others were informally organized. As someone has observed, Americans will give "to build something, to fight something, or to save something."[10]

America's "voluntary spirit" has, of course, been celebrated time and again as a reflection of participatory democracy and pluralistic expansiveness, cutting across class, racial, and ethnic distinctions.[11] Community action through voluntarism has by no means been monopolized by liberal cadres. For every civil liberties group that advocates an expansionist or activist interpretation of constitutional rights barring school prayer, capital punishment, or religious displays on public property, there has been a counterpart conservative citizens' movement that takes the opposing view. Pro-choice groups are more than matched by right-to-life groups. Thus, for those of conservative, liberal, or moderate political views, local initiative through voluntary action and philanthropic work remains one of the most accessible and direct means for redress of social problems. In many ways, our tradition of grass-roots voluntary action seems healthy indeed.

At the same time, though, such a view tends to ignore important nuances of our charitable tradition, including some thorny and persistent ideological contradictions. Philanthropists and "philanthropoids," often collaborators but sometime antagonists, continue to share ambiguities and struggle to define the nature of their respective missions in an imperfect world. The distinguished historian of American philanthropy, Robert Bremner, begins his own landmark study by calling attention to this fact. He then proceeds to identify one of the most persistent points of ambiguity that continues to dog our best philanthropic impulses.

> The word philanthropy and the ideas it carries with it arouse mixed emotions in American breasts. Many Americans have been concerned lest their countrymen's generosity be abused. But on a deeper level there is something about philanthropy that seems to go against the democratic grain. We may be willing to help others, but we are not humble enough to appreciate the efforts of those who would bend down to help us. . . . We expect rich men to be generous with their wealth, and criticize them when they are not; but when they make benefaction, we question their motives, deplore the methods by which they obtained their abundance, and wonder whether their gifts will not do more harm than good. . . .
>
> Conservatives denounce "sentimental humanitarianism"; and radicals sneer at the "palliatives" offered by "mere philanthropic reform."[12]

Venerated as a national institution but also sometimes taken to task, our voluntary sector is an important and durable social adaptation. At best it is a means for spurring social progress in a society committed to sustaining individual political, religious, and economic rights—a society also enamored with the romance of individualism and self-reliance. As an alternative to collective action through market forces or government, the philanthropic enterprise has counteracted the tendency of the market to be subservient to the dictates of individual gain and of government to bow to the will and goals of the politically powerful. As Bremner is quick to add: "Whether we approve or disapprove of philanthropy, the fact remains that it has been one of the principal methods of social advance."[13]

Another historian, Michael Katz,[14] has ably shown through his work *In the Shadow of the Poorhouse* that during more than two centuries of national life Americans have tended to worry a great deal about whether their efforts to relieve suffering and degradation would instead result in its perpetuation. The "hand-up, hand-out" controversy remains the intellectual pivot for public policy debates regarding the preferred response to poverty. It also continues to figure largely in discussions concerning appropriate interventions by the private, voluntary sector. Clearly audible in the waves of rhetoric that inevitably accompany quadrennial presidential campaigns, these debates tend to invoke the big issues about the role of government, business, and other institutions in relation to individual economic and social upward mobility. This is the dilemma that a newly elected President Reagan framed in terms of the choice between "a social safety net or an entangling web of dependency," and that George Bush sought to resolve by invoking the image of "a thousand points of light."

Predictably, this ongoing dialectic bounces back and forth about every other generation. Crises such as those seen in the 1890s, 1930s, and 1960s provided sufficient interim resolution to enable reform. But these resolutions of the tug between beneficence and self-reliance have been fleeting. With time, new problems and crises emerge, and the old, competing ideological positions inevitably reemerge. Do-gooders, apologists, and iconoclasts alike—including those in the philanthropic arena—continue to fight the same ideological battle over and over again.

A subtler but even more fundamental point of ambivalence

continues to haunt the American love affair with doing good: are we about the *relief* of suffering or *reform* of conditions that underlie the distress of the unfortunate? As far back as the biblical culture of Judea, concepts of *tzedaka*, or charity, and *tikun olam*, representing social justice and reform or "repair of the world," have coexisted uneasily. In a working paper entitled "Major Challenges to Philanthropy,"[15] Robert Payton redefined this dilemma several years ago by identifying our efforts to do good as having two primary but distinct thrusts: that of *compassion*, identified with relief and the giving of charity, and that of *community*, reflected in efforts at civic improvement, social change, and reform. Payton underscores the fact that philanthropy "introduces compassion into community, but—and this has become increasingly important in the modern era—it is also a goad to the public conscience."[16] In his view "the philanthropic tradition is not just acts of benevolence; it is also a powerful lever of social change. It is the voice of discontent and dissatisfaction as well as the expression of nurture and encouragement."[17]

Those who doubt the continued emphasis in the 1990s upon social reform through voluntary means need only familiarize themselves with some of the thousands of groups of the political left, right, and center throughout the United States that are devoted to action around a variety of reform causes. Some of these include civil rights, labor, education, environmental preservation, health, child welfare, and myriad local civic concerns reflected in the so-called "neighborhoods movement."[18]

The view of voluntary organization as a vehicle for activism stands in contrast to the robust ideological and pragmatic arguments of others in favor of the role of the locally based nonprofit as primarily provider of community services.[19] The dual, sometimes conflicting, traditions of social action and social provision that surfaced in the settlement and community action movements are very much with us and remain largely unresolved. And so while policymakers at some of our nation's foundations grapple with how to maximize the impact of relief efforts for the hungry and the homeless, "change not charity" remains the creed, and empowerment the policy, of alternative philanthropic enterprises such as the Funding Exchange.

A third and final thread of ambiguity weaves through the fabric of American social thought, and that concerns the meaning of fairness. Does our concept of fairness favor preserving individual economic initiative, or mandating some degree of redistribution? It is the liberal's dilemma wherein the imperative of equity butts against the prerogatives of efficiency.[20] Notions of individual economic initiative, a free marketplace, and property right continue to form the ideological bedrock upon which American public policy is built. As a vehicle for the expression of impulses toward charity and civic good, voluntarism, its values, and its institutions continue to provide a counterpoint to even more powerful notions of private self-interest that underlie the business ethic.

In his attempt to explain away the seeming contradiction with which individualistic Americans so often embrace collective life through associations, it was, of course, Tocqueville who conjured up the concept of "self-interest rightly understood." In doing so he provided a rubric for understanding the peculiar genius with which American society has so often reconciled incompatible ideals of economic freedom and worldly compassion.

Historically, a worsening of social conditions and a deteriorating climate for business have preceded every period of social reform, including the Progressive era, the Great Depression, and the Great Society. There is good historical evidence to support the theory that none of these waves of reform could have proceeded without the knowing endorsement of our economic establishment.[21] The efficiency versus equity argument still tends to provide the rhetorical basis for our ongoing social policy debate and our periodic struggle to redefine the true, long-term interests of America's corpus economicus. In between times, though, it is the institution of philanthropy that carries the torch for compassion, if not always outright reform.

Our philanthropic impulses, it follows, are governed by our own ideological ambivalence and buffered by prevailing beliefs about public policy and private interest. In recent years the close interrelationship between public policy and the so-called voluntary sector has become axiomatic.[22] Going far beyond matters of taxation and regulation, interdependence becomes apparent in the ways in which government relies upon private auspices to implement policy pertaining to such things as commerce, public safety, health and human services, community development, education, and the arts. This interdependence is documented in the degree to which nonprofit community service organizations depend on public dollars.[23] As Nielsen among others has noted, such views persuasively challenge the image of vaunted independence of a voluntary sector that has actually operated in close collaboration and in parallel with government since colonial times.[24]

In the United States, during the reform period of the 1960s and early 1970s, a more or less new class of community-based organizations grew up, as either a direct or an indirect result of the availability of funding and in response to expanded demand for certain kinds of activities. In keeping with our tradition of voluntarism—or perhaps as a reflection of the voluntary groups that were then spearheading social change through the civil rights movement—government began to make available large sums of money for the pursuit of public policy goals. At that time, federal agencies initiated categorical funding programs that were to depend largely on local, private organizations to implement models originally created under philanthropic auspices such as the Ford Foundation to combat poverty. Thus, under the Economic Opportunity Act, Manpower Demonstration Act, and Title XX legislation, among others, literally thousands of new nongovernmental organizations were formed.

For a variety of reasons, community-based organizations were viewed as the preferred vehicle for targeting critically needed programs to the poorest and most underserved populations and for filling gaps in existing local service networks. On one hand, the voluntary organization was rooted in traditions of mutuality, ethnic and religious cohesiveness, and a predominance of relatively parochial purposes determined by the collective needs of a participant constituency. This alone could have made the CBO a prototype for grass-roots participation in the planning of services targeted to particular populations, such as minorities and the poor. On the other hand, a long history of social action through independent voluntary groups could be seen to lend itself to the goal of "maximum feasible participation," a means of redressing the imbalance of political power, seen by many as an underlying cause of poverty.

Sociological studies of voluntarism conducted in the period following World War II tended to downplay the degree of participation of low-income and minority groups in voluntary organization life. In fact, a tradition of philanthropy, voluntarism, and mutual aid within America's black population may be traced back over 200 years to the founding of the nation's first black Masonic lodge in Boston in 1787. More recently, research has begun to document the extent to which blacks,[25] Hispanics,[26] women,[27] Asians,[28] and other constituencies of low-income status or limited political power have historically generated their own voluntary institutions to respond to indigenous interests and needs. In fact, research by INDEPENDENT SECTOR has demonstrated that proportionally, those of low- and moderate-income status tend to give well in excess of the affluent.[29] To some extent, the emergence of community-based organizations can be understood as an extension of those traditions.

Such documentation tends to bolster our faith in the efficacy of voluntarism as an institution and as a means for philanthropic work at the community level. Over the years in locales throughout the country, we have seen the emergence of innumerable community-based organizations that represent the interests of low-income communities; minorities such as blacks, Hispanics, Asian-Americans, and Native Americans; or populations that lack service resources particular to their needs, such as women, the elderly, and the disabled. During the 1980s these organizations have been augmented by groups that address the plight of the homeless and people with AIDS. Many began with a mission of advocacy, but progressively they also assumed important roles in bridging the gap in available human service and cultural resources for underserved populations.

This development has not come about without a price. To some extent, more lofty but also somewhat diffuse goals for social change were replaced by program goals and objectives detailing projected units of service. As chroniclers of the Great Society such as Ralph Kramer have pointed out, the failure to clarify service or reform as an overriding priority in the 1960s was exacerbated in instances where both types of goals were pursued under the same organizational umbrella.[30] Nowhere were these conflicting goals more apparent than in community action agencies and their administrative progeny, the so-called "target area organization" or "delegate agency." In time, though, increasing competition in the nonprofit marketplace would largely obviate that issue and render social action an activity only marginally sought after by public and private funders.

This writer's own observations of community action programs, women's centers, and other ideologically oriented groups begun during the 1970s reaffirm those perceptions of a shift. If increased financial stability was achieved by some groups that made it through the Reagan years, many also faced more difficulty in responding to changing social conditions and needs as a result of the imperatives of sustaining funding arrangements. For those especially who sought to sustain themselves through the grants process, the nature of funding opportunities was such that newly emerging groups were very often pushed toward a kind of formalization that entailed increased professionalism in management and on volunteer boards, accountability, and adherence to management strictures. They were also pushed toward providing "hard services" at the expense of change-oriented activities.

To some extent, funder interest may have always served to undermine groups that seek political change. Looking back at grass-roots civil rights groups in the 1960s, Garrow has argued forcefully that it was the visibility of mid-1960s urban unrest and the threat of insurgent group activity that prompted philanthropic interest on the part of foundations in funding civil rights.[31] He convincingly demonstrates, though, that foundation support ultimately served to co-opt and undercut advocacy efforts by small but vociferous organizations such as SNCC by targeting more acceptable organizations and activities such as voter registration carried out by NAACP.

Searching for Stability in the Charity Market

Although community organizations continually face increased demands for service, they commonly struggle to achieve financial stability and to find adequate resources to grow in response to changing community needs. For an agency with a small budget, adding and sustaining even one new staffer at modest compensation can be a challenge. Although not commonly thought of as such, agency growth requires capital and entails several dimensions of risk. Programs are the "profit centers" of the nonprofit environment, and adding programs does offer some opportunity to further spread overhead. However, any agency that undertakes new or expanded programming without carefully assessing the potential for ongoing support is perhaps assuming too much. To add a new service in response to perceived community need generally means increased operations costs, even if volunteers are utilized, since volunteers require selection, training, and supervision. It also means an increased administrative burden and new expectations in terms of program achievements and accountability.

That community-based organizations are constrained by their ability to access seed capital and an ongoing base of support is a function of the nature and size of resource markets open to them. In particular, CBOs are customarily unable to draw from two of the largest sources of revenue most voluntary organizations seek to cover core costs, individual donors and earned income.

Few within community-based organizations, especially in low-income areas, are able to identify or access the kind of donor constituencies available to more upscale nonprofits, though these are the key to building financial stability. In this respect they are quite unlike their counterparts in the development offices of universities, hospitals, national charities, and well-heeled cultural organizations. Commonly lacking are sufficient staff time, development expertise, and resources to mount even a modest campaign. In addition, some who might be able to seek individual donors are restricted by their United Way membership from doing so.

Neither does earned income hold much promise. Fees for service are rare in small community service groups. At one time a hope was to generate monies through the development of businesses that could also spur opportunity for low-income constituents.[32] For most CBOs, though, this has proved to be not only rare but also a wholly inappropriate kind of activity. It is not just that the goals of social advocacy and business are at odds; it is also that the small organization is unable to function successfully as a small business. As an astute community action agency director noted: "I think that is a poor emphasis for an agency like ours. I think there are many other organizations in this community and in other communities that are much better able to run [small] business incubators and do that kind of thing. . . . We're basically service delivery, and they're asking us to push in a direction where our expertise really doesn't lie."

Despite the obstacles, thousands of community organizations formed during the 1960s and 1970s did in fact survive the 1980s against all odds. The survivors have been able to demonstrate the worthiness of their constituency's needs, and their critical role in meeting them, when they have been lucky enough to be situated in a local or regional environment of sufficiently rich and diverse institutional funding opportunities. The reality is that community organizations are first and foremost creatures of the grants economy.

The survivors have also learned that philanthropy must be approached as a process of exchange, even if, from their own point of view, it tends to be a buyer's market. CBOs exist only inasmuch as they are able to mediate between community needs and the concerns of funders and to sustain a program array with a diversified base of resources. Often, their maturation as organizations is reflected in a kind of professionalization and authority structure best suited to making swift and appropriately competitive responses to sudden opportunities or changing conditions. Under a structure that typically provides for nominal board leadership but strong, entreprenerurial agency executives who have often been rooted in the "days of the movement," many organizations have survived, stabilized, and grown.

Thus, as we move into the 1990s, we find the imperatives of organizational survival in the philanthropic marketplace very much dictating the terms under which agencies and funders do business together. The savvy agency executive director today realizes that it is neither an indignant expression of entitlement nor strident ideological rhetoric but rather a demonstrable need for services and an incessant scanning of the grants economy that enable an agency to survive and grow. After nearly twenty years of building a stable base of public and private funding, one agency executive expressed a preoccupation that typifies her and her most successful colleagues: "This is what I spend most of my time in. I see myself as a sort of gadfly who's always looking for money, maintaining contacts, and looking for other ideas."

In working through the grants process, CBO managers must contend with a number of barriers to funding that mitigate the ability of even well-established community-based organizations to effectively respond to changing community needs. These include accommodating the predelictions, prejudices, and demands of prospective donors and overcoming constraints in the use of contributed funds.

First, funders tend to assess community problems slowly and "from the top down." This may result in a failure to acknowledge emergent issues and problems until they are well along. During the early 1980s, for example, there were few, if any, studies of homelessness and little institutional response until after 1985. The same can be said about services for people with AIDS. A survey of these areas of need suggests that mainly churches and emergent community groups have provided the first responses; earlier philanthropic and public support for their efforts might have done much to alleviate a great deal of human suffering.

Moreover, assessment of community need from the top down does not always yield valid information. Solutions promulgated by funders who are removed from firsthand knowledge of community issues can result in intense frustration for those closer to where the action is. Community agency directors constantly struggle with the challenge of articulating true community need in order to accommodate the priorities of funders. The difficulty of doing so is especially intense when the nature of intervention being touted by a funder smacks of cultural insensitivity or even cultural imperialism in the case where what are perceived as white, middle-class values are being imposed. Recalling her attempts to structure and raise funds for an employment readiness program for low-income Latina women, the same agency director quoted above exposes the phenomenon:

> I feel that sometimes people don't really understand the community and their needs. . . . It's very hard sometimes to get across to the educational institutions that these are welfare mothers. They should have an introduction in some-

thing they are familiar with and after they feel they have
their feet on the ground and are established, they can do
other things. But they need that introduction at the Center.
Then they can go to the Community College which is far
away. . . .

Sometimes [funders] will say, "We cannot hold their
hand, be baby-sitters," but this is not the point. They don't
realize that these are people who have not had the right
surroundings all their lives and they cannot cope with the
educational institutions. . . . For [our agency], which is a
very small community-based agency, to try to deal with [the
community college and funders] and to get sophisticated
programs for our community . . . I really have to prove myself to them, prove that we can do it. Sometimes I get tired
of it.

As with all nonprofits that raise funds, survival for
community-based organizations depends largely on making the case
for support. Unfortunately, an emphasis by funders on quantitative
measures often belies the reality of community problems and the
ability of grass-roots efforts to ameliorate them. Unemployment
figures, for example, basically ignore the structurally unemployed
who have dropped out of the labor force and the "pockets of poverty" that constitute a large portion of our emerging underclass.

At least one corporate giving officer has acknowledged not
only the professionalization of those who manage philanthropy but
also the rationalization of the grant-making process itself. This has
been expressed in attempts to make it a policy science that utilizes
tools such as cost-benefit analysis, quantification, and computer
modeling.[33] Since small organizations typically lack the means and
expertise to conduct extensive research on their own, they can find
it difficult to mount a sufficiently strong case for needed programming from the funder's point of view. A corollary to the cult of
numbers in assessing community need is the pressure to quantify
services, which has resulted from the mandate for heightened accountability in the age of scarce resources. Some types of critically
needed services resist quantification or are in response to quality-
of-life issues. For this reason, piggybacking unfunded service deliv-

ery by using staff time paid for by funded programs is ubiquitous in grass-roots groups.

Community organizations are faced with another factor that undermines their search for stability. This is the lack of willingness on the part of funders to support developmental and operational costs. As one commentator writing in *Foundation News* noted several years ago: "For smaller organizations, ability to meet these costs may mean the difference between life and death."[34] Funders sometimes refuse to pay even for administrative costs that are incurred in carrying out programs they fund. It is not just experimental projects that funders may see as time-limited that suffer from a lack of administrative support but also needed longer term interventions. Administrative costs, especially in terms of management staff, increase with every year. Support for these costs is hard to find.

Traditionally, United Way membership has afforded agencies more flexibility in the use of annual funding so that money can be applied to cover "indirect" costs. There is some movement away from core funding arrangements toward funding specific services that are justified by needs assessment. One of the top United Way chapters in the nation, United Way of Southeastern Pennsylvania, is now experimenting with a combination of member grants, "targeted care" grants, and service funding that is awarded competitively. Whether this will become widespread is uncertain, but the trend toward specificity is unmistakable.

Community-Based Philanthropy: A Tradition at Risk?

Though community needs seem to be continually expanding, community organizations that try to cope with those needs exist in a field that is already operating at a peak of competitiveness for available resources. Constraints on public funding suggest even greater pressures on private philanthropy as the years pass and increased competition between voluntary organizations for philanthropic dollars. For those organizations, old and new, what are the prospects for the future? Merely to leave their fate to "America's voluntary spirit" is naive, for this neither does justice to the complexities of modern voluntary organization life nor considers the subtleties of relations between benefactor and mendicant in the field of philanthropy. In terms of resources, will there continue to be a market of public and private support? Will it be accessible, inclusive, and sensitive to conditions in underserved communities of need? Or is the field of voluntary action becoming so complex and technical that those who are most in need of its benefits will be least able to master its subtleties? At least in the United States, there is reason to believe that such factors as pluralism, decentralized special-interest philanthropy, and economic self-interest may ultimately condition the field of opportunities for grass-roots initiative.

We are now witnessing the accelerated "pluralization" of American society. The U.S. Bureau of the Census predicts that by the year 2100, about a century from now, the racial composition of the nation will be 46 percent white, 28 percent Hispanic, 17 percent black, and 10 percent Asian.[35] Together, the Ford Foundation and National Science Foundation are presently studying the effects of how immigration is changing ethnic composition in seven major cities and the ways in which resettled populations become integrated into the fabric of community life. Not surprisingly, voluntary organizations, often indigenous ones, continue to play a crucial role in mitigating the adjustment of waves of new immigrants to the mixed blessings of life in the United States.

In theory, voluntary action, voluntary association, and the philanthropic impulse are key elements in sustaining a democratic society and in buffering pluralism. Undoubtedly, continued immigration will test the ability of our institutions to become even more pluralistic. It is also likely that both public funding and philanthropy will increasingly emphasize "multiculturalism." In practice, however, voluntarism and philanthropy themselves continue to exhibit some distinctly antidemocratic and unpluralistic characteristics and trends. For instance, a 1982 study by the National Puerto Rican Coalition reported that while Puerto Ricans represented about 2 percent of the nation's population, it was receiving less than 2 percent of foundation grants awarded.[36]

The obvious relative disparities in bargaining power between those who seek and those who have are still exacerbated by serious shortcomings of access and participation. Although minorities are heavily represented among the most needy and underserved groups, they continue to be few and far between in the fields of philanthropy and fund raising. This has not been true for women, who are increasingly found to occupy positions of responsibility and authority in both development work and corporate and foundation philanthropy. Blacks, Hispanics, and Asian and Native Americans have apparently not fared so well. A December 1987 headline in the trade journal *NonProfit Times* bore this headline: "Wanted: More Minorities for Top Fundraising Jobs."[37] The article that followed detailed the results of a study by the Council on Foundations that reported that minorities comprised only 4 percent of foundation chief officers and only 15 percent of all foundation workers. Of the latter group, most were not in policymaking but support staff positions.

Reasons cited for this included insufficient efforts to recruit minorities into competition for qualified candidates from commercial sector employers, but also little pressure within the field to promote affirmative action. Further, only recently and for the first time has the National Charities Information Bureau included affirmative action in its revised guidelines. This and other new efforts to stimulate recruitment and training by NSFRE, CASE, and the Ford and Lilly foundations may help to add color to what has traditionally been a mostly white field. Still, it suggests that from the funders' point of view, there may be considerable class and cultural barriers if community needs are continually assessed by people with limited firsthand knowledge. Given the nature of our most pressing social problems, one is compelled to wonder about the efficacy of promulgating white, middle-class solutions.

The Rise of Decentralized and Special-Interest Philanthropy

In part, the barriers to access in philanthropy have engendered alternative federated and workplace giving programs, as well as foundation-based vehicles for targeting particular constituencies. Far more significant, perhaps, are indications that for the first time in the United States, the structure of philanthropy itself is being successfully copied, if not expropriated, by and for those who have largely stood outside its decision-making processes. These structures have included special initiatives to amass alternative philanthropic funds for blacks, women, and Hispanics, as well as community foundations designed to target unmet local needs. Also included are the Black United Fund, more than sixty women's umbrella funding bodies, the Funding Exchange, networking philanthropies for social change, and a host of other alternative fund-raising vehicles.

In fact, so crowded has the field become that non-United Way workplace giving programs have been divided into "traditional alternatives" (those that raise money for health and human services, the arts, and international relief), and "nontraditional alternatives" (which support causes related to social action, minority rights, environmental reform, and the like). According to the National Committee for Responsive Philanthropy, which follows developments in alternative workplace giving, nontraditional programs such as National Service Agencies, the United Negro College Fund, and assorted social action and "community shares" solicitation programs raised a total of $22 million in 1988.[38]

The Black United Fund was begun about twenty years ago in an effort to challenge the hegemony of United Way over workplace solicitation. As a result of litigation the fund opened the way for participation in the Combined Federal Campaign and some 500 other federated campaigns across the United States that had previously been limited solely to United Way. Now some 300 groups participate in some sixteen locations across the country. However, many campaigns at the state level remain exclusionary.

The emergence of Womens Way in Philadelphia during the late 1970s was the first attempt of women organizing a fund to target women's human service needs. Its first campaign in 1977 raised $25,000 from some 500 donors. Slightly more than a decade later, it had raised over $1 million from nearly 7,000 donors. In the interim, Womens Way has been joined by the New York Women's Foundation and other groups in San Francisco, Minneapolis, and other cities. A current total of thirty-seven women's fund-raising and philanthropic groups comprise the National Network of Women's Funds, which is dedicated to "women helping women." These are not only coalitions begun by affluent women and professionals, but efforts often carried out in concert with grass-roots activists.

These and other alternative workplace campaigns have had a major impact on the efforts of United Way. There is now competition for the workplace dollar where heretofore there was none.

In addition to years of local pressure from groups that felt they had been excluded from the United Way family, the increasing aggressiveness of the new, alternative funds has publicly called into question the ability of United Way to effectively serve women and minorities. Surprisingly, recent evidence suggests that the competition from alternative funds may be helping rather than hindering United Way's own efforts. The National Committee for Responsive Philanthropy survey mentioned above showed multiple-charity workplace campaigns to have resulted in overall increases in giving for both United Way and nontraditional, alternative funds.

Not coincidentally, minorities, along with small businesses, yuppies, working women, and the affluent elderly, have come to be seen as a growth market for United Way and religious bodies. United Way in some regions has sought to bring more minorities into its professional and volunteer ranks through initiatives like the Hispanic Leadership Development Program. But it has moved even more determinedly to bring Latinos into its *donor* ranks through aggressive Spanish-language advertising. For religious auspices such as World Vision, these efforts are paying off. According to *Giving USA*, in 1988, Hispanics tripled their contributions.

Another result has been the popularization of the "donor option" movement within United Way itself. Again the result of some intense community pressure, donor option has enabled contributors to select from a list of approved charitable organizations to benefit from their gifts. Organizations, in turn, have been free to encourage prospective donors to earmark funds for them to receive.

In some places donor option has been so successful as to raise concern for the viability of the United Way model. In one of the top few United Way chapters in the nation, United Way of Southeastern Pennsylvania, donor option was implemented in 1981. In that year, 35,000 donors gave $2.9 million to 1,200 groups. By 1987, 102,000 had given $11.5 million to 3,800 nonmember agencies. Donor-opted monies had risen to 28 percent of the nearly $54 million raised in the metropolitan Philadelphia area.

Recently, United Way instituted a new system called "targeted care"; this offers several categories of need from which the prospective donor can select. Some community groups have charged that this constitutes a move by United Way to regain control over the allocation of funds that it lost to donor option. United Way officials contend that the new system is meant to provide added choice for contributors but allow greater flexibility in the allocation process.

For United Way, there is likely to be continued pressure from a variety of quarters. Certainly there will be more competition from newer, outside fund-raising umbrellas. Additionally, there is likely to be continued competition within United Way's local communities between well-established and well-funded but traditional groups and newer, emerging and poorly funded groups. No doubt, too, with an increase in volunteer participation and solicitation from minority groups, there will be continued pressures on United Way from within to be more responsive to particular minority service needs.

Workplace fund raising is not the only arena in which philanthropy is being challenged by alternative fund-raising and grant-making initiatives. The rise of a new breed of foundation has provided alternative sources of foundation support in more than 250 communities throughout the nation. While not a new phenomenon, the increase in the numbers of community foundations, with their fund-raising and grant-making capabilities, reflects a blossoming in recent years.

In some instances, the community foundation has reflected a certain coming of age for minorities. This has been the case with the launching of a new philanthropic venture in Puerto Rico. In 1984, the Ford Foundation identified one of the key obstacles to community development in Puerto Rico as being the lack of a vehicle for channeling philanthropic contributions into worthy community activities. Recognition of this led Ford to collaborate with the National Puerto Rican Coalition and others on the island in establishing the first foundation there, the Puerto Rican Community Foundation. Some of the other new foundations have been geared to particular concerns and causes, such as ACORN (which targets low-income community organizing and development), numerous conservancies, land trusts, and action-oriented environmental groups, and an explosion of local groups that raise funds for AIDS education and treatment.

At the least, foundation, corporate, and other institutional givers, such as religious bodies, can expect to come under continued public and "consumer" scrutiny. First, looking out on behalf of the unempowered are a growing number of watchdog and advocacy groups. Such groups as the Center for Community Change, the National Committee for Responsive Philanthropy (NCRP), National Council of La Raza, National Puerto Rican Coalition, and American Indian Movement among others have local counterparts. Many are comprised of a new breed of younger and better-educated nonprofit sector professional who often feels confident in challenging the established philanthropic order. Like the alternative funds, their efforts essentially reflect dissatisfaction with what is perceived as a large, bureaucratic, and entrenched philanthropic cartel. Their growing ability to monitor the field of philanthropy is exemplified by NCRP's current project, a two-year study to determine the extent to which corporate giving goes to support minority causes and issues.

Further, since the report of the National Committee on Public Needs and Private Philanthropy (the Filer Commission), concerted efforts have been made to stimulate scholarly research and reporting on a wide range of issues in philanthropy and voluntarism. This has resulted in the launching of numerous studies, with the promise of more to come in the years ahead. This means greater and more detailed study and analysis of the policies and practices of institutional philanthropy.

Finally, a small industry of trainers, consultants, and fund raisers who service community-based organizations has emerged. The existence of such entities as nonprofit management training and technical assistance networks, including the Support Centers, the Nonprofit Management Association, and others, suggests continued scrutiny and perhaps pressures by a cadre of professionals who are highly articulate and are often in key intermediary positions.

On the other hand, conventional funding bodies—foundations and corporations—have begun to coordinate their efforts on a local or regional basis, and sometimes a national one. In 1983, the president of the Council on Foundations, James A. Joseph, focused his annual address to the membership on trends he perceived to be shaping philanthropy in the years to come. He saw a key trend in decentralization altering the way in which grantor decisions would be made.[39] The devolution of philanthropic decision making is showing up in the formation of funding consortia to make a pool of funds available for targeting community needs closer to the source. Such is the purpose of new grant maker consortia like the National Community AIDS Partnership launched by the Ford Foundation. This newly created fund is to be administered by the National AIDS Network. The network is designed to channel support from major corporate and foundation donors to nine locally based grantors, who will in turn fund effective responses to AIDS-related needs at the community level across the country. Community foundations, nontraditional workplace solicitation programs, and other alternative funding bodies also reflect decentralization in their attempts to raise and distribute philanthropic dollars closer to the point of need.

Additionally, regional associations of grant makers, or "RAGS," have sprung up all over the country in recent years to coordinate local and regional philanthropic efforts. These may well work to the *disadvantage* of community organizations since their own programs may become less distinct in the company of so many others competing for limited pools of support.

From the perspective of those laboring at the grass roots, the phenomenon of decentralization may entail even more subtle changes, changes that could result in unexpected and welcome kinds of empowerment. Having survived years of inflation, heightened standards of accountability, government cutbacks, and the mentality of retrenchment, the activist-turned-manager cum social entrepreneur may well have exhausted the grants economy. In an era of large government deficits, the likelihood of substantial new government funding streams appears limited. Just as alternative funds are an expression of new capabilities and self-confidence for those who work on behalf of "have-not" constituencies, community agency leaders themselves are reaching for new means for generating support.

Increasingly, there is a willingness to network informally or form community coalitions. In many areas community agencies are networked by industry, having formed associations of those running day care, seniors' centers, housing groups, women's organizations, and legal aid and civil rights programs. In some instances the impact of coalition lobbying has been significant. For example, when the Title XX funding stream was being converted to the Adult Social Service Block Grant, coalitions of women's groups in Pennsylvania successfully lobbied a conservative state administration to set aside a special block grant just to fund women's shelters and rape crisis programs. Similar coalitions of blacks, Latinos, the disabled, AIDS victims, and the homeless have been developed to press government and private philanthropy for greater responsiveness to unmet community needs.

Moreover, what some community leaders may lack in 1960s-style political activism is being replaced by new forms of community agency entrepreneurship. Enhanced knowledge and nonprofit expertise are increasingly being coupled with technological advances—especially the availability and accessibility of personal computers—to reshape and expand the field of opportunity for their organizations. Spurred by economic necessity, aided by untapped special interest constituencies, and armed with a growing sophistication about nonprofit marketing and what inexpensive, in-house technology can do, community organizations are beginning to turn to some of the methods traditionally reserved for mainstream institutions. Using personal computers to invoke such tools as data base development, mailing list management, and desktop publishing, CBOs are beginning to look to minorities, women, and the baby boomers with activist social values for support.

Thus, in the 1990s professionalism, pluralism, and technology may well be combined to bring a sort of democratization to philanthropy at the community level. Whether that process will continue to reach to the grass roots is uncertain. The paradox is that once armed with knowledge, expertise, and technical capabilities, the advocates for the disenfranchised may become far removed from the source of their ardor. Whether we have sold out on mission or merely evolved our means remains an open issue. Just as with the growth of professionalism in community organizations, the advent of more accessible technology may well signify our having given up a portion of our voluntary soul. The danger, as always, is that the generation of organizations that grew out of the 1960s and 1970s will become just another layer of the nonprofit establishment that fails to recognize and respond to emergent community problems. And, too, along with the passing of senior community activists, there may well also pass a sense of moral commitment, that investment or psychic equity that has been blended with the more pragmatic imperatives of working the grants economy on behalf of the dispossessed.

Self-Interest Revisited

As a nation, the United States is steeped in the folklore of egalitarianism and worldly compassion. In the case of the disadvantaged or the dispossessed, we bear a special commitment to invoke justice by remediating conditions of inequality and inequity. Payton reminds us that "the asymmetries of the human condition, the mismatches of needs and resources, wants and abilities, desires and power, are corrected in three ways: by self-interest, by rights guaranteed by the state, and by philanthropy."[40] Americans stop short of redistributing wealth evenly, unwilling to level the playing field by any politically radical means.

Instead, faith persists that acts of voluntarism and compassion will render acceptable levels of justice and that the best thing we can do is to "help people help themselves." In doing so, we rely heavily on the strength of our diversity and the depth and breadth of our resources. As long as the economy generates a healthy surplus, we can continue to afford charity.

Meanwhile, philanthropic auspices seem forced to select ever narrowing spheres of focus and activity, with the lesser of evils becoming more and more difficult to discern. Another one of our major thinkers on philanthropy, Paul Ylvisaker, points out that philanthropy is increasingly called upon to spread its resources ever more thinly to accommodate government retrenchment and rising social needs. As times worsen, this rationing role becomes more difficult and more ominous but all the more crucial. Witness choices between urgent problems of hunger and nutrition, basic health, and the environment as opposed to such other important concerns as education, housing, arts and culture, and recreation. As a field, how will philanthropy face up to its own limitations in the face of ever increasing human suffering and need and the emergence of more and more "tragic choices" wherein solutions are optimal and never ideal? Ylvisaker offers a sober, but also noble point of view: "The challenge of philanthropy is to ensure equity by working toward fair shares of hardship as well as opportunity in a social context that is more and more tilting toward social Darwinism, and by taking on the burden of an outcome that is not always to the majority's advantage. That willingness to strive for equity, in bad as well as in good times, is the special mission of philanthropy."[41]

There is, however, a growing frustration felt by those who labor on behalf of people in need at the grass roots, a sense of having been worn down by the struggle to sustain public interest in an era of private priorities. That sense of frustration is coupled with some remaining energy and moral indignation but also with an understanding of how the levers of power work to make or retard change in our society. Listen to the words of Dan West, executive director of a major community action agency in the mid-Atlantic region, an articulate African American with thirty years of work in the civil rights and antipoverty movement:

> We had a meeting with the directors from the area and our concern was precisely how we can get our message out more effectively to the private sector—let people know who we are, what we do and what our needs are. . . . Yes, we're concerned and we're frustrated at our inability to do this on a local basis. It's easy to just work in a little bubble. . . .
>
> I don't disagree that it is essential that we balance our [federal] budget. But I work on a simple concept that a true measure of greatness and sensitivity of a nation and a democracy is how we treat the poorest and most needy of our people. We cannot sacrifice our poor people, and we're talking about a substantial percentage now. You just can't sacrifice them. . . .
>
> What can we do? We need to start something better than just our own individual thing. We have rich resources. We've got a lot of industry. We've got foundations, philanthropists. Some of us are good at tapping these resources and some of us aren't. We need to do it on a collective basis. . . . Let's work together and see if we can maximize

these resources that are around, because we can't depend on federal or state funds. If we can get the strong and clear support of the business community, the influential people, then the politicians will follow.

At the end of the 1980s, there was a sense that "the system" might be showing the kinds of stress that may well supercede the ability of voices like Dan West's to be heard by those in positions of real influence. A preponderance of deteriorating social conditions and a threatened climate for business seem to have preceded social reform in every era of American history wherein it occurred. The advent of such things as child welfare laws and public education, workers' compensation, social insurance, and civil rights legislation all entailed some realignment of political rhetoric, a new synthesis of traditional values and contemporary realities that served to redefine self-interest.

We may now be seeing the beginnings of a response to a number of domestic and international social problems. In the United States, if a "kinder, gentler nation" comes about, it is likely to be at least partly a function of concern for impending labor shortages and a need to compete more effectively with a trained work force in the new international economic order. And it is likely to reflect a recognition of the economically high cost of inattention to social problems. Internationally, a more humane order that seeks to relieve the misery of the less developed nations—the Third World— may well reflect a recognition of the need to seek new industrial and consumer markets. The underlying sensibility was well articulated by a corporate community relations officer who said that "the wave of the future isn't checkbook philanthropy. It's a marriage of corporate marketing and social responsibility."[42]

In any hypothesized outpouring of concern for human suffering, with few notable exceptions, the predominating posture of the corporate world can be expected to set the tone in large measure for both public policy and private philanthropy. Philanthropy itself is likely to remain a risk-averse exercise until the political-economic order on which it is founded is in jeopardy. And then it is likely to function in a conservative and self-serving manner. Was it not a certain conservatism, after all, that characterized the underlying thrust of public policy and philanthropic largesse during the Progressive era, the New Deal, and the Great Society?

In seeking to identify important issues for the years to come, we find that history continues to provide good clues. The recurring equivocations of American political and social philosophy are continually evident in American philanthropic and voluntary life. Considered from any angle, philanthropy is a value-laden enterprise. Thus, some of our best thinkers still struggle to define what really constitutes benevolence and to set the agenda for the public good.

Other chapters in this volume demonstrate that "making the case for support" inevitably invokes the values and moral concerns that underlie personal and institutional choice. Dichotomies such as hand-up versus hand-out, community versus compassion, and equity versus efficiency are like stress cracks in the foundation of our collective ideological house. For philanthropists and philanthropoids alike, it is always much harder in times when the nature of good work remains uncertain and when ideology itself must be swayed. This contentious, peculiarly American scenario is likely to persist in the years ahead. As the unvindicated but nevertheless visionary writer Edward Bellamy suggested just over a hundred years ago, we can often learn a lot about where we are headed by looking backward.

Notes

1. William Julius Wilson, *The Truly Disadvantaged*. Chicago: University of Chicago Press, 1987.
2. Lester Salamon, "The Voluntary Sector and the Future of the Welfare State." *Nonprofit and Voluntary Sector Quarterly*, 1989, *18*, 24.
3. American Association of Fund-Raising Counsel, *Giving USA*. New York: American Association of Fund-Raising Counsel, 1989.
4. Ann Lowrey Bailey, "Companies' Giving Programs in Turmoil in Fever of Mergers and Acquisitions." *Chronicle of Philanthropy*, Nov. 22, 1988, *1* (3), 1 ff.

5. Larry Sterne, "Religious Giving is a No-Growth Field, New Survey Says." *NonProfit Times,* Nov. 1988, 2 (8), 1 ff.

6. Teresa Odendahl, *America's Wealthy and the Future of Foundations.* New York: Foundation Center, 1987.

7. Conference Board. *Survey of Corporate Contributions, 1988 Edition, 1986 Data.* New York: Conference Board.

8. American Association of Fund-Raising Counsel.

9. "Future CEO's Less Committed to Philanthropy." *NonProfit Times,* Nov. 1988, 2 (8), 1 ff.

10. Richard Gaylord Briley, Keynote Address given at the Direct Marketing Association's Non-profit Day '88, New York City. Quoted in *Fundraising Management,* Oct. 1988, p. 5.

11. Jon Van Til, *Mapping the Third Sector.* New York: Foundation Center, 1988, chaps. 1 and 2.

12. Robert H. Bremner, *American Philanthropy.* Chicago: University of Chicago Press, 1960, p. 2.

13. Bremner, p. 2.

14. Michael B. Katz, *In the Shadow of the Poorhouse: A Social History of Welfare in America.* New York: Basic Books, 1986.

15. Robert Payton, "Major Challenges to Philanthropy." Working paper presented at the annual meeting of INDEPENDENT SECTOR, Washington, D.C., Aug. 1984.

16. Payton, p. 24.

17. Payton, p. 119.

18. Two studies that focus on grass-roots activity are Harry C. Boyte, *The Backyard Revolution: Understanding the New Citizen Movement.* Philadelphia: Temple University Press, 1980; and Robert Fisher, *Let the People Decide: Neighborhood Organizing in America.* Boston: Twayne Publishers, 1984.

19. Several leading theorists who have argued the utility of community organizations providing personal human services and other services include Amatai Etzioni, "The Untapped Potential of the Third Sector." *Business and Society Review,* Spring 1972, pp. 39–44; Ralph Kramer, "Voluntary Agencies and the Personal Social Services." In W. W. Powell (ed.), *The Nonprofit Sector: A Research Handbook.* New Haven, Conn.: Yale University Press, 1987, pp. 240–257; Peter L. Berger and Richard J. Neuhaus, *To Empower People: The Role of Mediat-*

ing Structures in Public Policy. Washington, D.C.: American Enterprise Institute, 1977; and Robert L. Woodson, "The Importance of Neighborhood Organizations in Meeting Human Needs." In J. A. Meyer (ed.), *Meeting Human Needs.* Washington, D.C.: American Enterprise Institute, 1982, pp. 132-149.

20.	Arthur Okun, *Equality and Efficiency.* Washington, D.C.: Brookings Institution, 1975.

21.	Compelling historical evidence and arguments of this sort have been offered by Gabriel Kolko, *The Triumph of Conservatism.* New York: Free Press, 1963; James Weinstein, *The Corporate Ideal in the Liberal State.* Boston: Beacon Press, 1968; and Sidney Fine, *Laissez-Faire and the General Welfare State.* Ann Arbor: University of Michigan Press, 1976.

22.	Susan Ostrander, Stuart Langton, and Jon Van Til (eds.), *Shifting the Debate: Public/Private Sector Relations in the Modern Welfare State.* New Brunswick, N.J.: Transaction Books, 1987.

23.	Lester Salamon, "Partners in Public Service: The Scope and Theory of Government-Nonprofit Relations." In Powell, pp. 99-117.

24.	Waldemar Nielsen, *The Endangered Sector.* New York: Columbia University Press, 1979, esp. chap. 2; Clark Chambers, "The Historical Role of the Voluntary Sector in Human Service Delivery in Urban America." In Gary A. Tobin, *Social Planning and Human Service Delivery in the Voluntary Sector.* Westport, Conn.: Greenwood Press, 1985, pp. 3-28; and Peter Dobkin Hall, "A Historical Overview of the Private Nonprofit Sector." In Powell, pp. 3-26.

25.	E. Franklin Frazier, *The Negro Church in America.* New York: Schocken Books, 1974; John Hope Franklin, *From Slavery to Freedom: A History of Negro Americans.* New York: Knopf, 1980, chap. 16; Roosevelt Green, "A Functional Analysis of Black Churches: Contributions to the Community." *Proceedings of the Thirteenth Annual Meeting of the Association of Voluntary Action Scholars,* New Orleans, La., Oct. 6-9, 1985, pp. 135-149; and Emmett D. Carson, "Despite Long History, Black Philanthropy Gets Little Credit as 'Self-Help'

Tool." *Focus: The Monthly Newsletter of the Joint Center for Political Studies,* June, 1987, pp. 3 ff.

26. Sylvia Alicia Gonzalez, *Hispanic American Voluntary Organizations.* Westport, Conn.: Greenwood Press, 1985, pp. 162–167.

27. Kathleen D. McCarthy, *Noblesse Oblige: Charity and Cultural Philanthropy in Chicago, 1849–1929.* Chicago: University of Chicago Press, 1982; and Anne Firor Scott, " 'To Cast Our Might on the Altar of Benevolence . . .' Women Begin to Organize." Working paper, Center for the Study of Philanthropy and Voluntarism, Duke University, Jan. 1988.

28. Rosalyn Miyoko Tonai, "Asian American Charitable Giving." University of San Francisco Institute for Nonprofit Organization Management, Working Paper Series no. 4, 1988.

29. This finding was the result of a survey carried out in 1988 by the Gallup Organization on behalf of INDEPENDENT SECTOR and reported in the *NonProfit Times,* Nov. 1988, 2 (8), 1.

30. Ralph Kramer, *Participation of the Poor.* Englewood Cliffs, N.J.: Prentice-Hall, 1969, pp. 3–5.

31. David J. Garrow, "Philanthropy and the Civil Rights Movement." Center for the Study of Philanthropy, City University of New York, Working Papers, Oct. 1987.

32. Charles Cagnon, *Business Ventures of Citizen Groups.* Helena, Mont.: Northern Rockies Action Group, 1982; James C. Crimmins and Mary Keil, *Enterprise in the Nonprofit Sector.* Washington, D.C.: Partners for Livable Places/Rockefeller Brothers Fund, 1983; and Edward Skloot, *The Nonprofit Entrepreneur.* New York: Foundation Center, 1988.

33. Jerry Welsh, corporate social relations director at American Express, quoted in *Wall Street Journal,* June 21, 1984; quoted in Payton, pp. 80–81.

34. Joseph Foote, "Grantees' Overhead Costs: Should Foundations Pay?" *Foundation News,* May/June 1983, pp. 51–55.

35. Kathleen Teltsch, "In Queens, a Preview of Future Cities." *New York Times,* July 20, 1988, p. 22.

36. National Puerto Rican Coalition, *U.S. Foundations' Responsiveness to Puerto Rican Needs and Concerns: Foundation*

Giving to Puerto Rican Organizations 1979–81. Alexandria, Va.: National Puerto Rican Coalition, 1982.

37. Larry Blumenthal, "Wanted: More Minorities for Top Fundraising Jobs." NonProfit Times, Dec. 1987, pp. 1 ff.

38. National Committee for Responsive Philanthropy, Report on a Survey of Non-Traditional Workplace Giving. Washington, D.C.: NCRP, 1988.

39. James A. Joseph, "Six Trends Shaping Philanthropy's Future." Address to the 34th annual conference of the Council on Foundations. Foundation News, May/June 1983, pp. 22–24.

40. Payton, p. 38.

41. Paul Ylvisaker, "Philanthropy as Triage." Foundation News, Mar./Apr. 1982, p. 10.

42. Jerry Welsh, quoted in Payton, p. 66.

PART THREE

Strengthening
Philanthropic Practice

Chapter 7   *Robert L. Payton*

Teaching Philanthropy, Teaching About Philanthropy

Starting Point[1]

Personal observation over many years and in many different settings has persuaded me that voluntary service appears to work for the benefit of those served—at least in most cases, though by no means all. I am even more convinced that voluntary service, when it is driven primarily by a concern for others, is an enriching, rewarding, deepening, maturing experience for those who engage in it.

Many examples that come to my mind are spontaneous acts of generosity and self-sacrifice; much more impressive are those that show persistence over time. The most impressive example out of my own experience is the missionaries I met in some of the remotest parts of Africa who devoted their lives to nursing daily the wounds of lepers. Most of us know at first hand of cases in which the service of one person inspired others to follow suit. The son of friends of ours recently returned from a summer's service as a volunteer in a hospital for the terminally ill in India, "called" there by what he had heard about the work of Mother Teresa.

The Uses and Abuses of Philanthropy

I have also more than once observed the exploitation and misuse of volunteers, sometimes for purposes of simple monetary gain and sometimes in the service of ideology. I have seen self-styled volunteers whose principal interest seemed to be their own vanity; I have seen others make empty promises (I confess to some of my own); and others have used voluntary service as a means of seeking social prominence or of imposing their own will on an organization or even on a community. Novelists and essayists of diverse persuasions have long mocked and ridiculed the smug and self-satisfied do-gooder. The academic culture of recent decades is one in which it is assumed that honorary degrees are bought by money or influence rather than earned by merit. Boards of trustees are often seen as cabals of alien influence engaged in a war against scholarship. Many people—especially young people—are taught to be cynical rather than idealistic about voluntary service.

On the other hand, the academic world welcomed and even embraced (as I did) the idealism proclaimed by the Kennedy administration in creating the Peace Corps. (The present leadership of Campus Compact refers back to that innovation the way an earlier generation praises the Civilian Conservation Corps.)

These public models of public service reveal the complexity of motivation: we want to help our young people become more self-sufficient and responsible; we want to address important social or economic needs; we want to carry our values to the world. However, arguments for voluntary service, like arguments for higher education, can also be cast in negative terms: as a means of keeping excess bodies out of the labor market; as a way to subsidize intellectuals in order to seduce them away from the barricades, or to advance American political interests abroad (even as a means of covert intelligence, the most common anti-American canard of the 1960s and 1970s). Some feminists argued against voluntary service on the grounds that it is a device of exploitation and marginalization of women in the economy. Even the missionaries in those leper hospitals in the mountains of north Cameroon are seen by some not as angels of mercy but as self-righteous ideologues imposing their religious doctrines on defenseless people.

Thoreau warned us: "If I knew for a certainty that a man was coming to my house with the conscious design of doing me good, I should turn and run for my life."[2] That not only warns the recipient of assistance, it warns the potential volunteer: who would want to be in a role that causes others to run away? Veblen warned us that if we let businessmen into the governance of our universities, they will turn them into temples of greed rather than temples of learning. Why let people insinuate themselves into the life of the university under the guise of well-meaning volunteers? Emerson warned us not to waste our money on unknown savages half a world away.[3] Why would anyone volunteer to help the hungry in Ethiopia or the oppressed in South Africa when there are hungry and oppressed here at home? Should students heed the call of Oliver North or Noam Chomsky? At the libertarian end of the ideological spectrum, Ayn Rand warned us that philanthropic values are soft and enervating. The ideological right (left) has charged that the ideological left (right) has seized control of the philanthropic foundations, and so has set out to create its own; that nonprofit organizations are using the exemptions of philanthropy to advance their liberal-leftist (conservative-rightist) political ends—and so it is necessary to retaliate in kind. The young people are the target: the war is not a battle for our own souls but for those of the next generation.

And so on. The quality of discourse about philanthropy is low. It is usually underinformed, and it is often driven by ideological bias. Discourse about voluntary action for the public good is lost in a fog of technical debate about tax deductions for nonitemizers or about unrelated business income.

Teaching Philanthropy

In the midst of what could plausibly be called confusion, what should undergraduates know about the philanthropic tradition and, more specifically, about voluntary service? The argument of this chapter is (1) that philanthropic action *should* be taught, (2) that teaching about it should be honest and balanced, and (3) that instruction should reflect practice and vice versa.

I take literally the rhetoric of the liberal arts. The liberal arts should help students learn how to be free. The liberal arts should help students to identify and to root out their prejudices. Students should learn from the liberal arts how reason can master passion. People like me have believed and argued most of our lives that the liberally educated person will be a person of good character, not simply smart or clever or well-informed or fashionably *au courant*. The problem has been that when looking at ourselves and at others around us, we are acutely aware that the ideal of liberal education is seldom realized. I and many of my so-called "liberally educated" friends often prove to be illiberal, closed-minded, self-centered, and self-serving.

Our failings have not caused me to abandon the ideal of liberal education any more than the failings of Christianity or the evils of the world have caused me to abandon my faith. The saving phrase is "on the average"—as Howard Bowen argued, the outcomes of a college education are revealed *on the average* to be an improvement in social values as well as the ability to solve problems and to make a living. It is not clear whether graduates of St. John's College are "better people" than those who were educated at the University of Maryland. It would be hard to demonstrate a causal relationship between undergraduate business education and hedonism, either, for that matter. The rough assumption would appear to be that intellectual training has *something* to do with behavior.

I don't expect to find reliable, empirically grounded research that will settle the problem. What I am interested in are the practical questions of how to attract students into the tradition of voluntary service and how to help them perform that service at a high moral level. That suggests that part of the educational purpose I have in mind is teaching philanthropy, teaching *applied* philanthropy, if you will. If I turn to the apparatus that exists on most campuses, I will find administrative units whose function is to "facilitate" voluntary service. Madison House at the University of Virginia, for example, attempts to recruit students into voluntary service and to match them with the needs of local nonprofit agencies and organizations. The Volunteer Students Bureau at Indiana University does the same thing, as do similar programs at Washington University and at Hofstra University (to mention four institutions I have been associated with). The institutional assumptions underlying such efforts—rarely examined systematically—are that student volunteers can provide useful service that might not be provided at all without their help and that the students themselves will benefit from their service as volunteers.

Organized voluntary service on American campuses is as old as American higher education. Some of the voluntary organizations (especially the church-related ones) have been around for more than a century. The late nineteenth century in England and in the United States saw efforts to create student enclaves in poor neighborhoods (Toynbee Hall in England recently celebrated its centennial). Students were to bring the higher culture to the lower classes, just as older intellectuals brought philosophy to labor union halls. (Will Durant gave the lectures that became *The Story of Philosophy* at Union Square in New York City.[4])

All these things can legitimately be called "teaching philanthropy." It is taken for granted that colleges and universities should encourage students to become involved in voluntary service. "Service to what?" can be answered in innumerable ways. Students act as Big Brothers and Big Sisters; students sit with Alzheimer's victims; students organize and staff shelters for the homeless and serve food to the hungry; students raise money for art films and blood drives and cancer research and Afghan refugees; students fast, march, sit in, sing, and pray for human rights and civil rights and animal rights; students design posters and stuff envelopes and repair toys and collect canned goods and used clothing and signatures on petitions; students run long distances, crowd into small cars, dance until they drop, wear rhetorical T-shirts, and wear costumes to celebrate ethnic diversity. Some students build shanties in protest of apartheid in South Africa, and other students tear them down in defense of tradition in America; some students hand out literature denouncing abortion, and others distribute condoms to prevent AIDS. Students staff the booths of art fairs and book fairs and help alumni in telethons to increase annual giving from alumni and even parents.

The blurring of the sectors is also evident. Students are encouraged to serve as volunteers in programs supported by public agencies. (Three-fifths of the states have "volunteerism" departments.) Much of the rhetoric in behalf of voluntary service stresses "community" service, allowing for public as well as nonprofit voluntary service, and for paid service comparable to the rewards offered, for example, by ROTC. The study of philanthropy is no place for conceptual purists.

Many students "don't have the time" for such things. Some are indifferent or uninterested. Many other students, however, work full-time and go to school and study in the hours they are not working. Some students are parents who are torn between buying books for their own education and buying new clothes for their children. Many students do not live on campus and rarely see much of it beyond the buildings where their own classes are held. They feel lucky when they have time to spend in the library; the student union is a foreign land. They don't know many other students and often never hear about the opportunities and challenges publicized by campus organizations. They don't have time for public lectures, much less rock concert fund raisers. Most of them feel that the campus is designed for young people who have time and money to spare, not for people like themselves who see it as an obstacle to overcome on the road to a (somewhat) better job. Some of them are themselves regular recipients of charity, public and private.

Liberal education was designed for young people who could afford it, those who could spend four years in college and reach voting age without learning a trade. It has rarely been designed for the increasing numbers of older, poorer, and less-advantaged people who have become the moral mission of higher education during the past twenty years.

My observation has been that voluntary service is also most often designed for those who can afford it, for those who have the time (who can meet their educational requirements for graduation and have time left over), and for those who can afford not to take a part-time job to pay their tuition. And, as in all other areas of human affairs, some people simply make fuller use of their time than others.

Both liberal education and voluntary service can be seen (in the context of higher education) as the products of a time when a college education was a privilege of upper economic status. The liberally educated person was a gentleman or a lady; the volunteer was someone "better off." In many places, voluntary service was part of the learning expected of members of fraternities and sororities. The liberally educated volunteer was the model of the educated person, just as the liberal arts college was the institutional model of higher education.

Cultural Resistance to Teaching Philanthropy. If the tradition had its roots in economic and social classes, it also had deep religious ties. Some of the strongest voluntary organizations on campuses were arms of religious denominations: the Campus Y, Hillel, Newman, and so on. Most students came to college not yet disabused of their religious upbringing. Most of them had participated in religiously sponsored voluntary service. Very often antireligious sentiment in the classroom undermined proreligious activity outside it.

If social, economic, and religious factors were evident, so were political ones. Campus life encouraged involvement in campus political organizations. Depending on the campus, the political range reached as far left as Young Socialists and (somewhat later) as far right as Young Americans for Freedom. The politicization of veterans organizations during the peak years of veteran enrollment probably left its mark on all voluntary organizations. The history of the McCarthy era and that of the Vietnam War provide rich opportunities to see how ideology can penetrate philanthropy and turn it to its own ends. In the former period every organization was fair game for ideological prying and purification. In the latter period established voluntary organizations were repudiated along with the rest of mainstream institutions of the land.

One of the most interesting and difficult issues is the growing intellectual and cultural hostility toward religion, and with it hostility toward the organizations sustained by religious sponsors. One chose sides outside the classroom on the basis of arguments made within it. From a generally held view that American society was a religious society without an established church, the common academic view came to be that America was a secular society. From a proreligious culture to a culture that was tolerant of religious and nonreligious points of view—and that academics were hesitant to attack—the campus seemed to move steadily toward a culture that pushed religious influence to the margin and to lower status.

The central tendency of voluntary service shifts over time. The campus changes did not take place in isolation: new political issues emerged, and institutional leaders modified their opinions. Intellectual positions and values changed. The principal philanthropic shifts from between, say, the mid-1950s and the early 1970s seem to be from relief to reform, from social to political action, from

174   Critical Issues in American Philanthropy

service to advocacy. At this point, the 1980s seemed to show greater stability but less coherence than either of the earlier periods.

Liberal education in the 1950s was neatly packaged in programs of general education—core courses and required readings common to most students. The breakdown of consensus on the curriculum (whether the consensus had been earned by persuasion or imposed by authority) has been paralleled or followed by the breakdown of intellectual consensus. The curriculum became confused because the faculty was confused. The curriculum has been deconstructed, as it were; and as with deconstructed literature, no one seems sure whether there is anything left.

A New Field Emerges. In such a setting, new opportunities have arisen for new fields. Although departments remain strong politically, they are now the academic equivalent of the big city political machines of the early twentieth century. And like the political machines of the early part of this century, they find themselves increasingly out of step with reality. The political boundaries remain, but the intellectual boundaries have begun to fall. Startling new liaisons are arranged (biology and engineering, ethics and business, philosophy and technology, literature and politics). New fields appear out of liaisons between outside organizations and academic allies (Afro-American studies, women's studies, environmental studies, energy studies). Occupational opportunities spawn still others (criminal justice, medical technology, even nonprofit management).

"Philanthropic studies" today emerges in all of these channels, pushed, pulled, and parachuted in. The actors have changed, the instruments are different, the motivations are complex, the objectives are unclear. The scattered and fragmented and undernourished campus voluntary organizations are not the force behind philanthropic studies. There is no observable rising demand from undergraduates to understand the theory and history of voluntary service or the American philanthropic tradition. This is largely a movement from outside, and from the top down, a leadership trying to reestablish contact with its neglected allies.

The emergence of philanthropic studies comes at an important time. The common opinion is (1) that our young people are in trouble: their education seems to be less good in some important ways than it was in the past; (2) many of them are self-centered and self-indulgent to the extent that they will not make good parents, good employees or good citizens; (3) at a time when the needs for greater public and community service are called for, young people have been permitted or encouraged to think first or even exclusively of Number One; (4) ancient and persistent problems like homelessness are more visible than they have been in twenty years; modern and baffling problems like AIDS and drug abuse threaten the students themselves as well as anonymous strangers.

Those widely shared concerns are matched with a sense of rediscovery of America's honored tradition of voluntary association and voluntary service. The tradition receives bipartisan praise and ecumenical blessing. Government and the marketplace encourage it. Even scholarly research seems to justify it: altruistic behavior is a positive formula for psychological well-being and spiritual enrichment. Young people need it; the country needs it.

And, of course, there is evidence that recipients need it, too. There are more aged to care for, more small children in need of love and attention, young artists to encourage, young scholars to support. The society seems to produce a large disposable surplus, resources that could be captured in new taxes or that could be seduced by charitable appeals. Some will argue that we need new taxes to provide additional social and cultural and educational services and opportunities. The consensus seems to be that it would be better if all of us contributed voluntarily more of our individual or family surplus to good causes. It seems to be true that most of us have more money to give than we are now giving and that we have more time to give in service than we are now giving.

However, the retrenchment of the public sector because of the relative decline in tax revenues is paralleled by an increasingly narrow fixation on a short-term bottom line in the private sector. The third sector is thus implicitly called upon to expand to make up for the other two. If health costs are rising beyond our ability to pay, for example, the only way a high quality of health services can be paid for is by increases in voluntary contributions and voluntary service. The day may soon come when American cities will begin to look like the new urban communities in fifteenth-century England. Government could not pay for bridges or roads and so merchants and tradesmen built them. Philanthropy may one day be called upon to rescue us from toxic waste and municipal garbage.

Pressures and Obstacles. The emergence of philanthropic studies has diverse internal and external pressures behind it. Academically, every new field represents a new array of personal and professional opportunities, and some will wish to advance the study of philanthropy because it will help their careers. Some are attracted to it because it is in such a rudimentary conceptual state that it is difficult to separate good thought from bad. On the other hand, every new interdisciplinary field shakes up one or more of the self-satisfied or ossified disciplines. Every new field offers—for a while—opportunities for young scholars to make a name for themselves quickly. Every new field brings with it new publications, new scholarly associations, new networks. American higher education is like a Middle Eastern bazaar, with new traders arriving in an endless stream to display their wares, claiming new space or simply elbowing aside those who arrived earlier.

For all that, every new field is a high-risk venture. Conceptual uncertainty can kill a new field before it is strong enough to compete evenly with those who got there earlier. (One recommendation is to bluff it out; don't let anyone know you harbor doubts about what you are doing. Arrogance is presumably a more useful virtue than is humility.) Lack of a place in the structure makes every new field a threat to limited, inadequate resources. On the other hand, an existing large and well-funded profession can absorb a new field and smother it, or relegate it to apprentice status. Ambitions for new fields are usually higher than can be realized in academic time—developing new courses and programs is a painfully slow process when it is done well. It also seems to be true that many of the mechanisms of program and course review are designed to screen out the unorthodox and innovative as well as the inadequate.

Thus every new element of opportunity and progress will be weighted against a past practice, a past failure, an archaic doctrine. For those who fancy such fashions, philanthropic studies offers an exercise in weighing costs and benefits.

And then *money*. Without financial resources, it is difficult if not impossible to bring new fields into being. Governmental and corporate support have joined with foundation grants in recent decades to build academic scientific research into a vast enterprise. Most programs began with soft money and have either laid claim to hard money or failed to survive. Scholarships, fellowships, research support, space and equipment, library acquisitions, released time—all are important and all cost money. The dramatic new fact is that foundations and corporations, even individuals, have begun to invest in the study and practice of philanthropy. For the first time, resources are beginning to become available for the development of academic programs in philanthropic studies.

Teaching About Philanthropy

Four facts are vitally important for those who wish to teach about philanthropy. (1) The first fact is that philanthropy, at this stage in its development, is not a discipline. It may be thought of as parallel and analogous to politics and economics, but it does not yet have a clear conceptual shape. It is less defined, more like esthetics. As a field of study, philanthropy is already moving toward status as a profession. Applied philanthropy has put down its roots in business (as nonprofit organization management, arts management, and so on), in law (legal and tax aspects of philanthropy), in social work and in nursing (welfare policy, the "caring arts"), in public policy and environmental and public affairs (tax policy, welfare issues, trade-offs of technology).

Fund raising, the least respected field of all, is endemic to applied philanthropy. Because *every* field needs resources, people in such fields as physics and biochemistry and artificial intelligence and foreign languages come together (however reluctantly) to learn about how to raise money.

(2) The second fact of teaching about philanthropy is that it serves two groups of students: those who want to learn how to apply philanthropy (largely people with a professional interest in the field) and those who might enter into the liberal study of the organization, methods, and principles of philanthropy. All of us drawn to philanthropic studies should be trying to blend those two educational purposes. Only a few will consciously want to do both. Practice should indeed be informed by theory and history. Academic

study should indeed be informed and tested by experience. We do not yet know how to do that.

Thus far the only substantial effort to link theory and practice appears in the efforts of practitioners to learn about what they call "ethics." Like most people, and unlike most philosophers, philanthropic practitioners think of ethics as a monolithic concept. Ethics courses (taken by only 5 percent of undergraduates, by the way), in contrast, present the subject as a cluster of three to five conceptually incompatible approaches. The ethics of philanthropy offers an immediate opportunity to test the blending of ethical theory and practice. Much can be learned at the outset from those pioneers who have brought business ethics and medical ethics into professional consciousness.

Experience precedes theory. Every student brings personal experience of philanthropy acquired long before college. If students are encouraged to reflect on their own involvement in philanthropy—as donors and fund raisers and volunteers—the subject will be more interesting and more relevant. The problem is that we do not start with a mass of empirical data about the past experiences of students in philanthropic action. As far as I know there are no studies of what students think about their experience of going door-to-door for UNICEF, or about the appeals they heard as part of the Live Aid concert, or about how they were treated when they showed up to volunteer to raise money for cancer research. The socialization of the young into the practice of philanthropy seems to have been mechanical and manipulative—or wholly unstructured—rather than educational. I do not think we have information that will tell us whether those door-to-door solicitations build positive attitudes toward voluntary service or not. We may not even draw on the backgrounds of our own students: what was their own childhood introduction to philanthropy, and how does it influence their current activity (or lack of it)? Were enough of us to accumulate such information over time scholars might be able to interpret it to reveal important insights into the way experience shapes later learning.

A first principle of teaching philanthropy should be to ground the subject in personal experience and to compare the experience of one's own students with the experience of others who have engaged in the same kinds of activity.

(3) The earlier parts of this chapter talk about the number and diversity of student opportunities to practice philanthropy. There is presumably pedagogical value in the immediacy and convenience of evidence of philanthropy in action. The third fact about teaching philanthropy is that it is regularly in the news. Every daily newspaper carries reports of reform efforts, fund-raising benefits, relief crises, memorial services for people whose obituaries give pride of place to their voluntary service. H. Richard Niebuhr's persistent ethical question is "What is going on?"[5] Alas, Jim and Tammy Faye Bakker were part of *what is going on* in American philanthropy. The current debates about the unrelated income of nonprofits is part of what is going on. The abuse of tax-exempt status to direct private funds to support the Contras is part of what is going on. Mother Teresa is part of what is going on. Auctioning dates with handsome young bachelors for charity is also part of what is going on.

(4) The fourth fact about teaching philanthropy is that the field contains many actors and organizations, and a bewildering range of acronyms. It is important to impose order on this apparent chaos, usually by asserting a working definition: in my case, "voluntary action for the public good," with some sense of the historical usage of the two most common terms, *charity* and *philanthropy,* the difference between them and their dilution into labels for the whole array of activity under consideration. The conceptual division of American society into three sectors is another arbitrary but useful ordering device. Widely diverse behavior is then forced into several awkward but generally accepted categories: the purposes that are claimed as the goals of philanthropy, the sources of funds, and the numbers of volunteers and associations.

I cannot presume to make suggestions about how the ideas and facts about philanthropy should be brought into existing courses in economics or psychology or marketing or the history of science or so on. Nor can I make useful suggestions about how to teach courses about philanthropy in the various disciplines and professions. The focus here is on interdisciplinary courses in philanthropy that might be offered as part of the general education of undergraduates.

One Man's Approach

All of my formal "teaching" about philanthropy thus far has been in the form of seminars, most of them with scholars and professionals. With dozens of lectures, perhaps hundreds, behind me, I approach my first engagement with undergraduates with some sense that the gap between my knowledge and theirs is probably much narrower than it is in many of the courses they take. That is an advantage rather than a barrier. The question is whether teaching about philanthropy to adult college graduates who know little about the philanthropic tradition is different from teaching undergraduates who know even less about it.

My own approach is more humanistic than scientific or professional. It tries to sort out what we mean when we talk about "philanthropic values." The subject is for me an inquiry into the history of ideas, the study of a historical tradition that has immediate and important consequences in its modern expression.

That means that I think that we should *use* history to teach about philanthropy and *use* philosophy to teach about philanthropy. We should feel free to borrow (if not shamelessly, at least unapologetically) from economics and political science and law. We should wander into comparative religion and comparative politics and comparative institutions. I hope that we are also willing to draw material from unreliable sources like novels and personal journals and daily newspapers in order to make the practice of philanthropy more visible. We should be willing to test theoretical models (collective choice, for example) against the experience of applied philanthropy to try to determine whether the theory is inadequate or whether we are wearing ideological blinders.

My purpose is to engage students in thinking about philanthropy, to link it to their own observation and to their own experience, without either discarding or overvaluing my own experience. Some of us must be willing to proceed on the corrigible conviction that "philanthropy" is a useful concept and that voluntary service and voluntary giving are marks of the virtuous person.

The guiding pedagogical philosophy that I seek to employ is "exploratory discourse." That suggests a structured discussion drawing on diverse facts and values and opinions rather than a lecture transmitting securely grounded information. The substance of philanthropy is not fixed but dynamic. Inquiry into philanthropy is the continuing exploration of open-ended social issues: poverty, patronage, paternalism, public goods, all arising out of widely shared experience.

Philanthropy is above all a tradition, and in a sense the embodiment of the idea of tradition—of serial reciprocity.[6] That does not mean that philanthropy cannot be studied out of its historical context. It simply reinforces the notion that theory and practice over time have to be brought together sooner or later.

Were I prescribing a core course in the study of philanthropy for all undergraduates, my recommendation would be less ambitious. First, I would start with facts, events, and familiar practices. I would attempt to show how they fit into the taxonomy of tax-exempt organizations. I would argue that that is one way of describing the subject at hand. Second, I would ask the students to begin by reading about the history of American philanthropy, using selections either from Brian O'Connell's *America's Voluntary Spirit* (Foundation Center, 1983) or from Robert Bremner's *American Philanthropy* (University of Chicago Press, 1988) or both. Those two steps would provide a sense of what "philanthropy" is about and some awareness of how we got where we are. I would try to include some reference to the Western tradition of philanthropy, arguing that it is the tradition that is clearly dominant in our culture. I would also make reference to the presence of philanthropic practices in other, non-Western cultures (and prepare to be chastised again for making too much of American distinctiveness). I would also try to introduce questions about philanthropy in socialist and capitalist societies that either suppress philanthropy or deny its importance. The question should be asked: If the United States relies more heavily on voluntary action for the public good than do other societies, what difference does it make?

A third step would be to propose some of the "principles" (the quotation marks are meant to emphasize the lack of consensus) of philanthropic practice: serial reciprocity, for example, or the bias toward the poor. A fourth step would be to examine some of the most familiar philanthropic values, such as respect for the recipient or the importance of public recognition or anonymity for the donor.

The emphasis on history and tradition does not mean to begin with traces of philanthropic action in ancient Egypt. It may mean working backward from the present. It may also mean working from the American experience toward non-Western cultures. To stress the historical also risks rejection by a student population largely without historical consciousness, but I do not intend in my own teaching to abandon the effort to make history a central part of education. I would rather try to find ways to start with the present and work backward, hoping that curiosity might grow rather than wither in the process. One might begin with the worldwide series of fund-raising concerts sponsored by Amnesty International, for example, baldly capitalizing on the appeal not of human rights but of rock music. One might ask about the role of philanthropy in the emergence of human rights as a social movement. One can move in that same path back to the 1985 Live Aid concert in behalf of famine victims in Africa and from there to the Bangladesh concert a decade earlier and from there toward the involvement of entertainers in raising funds for Liberty Bonds in World War I. The cause of relief for famine victims is as old as history itself; when did entertainers become involved? Should entertainers make their talent available for chauvinistic appeals as well as charitable ones? (My approach asks a great many "should" questions.)

I do not assume that the majority of undergraduates taking a first course in philanthropy will be ready to plunge into studies of the differences between charitable practice in England and the United States in the late nineteenth century, or to analyze changes in the definition of charity and philanthropy since the Statute of Charitable Uses of 1601, or the correlation between changing rates of church attendance and voluntary service. There might be more interest in exploration of the past when it raises awkward questions about the current style of large-scale fund raising and consciousness raising. Many students of philanthropy, practitioners as well as scholars, are deeply concerned about the depersonalization of philanthropic values as fund raising and promotion of causes grow in scale and technical complexity. Philanthropic values imply (and sometimes assert) a higher morality than marketplace values. In addition to truthfulness, a value praised (by lip service) in both sectors, there is an explicit assertion of concern for the well-being of others in philanthropy that is supposed to be different from the self-interest of the marketplace. I use phrases like "supposed to be" because there are those who will argue differently: that self-interest drives philanthropy like everything else, or even that the entrepreneurship is intrinsically altruistic. Others will argue that philanthropy is not necessary in a just society and that we should therefore devote our efforts to reform or even to revolution to achieve justice (and that justice is the supreme value).

Throughout our courses we should encourage students to think about their future personal involvement in philanthropy, either as volunteers or as prospective employees. All students will turn out to be one or the other, as well as beneficiaries of the voluntary action of unknown benefactors, past and present.

The informal sketch for an introductory course in the philanthropic tradition that follows was designed for the honors program in Political and Social Thought at the University of Virginia.

The Philanthropic Tradition:
An Introduction to Voluntary Action for Public Purposes.

Course Outline

This interdisciplinary course will examine the core values of philanthropy and the principal patterns of philanthropic behavior and organization with particular emphasis on the Western tradition and the American adaptation of it. American practice extends from interpersonal assistance to large-scale enterprise, from efforts to shape the social and moral agenda to the provision of cultural services in museums and theaters. Individuals are encouraged, urged, implored, and pressed to contribute their time, their money, and their enthusiasm. The scope and complexity of the philanthropic "system" is praised and criticized for its organization, its purposes, and its results. The course will, as a consequence, also examine the principal critiques of voluntary philanthropic action. Students will be expected to draw on their personal experience as participants in the work of nonprofit organizations.

I. Overview

Contemporary definitions of philanthropy in terms of a third sector of voluntary service, voluntary association, and voluntary giving. The place of philanthropy in the other two sectors (the economic and political).

Readings: Merle Curti, "Philanthropy," in *Dictionary of the History of Ideas*, vol. III, pp. 486–493, Scribner's, 1973. James Douglas, *Why Charity? The Rationale for a Third Sector*, pp. 11–33, Sage, 1983. Robert L.

Payton, "Gleanings," in *Philanthropy*, Macmillan, 1988. (Additional selections from Burton Weisbrod, *The Nonprofit Economy*, Harvard, 1988; Michael O'Neill, *The Third America*, Jossey-Bass, 1989; Richard Magat, ed., *Philanthropic Giving*, Oxford, 1990.)

II. The Core Values of Philanthropy

Philanthropy is often traced to its religious origins in the ancient world of the Middle East. Its secular origins are usually found in the philosophies and institutional innovations of classical Greece and Rome. Benevolence and humanitarianism blend religious and secular values in the emergence of new philanthropic institutions and practices in Elizabethan England and prerevolutionary France. Other core values, such as the concept of serial reciprocity, differ among cultures (for example, in gift exchange). The modern synthesis of charity and philanthropy appears in the latter decades of the nineteenth century in England and the United States and expands ambitiously in the United States during the first half of the twentieth century. Voluntary action diminished throughout western Europe during the rise of the welfare state, calling into question the legitimacy as well as the effectiveness of voluntary initiatives for the public good. Recent American experience reveals a loss of confidence in public welfare and— perhaps—a diminishing commitment to philanthropy.

  Readings: Selections from Deuteronomy, the Prophets, Matthew, Maimonides, Thomas Aquinas, Butler; selections from Aristotle, Cicero, Seneca; selections from Smith, Hume, Mandeville, Tocqueville, W. K. Jordan, Lord Beveridge, Owen, Boulding. Charles S. Loch, "Charity and Charities," in the eleventh edition of the *Encyclopaedia Britannica*, 1910, published in expanded form as *Charity and Social Life*, 1910, remains the only historical overview of philanthropy other than the short Curti essay mentioned above. Also Payton's "Philanthropic Values," in Magat, *Philanthropic Giving*, cited above.

III. Philanthropy as a Virtue

The Western tradition reveals concurrent streams of philanthropic behavior: one emphasizes community and the participation of individuals in philanthropy through organizations (especially the church); the other stream grows out of Western ideas of individualism and is reflected in values of personal responsibility, stewardship, and praiseworthy action that goes beyond what is expected. The place of philanthropy (charity, benevolence, generosity) among the virtues brings out the difficult problems of balancing generosity and prudence, charity and justice.

  Readings: Selections from Aristotle on virtue in the *Ethics*, David Hume on benevolence in the *Essays*, Adam Smith on benevolence in *The Theory of Moral Sentiment*, John Dewey on virtue in his *Ethics* (with James Tufts), Walter Lippman from *A Preface to Morals*, James Wallace's contemporary academic analysis of generosity in *Virtues and Vices*, and Judith Shklar's contrasting reflections on *mis*anthropy in *Ordinary Vices*.

IV. Philanthropic Institutions

Organized philanthropy has played an important role in the development of social and cultural institutions, from the establishment of temples and churches, hospitals, schools, theaters, and the complex problems of their maintenance and support (raising questions of legal constraints on bequests, endowments, and the mixing of private and public funds).

Readings: A. R. Hands, *Charities and Social Life in Greece and Rome;* Jacob Neusner, *Tzedakah;* Brian Tierney, *Medieval Poor Law;* readings on Byzantine and Confucian philanthropy; the 1601 Statute of Charitable Uses; "The Taxonomy of Tax-Exempt Organizations," INDEPENDENT SECTOR, 1987; Walter Trattner, *From Poor Law to Welfare State;* Paul Barker, *Founders of the Welfare State.*

V. The Critique of Philanthropy

Throughout the history of philanthropy, concerns have been expressed about both its methods and its consequences. For example, the ancient Judaic and early Christian literature is sensitive to the dignity of the recipient as well as to the sin of pride on the part of the donor. The institution of the dole in Greece and Rome raised questions about "pauperization," an important unintended consequence of social action in behalf of the poor. Philanthropy allegedly serving as a device used by the rich against the poor and as a means for those in power to extend and retain that power has been a commonplace in Marxist literature. Modern variations appear in language of "domination and dependency," as well as false consciousness. Modern economic and political analysis has amplified the power of rational self-interest in ways that suggest that philanthropy must be coerced (in theories of collective or public choice). Philanthropic action also brings out two modern themes of *rights* and *basic needs*. The underlying structural tension in the Western philanthropic tradition is the movement from charity to justice, from considering basic needs as basic rights.

Readings: Hands (*Charities and Social Life in Greece and Rome*) notes the emphasis on community values in the classical world as well as the importance of individual honor and its recognition beyond the grave. W.E.H. Lecky, *History of European Morals* (1869) is representative of nineteenth-century rationalist approaches; Michael Ignatieff, *The Needs of Strangers* offers a contrasting contemporary view; Albert Memmi on *Dependence* is a critique from a French sociologist writing from an anticolonial perspective; Martin Anderson's *Welfare* portrays a contemporary argument against pauperization as the result of public charity. (Anderson was Reagan's domestic policy adviser during the first term.) Marx discusses philanthropy briefly in the *Economic and Philosophical Manuscripts;* Iain MacLean provides an accessible introduction to *Public Choice; Basic Human Needs* identifies a popular concept among those active in economic development in underdeveloped countries.

VI. Philanthropy in Action

The philanthropic response to the Ethiopian famine provides a recent and graphic illustration of a set of issues central to charity and philanthropy abroad. The response also brings out the American style of philanthropy, with its use of popular entertainers and communications technology.

Readings: Robert L. Payton, "Philanthropy in Action," in *Philanthropy: Four Views* (the Social Philosophy and Policy Center and Transaction Books, 1988); Peter Singer and Onora O'Neill are contemporary philosophers who have written on responses to famine; Garrett Hardin is well known as an opponent of famine relief on moral grounds; the economist Amartya Sen has written extensively and helpfully on famine. Roger Riddell has written a thorough review of the issues from a development perspective in *Foreign Aid Reconsidered*.

VII. Philanthropic Studies in the University

The perspectives of the disciplines and professions are examined. Also addressed is the place of philanthropy in studies of literature, philosophy, religion, history, psychology, economics, anthropology, sociology, political science, law, business, social work, and education.

Readings: There are suggestive analogies in the literature surrounding the emergence of sociology a century ago and around the emergence of women's studies, Afro-American studies, and other interdisciplinary "fields." Higher education itself has emerged as a field and is described in *The Academic Revolution* of David Riesman and Christopher Jencks. Talcott Parsons's *The American University* is immediately relevant to this topic, and his conceptual framework may be particularly valuable in philanthropic studies generally.

VIII. Voluntary Service

The ultimate objective of the course is to enrich the understanding of social justice and individual responsibility. Students will be encouraged to reflect on their personal experience and to relate that to their own personality, character, and sense of virtue.

Exercise: Students will be asked to take the Myers-Briggs Personality Type Inventory. The test will be given at the beginning of the course and presented to the students at the conclusion of the course. The purpose of the exercise is to help students relate their personal preferences to their participation in voluntary action and to their ability to work with others in voluntary settings.

Students will be able to offer a ten- to fifteen-page paper based on a description and analysis of their voluntary service or on more traditional scholarly research. A one-page description of the paper will be submitted for approval beforehand. There will also be a midterm and a final exam. The grade will reflect class participation, exams, and the paper and will give equal weight to each.

Notes

1. *Philanthropy* is defined here as embracing voluntary service, voluntary association, and voluntary giving.

2. Henry David Thoreau, "Economy." In *Walden*. Princeton,

N.J.: Princeton University Press, 1971. (Originally published 1854.)

3. Ralph Waldo Emerson, "Self-Reliance." In *The Essays of Ralph Waldo Emerson*. New York: Berner, 1944. (Originally published 1847.)

4. Will Durant, *The Story of Philosophy*. New York: Simon & Schuster, 1926.

5. H. Richard Niebuhr, *The Responsible Self: An Essay in Christian Moral Philosophy*. New York: Harper & Row, 1963, p. 60.

6. *Serial reciprocity* is Kenneth Boulding's term for repaying the debts that we owe to our parents by what we give to our children. See *The Economy of Love and Fear*. Belmont, Calif.: Wadsworth, 1973, pp. 26–27.

Chapter 8   *Elizabeth T. Boris*
                                             Teresa J. Odendahl

Ethical Issues in Fund Raising and Philanthropy

This chapter explores the application of ethics to philanthropy at the operational level in the realms of governance, fund raising, and public accountability. Our premise is that many decisions made on a daily basis in this field have ethical dimensions that are not recognized as such. Our goal is to call attention to some of these areas and to examine the implications from the perspective of ethics.

Philanthropic ethics is a relatively new and unexplored area that is beginning to attract attention, though seldom in a systematic or comprehensive way. The concepts of philanthropy and ethics are complex and mean different things to different people. As Paul N. Ylivsaker has commented, "When you put two words like ethics and philanthropy together, you are in trouble; each of them resists definition, and when combined, they can be totally elusive."[1]

Other chapters in this volume explore the various meanings of *philanthropy* in some detail. We use the term in its most inclusive sense, as private money and volunteerism for the public good. Philanthropy covers local, national, and international activities and nonprofit institutions as diverse as advocacy efforts, the arts, community and neighborhood groups, foundations, hospitals, museums, religious organizations, and schools and universities. Philanthropy is also the province of large and small donors. All of these entities exist in a complicated web of interdependent relationships and multiple roles that also involve business and government in providing services for our society.

Ethics is the discipline that deals with what is good and bad, a set of moral principles, or a theory about ways of acting based on common values. In this chapter we will not discuss the various philosophical approaches to ethics reflected in the writings of the great philosophers.[2] Behaviors that exemplify the values of honesty, justice, and equity are those we refer to as ethical. They embody fairness and the universal golden rule. This view of ethics reflects Judeo-Christian and democratic values: it couples respect and compassion for the individual with responsibility for the impact of one's actions on the community.

In a basic sense, ethics is a concern with choices and operates beyond the realm of the law. Making choices between culturally defined good and bad actions may be easy, although it may require courage. Ethical choices become most difficult when competing values are at stake, for example, privacy versus disclosure, or when there is a need to assign priorities among important values such as educating or healing. In many instances there is no simple right answer, and ethical behavior consists of carefully weighing competing claims and making reasoned decisions within a framework that considers the impact on individuals, the organization, and the community.

Conversations about philanthropic ethics often become entangled in the positive value of the work because philanthropy is often considered synonymous with "doing good" or being ethical. According to Robert L. Payton, "[I]t is within the philanthropic tradition that the moral agenda of society is put forward."[3] Is the philanthropic sector somehow different from other areas of society? Should we assume that philanthropy embodies higher standards? Since the goals of philanthropy are usually considered worthy and above question, the ethical implications of the means are not often seriously examined. Compared to business ethics or government ethics, the literature on philanthropic ethics is sparse and not well developed.

Michael O'Neill argues persuasively that managing any organization, private, public, or nonprofit, requires moral responsibility to enable that organization to meet its goals, whatever they are.[4] Choosing among competing values is no easier for nonprofits than for business or government, although the framework of expectations about ends is different. In business, profit and the satisfaction of customers may be paramount; in government, public interest and the well-being of the citizen and the state may be the primary objectives; in nonprofits, public interest and the well-being of the clients or those people or ideas served may be most important. If philanthropy is a form of public service, then ethical choices in philanthropy should enhance civic life and advance the values of democracy.

In addition, one can argue that society expects educators, ministers, nonprofit social service providers, and volunteers to be role models of moral responsibility. For example, in recent cases people seem more shocked by the improprieties of religious leaders than of Wall Street investors or politicians. Trust and stewardship, perhaps to a greater extent than in other sectors, characterize the expectations of philanthropic behavior. Thus one might expect ethics to be a guiding force in the organizations of this sector and a topic worthy of extensive examination and discussion.[5] In the following sections we address some of the issues involved in three important areas: governance, fund raising, and public accountability.

Governance

Philanthropic entities are generally governed by voluntary boards of directors who are charged to serve the public interest. In addition to the legal duties of due care and fiduciary responsibility, the board approves policies and procedures that ensure that the organization operates efficiently, effectively, and ethically. While practices vary, the board usually hires the executive, helps to raise funds, and oversees operations. If there are no employees, the board members may act as staff, running the organization themselves.

Operating Philosophy. The board is responsible for adopting and periodically reviewing the overall mission and goals of the nonprofit organization. Over the course of time, a board may have to make difficult choices about the continued relevance of the organization itself or its programs. Operating philosophies that have a basic orientation toward justice, respect, equity, and accountability, both inside and outside the organization, demonstrate ethical sensitivity. But implementing such ideals may raise ethical dilemmas. For example, productions of arts organizations with high expenses may be priced out of the reach of many in the community. In such instances, steps might be taken to raise additional monies, to lower admission fees, or to develop special programs accessible to the broader community.

In our view, policies and procedures should self-consciously address the question of access to services or grants. Boards should be aware of the moral dimension and long-term implications of choices about the quality of programs, as well as the numbers of people and segment of the population that are served. This is as relevant for a college or university as it is for a fund-raising intermediary like United Way, a hospital, or a small nonprofit service agency. For givers, both foundations and intermediaries, this means a fair process that provides a thorough pre-grant review without interfering in the program, subverting the mission, or imposing excessive constraints on the use of funds. For service organizations, it means a fair process to determine whom to serve with what programs. What are the most pressing needs? Who is underserved?

In the spirit of public trust, an organization should attempt to ensure that it does no harm through its services, programs, or grants. The board is responsible for assessing the benefits and costs to society of the activities it undertakes. For example, a foundation working on urban redevelopment must weigh the costs of displacing individuals and families in the short term against the potential long-term benefits of the renovation project. Will those displaced have adequate housing? Will the project benefit them? A concerted effort to weigh the implications of the choices and consider alternatives characterizes ethical sensitivity.

An essential, but often unarticulated, part of an organization's operating philosophy is its attitude toward those it serves (students, patients, clients, patrons) and toward its colleagues in similar endeavors. Respect for the individual and disclosure of pertinent information are two basic requirements. How much control of the individual client or grantee organization is really necessary to provide effective services or a successful grant project? The criticisms of arrogance, paternalism, and elitism that are sometimes leveled at nonprofit organizations should be considered seriously. Has the organization lost its compassion? Is anyone listening to individual members or involving them in improving the services or making the services more respectful of personal dignity? Considering such questions at regular intervals can be an effective means of ensuring that an organization remains true to high standards of responsibility and service.

Board Operation and Composition. Trustees are responsible for developing clear policies and procedures as well as overseeing their implementation. This responsibility extends to their own performance and tenure. One such policy involves actual and apparent conflicts of interest. A director whose business provides services must carefully consider the ethics of, for example, bidding for a contract with the nonprofit group he or she serves. If the director were to benefit financially from such an arrangement, this might be viewed as compromising his or her objectivity and a clear conflict of interest. But what if the director were willing to provide the service for free or at cost? Even if the nonprofit would receive a benefit and the trustee would not realize a profit, might his or her objectivity still be compromised? Or might there be other benefits for the giver such as visibility? To outsiders such a relationship might appear to be a conflict of interest and might damage the nonprofit's reputation. In addition, might such a gift undercut a business competitor, or might it be a charitable contribution for the trustee? Does the resolution depend on how badly the nonprofit needs the service or how many more clients could be served?

In accordance with democratic values, a board should have a process for selection of board members and reflect in its composition the diversity of the community served. Self-perpetuating boards often lead to charges of "cronyism," as John Nason notes in his excellent publication on board selection among foundations.[6] Women, people of color, ethnic groups, the disabled, and others add important, often neglected perspectives to governing boards and advisory committees. Individuals with the necessary financial and program skills (and training) help the organization carry out its mission. A nonprofit group that serves a primarily Hispanic community gains necessary insights when at least some board members are Hispanic, speak Spanish, and understand the culture. While inclusiveness might seem like a pragmatic operating principle, debates on this issue often take the form of weighing competing values—excellence versus inclusivity. Addressing the issues openly and dispelling stereotypes involves a commitment to fairness and an ethical perspective.

Oversight of Employees. The board has a moral responsibility for the working conditions and well-being of employees. This responsibility extends to both material rewards and less tangible factors such as leadership and morale. When a nonprofit has a paid staff, providing a policy of equal opportunity and affirmative action in recruitment and promotion encourages the same values of diversity that are helpful on a board. A higher proportion of women and minorities work in nonprofit agencies, but generally at low wages. Establishing adequate salaries, benefits, and personnel policies that include fair processes for employee grievances is within the purview of the board. This can be particularly difficult because it involves the gray area of overlapping board and staff responsibilities.

A fair procedure for valuing specific job duties to determine salary levels is an ethical issue. On the one hand, there is general agreement that the expertise and dedication of nonprofit employees must be adequately rewarded; on the other, there is a perception that public service work should not be highly compensated or reach levels common in private corporations. Paradoxically, there seems to be tolerance of salaries for top positions that are much higher than those of other employees or of public officials. And as in the business sector, large successful organizations can afford to reward employees at higher levels. Boards are increasingly going to have to wrestle with the ethical implications of their salary structures, in terms of the staff they wish to hire and retain, the clients they serve, the needs of the society, and the perception of public service that they wish to convey or promote.

In some cases the services that a nonprofit group can undertake may be limited by excessive salaries. In other cases, services may be maximized and costs may be minimized through very low wages;

but these wages may be so low that the employees must live in poverty. Service decisions should be based on a conscious trade-off among competing values: maximizing services or minimizing fund raising versus employee wages. Contributing to the ranks of the working poor is a decision that the board should not make lightly. And in a humane workplace, special employee needs such as day care and parental leave must also be considered.

The notion of "professionalism" enters into this discussion at several levels. The board is responsible for general oversight of employees and should ensure that staff members are trained adequately for their work. But board members may not necessarily have the qualifications for technical oversight of the staff. For example, should a responsible agency that provides counseling to clients have psychiatrists or psychologists on the board or in an advisory capacity? On the whole, most paid service providers and some intermediaries are more likely to have professional credentials related to their work than are the volunteer board members who oversee them. Most religious organizations require specific education for ministers, priests, and rabbis. The state regulates some mental health professionals and social workers. An ethical consideration is whether board or staff ultimately determines policy and directs the organization. How are differences that involve professional expertise decided? Perhaps a value of nonprofit groups is that boards with general perspectives and professional staffs with technical expertise may mutually develop creative approaches to problems.

A related issue concerns the qualifications of institutional or individual funders to make decisions about the technical ability of service providers and the worthiness of projects. Some individuals employed by or on the boards of grant-making organizations may have specialized expertise, but often they are generalists. (The use of consultants or advisory panels may provide needed expertise.) But an opportunity to receive informed and fair consideration of proposed projects is an ethical issue. Although organizations such as the Council on Foundations, the National Network of Grantmakers, the Philanthropic Roundtable, and regional associations of grant makers all contribute to the professional development of grant makers, there is little systematic training and no credentialing in the process of grant making.

Oversight of Volunteers. Volunteers are an essential resource for many nonprofits and an important way of involving citizens in their communities. Board members are themselves volunteers, as are unpaid workers at every level. Decisions about recruiting, training, and using volunteers involve ethical choices at many levels. Policies to train and use volunteers effectively and with dignity should be developed and implemented. If volunteers are an important part of an organization, their work must be evaluated along with that of the paid staff if the overall impact of the agency is to be accurately assessed. Inadequately trained volunteers may do more harm than good, and if such volunteers are also important donors, the organization may be reluctant to apply its usual standards to them. Such situations raise ethical dilemmas that must be resolved. Matching volunteers with assignments that are appropriate to their skills is a part of responsible management.

Fund Raising

Fund raising is central to the ability of nonprofit organizations to meet their goals. Private contributions from individuals and institutions, however, represent only about 27 percent of income in the field. Government grants and contracts add another 27 percent to the budgets of nonprofits. An increasing proportion of the revenue of nonprofit groups, almost 38 percent, is derived from dues, fees, and charges. The remaining receipts are from endowment and investment income.[7] Each of these income sources has its own set of problems and choices that boards must resolve. Ultimately, boards must develop a mix of strategies that permits the organization to obtain the necessary revenues and to operate with integrity.

The Appeals. There is a host of methods used to raise funds for nonprofit organizations, and more seem to be developed each year. These include appeals to the general population through direct mail, telephone, television, and door-to-door canvassing; personal solicitation of major donors and organization members; special events such as charity balls, dinners, and concerts, as well as runathons and walkathons; and formal grant proposals to foundations and government agencies.

A variety of potential conflicts and ethical dilemmas can arise in each of these contexts. Some methods are more effective and/or costly than others. Some are more intrusive. Because revenue is both difficult to obtain and essential to ongoing operations, fund raising may begin to shape an organization's mission and dominate its activities. Program staff may be pressed into fund-raising roles, and the mission may be shifted into areas that have greater appeal to donors. These are choices, often with ethical components, that the board and staff should confront and decide with clear understanding of the impact on the organization, its mission, and those its serves.

The need to attract attention and persuade a giver to contribute to one particular program rather than another may lead to competition among organizations, overdramatization of causes, and a less than fair presentation of the facts. In order to demonstrate need and open pocketbooks, the appeal is often emotional, such as using photographs of starving children. False and misleading appeals are on their face unethical and perhaps illegal. To protect the credibility of the agency and the field, nonprofit boards must take a stand against shading the truth and manipulating potential donors. Boards are responsible for the policies that undergird the fund-raising appeal. Those policies should not be left to the fund raiser. They should reflect the character and integrity of the organization and the sector of which it is a part. Clearly presented information that informs the donor about the program and how the money will be used is required.

A successful appeal for a particular program may tempt an organization to use some of that money for less popular programs or for the more difficult to fund general operating expenses. Issues of openness, accountability, and survival may be at stake in such cases. Honesty and disclosure are the ethical precepts that can help boards make choices that will not betray public trust.

Conflicting issues of privacy and free speech are raised by some fund-raising methods, and these promise to become even more controversial in coming years. Boards are going to have to weigh the success of intrusive fund-raising methods against the impact on the potential donor and the public perception of the organization and of philanthropy. The specter of citizens asking to be shielded from philanthropic appeals that reach into their homes via telephone may haunt the field in years to come. Efforts to develop a code of ethics in telemarketing reflect not only the need for standards but increasing regulatory pressure.[8]

Commercializaton. Shrinking dollars and rising needs have caused many nonprofits to look outside traditional philanthropy for funds. Charges, dues, and fees may be introduced or increased when revenues are needed. Fees raise a number of ethical questions: Is it ethical for a nonprofit to exclude those who are not able to pay? What if the alternative is the inability to provide any services at all? Is "creaming" (serving only those who can afford to pay the most) ethical? Who should serve those who cannot afford to pay?

A variety of entrepreneurial schemes to generate necessary income involve unrelated business activities. Such activities may commercialize nonprofits and divert their energies from their primary mission. In addition, nonprofits may find themselves in competition with profit-making enterprises. This is currently a serious issue that is having an impact on the whole field and may result in significant regulatory consequences.[9]

Under what circumstances, for example, is a nonprofit community agency that provides recreational programs unfairly competing with for-profit health clubs? Do nonprofit organizations have an obligation to serve low-income clients? If they do not or if they cannot justify their lower fees in contrast to profit-making entities, is that an adequate justification for removing their tax-exempt status? These are questions currently being resolved by the courts. But the principles involve ethical choices about how to raise revenue and what sectors of society to serve. Actions that contribute to the perception that philanthropic agencies are profit-maximizing entities undermine the legitimacy of the sector. Boards and staffs of philanthropic agencies should recognize the ethical as well as the fund-raising dimensions of these types of activities.

"Cause-related marketing" is an increasingly popular fund-raising and marketing strategy that has provoked a great deal of feeling, both pro and con.[10] Initially, in this type of advertising, certain major credit card companies endorsed particular charities and contributed a proportion of the total expenditures of card-

198 Critical Issues in American Philanthropy

holders toward those causes. Since the concept was introduced, it has spread to the marketing of other products and services where companies promise to give, for example, one cent to charity for each unit of product sold. The concept is controversial because of the many serious questions it raises: Is this approach mutually beneficial to nonprofits and businesses? Does it undercut charities that are not selected for promotions? Does a nonprofit become identified with a corporation and its products? Is it perceived as endorsing the company's products? What is the impact on the scope of corporate philanthropy and on the general concept of the social responsibility of business? Is a corporation fulfilling its social responsibility by participating in cause-related marketing? Is this charity or is it business?

Maurice Gurin argues that cause-related marketing is business.[11] The company receives a business deduction, and the charity receives a piece of the profits that is unrelated business income. Gurin sees this as an unwarranted commercialization of philanthropy that helps corporations target desirable segments of the market for their advertising while putting nonprofits in the position of converting their donors to customers of a particular business. Not only is this questionable from an ethical perspective, but he maintains that it is bad management. In the long run corporations go on to other markets and the charity must dissociate itself from the product and rebuild its donor base. Philanthropy may be trivialized and the value of its contributions to democratic life overshadowed by being used in marketing campaigns.

Others, including Philip Webster, argue that cause-related marketing is a productive partnership for both business and philanthropy. It brings visibility to the cause and is effective in raising the dollars so badly needed.[12]

Is the commercialization of a charity in its best interest or in the best interest of the sector? The issues are not simple, and the long-term consequences may be profound. Boards are urged to consider very seriously their stewardship responsibilities for future generations when making decisions about cause-related marketing.

Costs. The level of fund-raising costs is increasingly a concern. States, local communities, and watchdog organizations are involved in trying to set limits for reasonable expenses. Should nonprofits agree to pay commissions or bonuses to fund raisers on the basis of the amounts contributed, or should they negotiate a flat fee? For example, a major university may hire a development expert to implement a capital campaign for a 5 percent commission. If the campaign successfully raises $50 million, then the consultant has earned $2.5 million for the work. If the campaign fails, the consultant gets nothing with a commission arrangement, but he or she still gets a fee when working on a flat-fee basis.

The uses of commissions, bonuses, and gifts must be carefully assessed in light of the costs to the organization and the commercialization of its mission. This is both a cost-benefit issue and an ethical question. Though not completely resolved, there is a consensus, at least among the major fund-raising organizations, that commissions are not ethical. Recently, however, both the American Association of Fund-Raising Counsel and the National Society of Fund-Raising Executives took out of their ethical codes the prohibition against working for a commission on the advice of their counsel. Such a prohibition, it was argued, could be viewed as a restraint of trade.

It is too soon to know whether this change will affect the norms. It appears that the technologies of telemarketing, direct mail, and other forms of fund raising are increasingly conducive to percentage contracts. These methods are also amenable to high-pressure tactics, particularly if the solicitor is paid on commission. Paid solicitors may usurp the role of volunteers and in the process mute the message and personal appeal of the organization. Neither the sector nor the public is well served by fund-raising campaigns that produce a handsome return for the consultant and little for the charity. In addition to undermining public trust, the agency's financial integrity and management oversight are called into question.

Standard-setting bodies such as the National Charities Information Bureau (NCIB) and the Philanthropic Advisory Service of the Council of Better Business Bureaus also monitor fund-raising costs. For example, the newly revised NCIB "Standards in Philanthropy" now specify that at least 60 percent of annual expenses be applied to the organization's program. Attempts by various states to legislate limits on fund-raising levels, however, have been struck down by the courts, leaving appropriate costs in the realm of ethics, at least for now. The issue has entered the public policy arena, however, and will probably take on added importance in years to come.

The arguments against high fund-raising costs may at times be frustrating to nonprofit executives. Such costs may be viewed as an investment that, though expensive, may pay off handsomely in higher revenues. In the same vein, foundations and other endowed organizations, by trying to keep administrative expenses low, may choose to incur lower investment costs than others who pay for high-performance asset managers. If the higher costs result in greater gains, is there an ethical problem? These issues involve conflicting values and expectations that must be discussed openly and resolved by boards and staffs of nonprofits. How donated money is used involves trust and disclosure. Confidence built up over years can be destroyed by methods that appear wasteful or enriching for the organization's managers.

Public Accountability and Standards

Accountability is an overarching issue that we touched on in the earlier sections of this chapter. We raise it again here because we feel that ethics and accountability are intertwined at many levels. Ethical discourse often arises in the context of assessing an organization's responsibility to inform the public, donors, and those served directly. A policy of full disclosure of financial and program information is not only an accountability mechanism; the flow of information permits ethical considerations to be raised and discussed both internally and externally. Disclosure is the keystone of trust and stewardship upon which the sector is built. The requirement of disclosure is particularly compelling where it affects access to and oversight of the organization. Nevertheless, there is often a need to protect the confidentiality of clients and the privacy of donors. In what circumstances, then, should the identity of givers, intermediaries, or providers remain confidential?

Funders help themselves, intermediaries, and providers when they acknowledge and disclose (often in an annual report) information such as former grantees, funding areas, philosophy, and size and number of grants. Inappropriate applications can thereby be limited. In the same manner, intermediaries and providers are responsible for giving full and honest information in such areas as overhead, numbers of people served, effectiveness, and even past failures. The philanthropic community is served by having such information guide its decisions.

Evaluation. Governing bodies are in a better position to decide whether changes in policies, procedures, or leadership are necessary if they systematically assess the services they provide and also their operations on a regular basis. Evaluation is an integral part of effective management and helps to answer three pressing questions: Is the organization fulfilling its mission? What impact is the organization having? What factors must the organization consider to maintain or increase that impact in the future?

Since evaluation is a relatively undeveloped area in philanthropy, many other questions arise: How does the individual evaluate personal giving? Who should undertake evaluation of an organization, an insider or an outside expert? Who should see evaluations? Should evaluations of grantees or staff members, for example, remain confidential? How should evaluations of boards be handled? Issues of confidentiality, of protecting reputations, of due process, and of the validity of the methods themselves are involved. Many of these and related questions must be considered if nonprofits are to be effective, yet the organizations must remain sensitive to the competing values involved.

Relations with the Community. Realistic public policy often depends on input from groups that have had experience in particular areas. Nonprofits can promote better ways to solve problems by informing the larger community of their work—both the successes and the failures. They can provide useful models and help shape answers to issues such as the effectiveness of competitive as compared to cooperative efforts to meet certain goals. Both the political and business arenas need to be informed about the role that nonprofits play in current-day America. Mythical visions of charity may be useful in some situations, but a realistic appreciation of the potential and limitations of nonprofits will serve society better.

Nonprofits also have the responsibility of being good citizens in their communities. Churches, hospitals, universities, and agencies all have an impact on the local economy and quality of life. Working together to face and solve problems is a vital contribution to the civic community.

Are ethical standards desirable or possible? Is self-regulation the best approach? Does organized philanthropy merit more scrutiny than individual giving? There are no easy answers. Standards are useful, indeed necessary, because they help focus sustained attention and reasoned debate on the confounding issues that arise. They both reflect and promote consensus on appropriate behavior. The impetus for adopting standards may also involve outside interest and pressure, often from those who would legislate more restrictive standards.

Yet the issues we have addressed go beyond standards, helpful and necessary as they are. Basic philosophical issues concerning values and priorities must constantly be measured against the requirements of fairness, disclosure, equity, and justice if philanthropic institutions are to maintain public trust and serve the common interest effectively.

Notes

1. Paul Ylvisaker. From a speech delivered to the Associated Grantmakers of Boston, 1982.
2. For a review of the ethical writings of the great philosophers see Oliver A. Johnson, *Ethics: Selections from Classical and Contemporary Writers.* (3rd ed.) New York: Holt, Rinehart & Winston, 1974. A monumental overview of both classical ethical thinking as it relates to philanthropy and recent literature from a variety of fields is covered by Virginia Hodgkinson, *Motivations for Giving and Volunteering: A Selected Review of the Literature.* New York: Foundation Center, 1991 (forthcoming).
3. Robert L. Payton, "Philanthropy as Moral Discourse." In Leslie Berlowitz and others (eds.), *America in Theory: Theory in America.* New York: Oxford University Press, 1989.
4. Michael O'Neill, "Management and Responsibility in the

Nonprofit Sector." In *Working Papers from the 1988 Spring Research Forum*. Washington D.C.: INDEPENDENT SECTOR, 1988, pp. 116–129.

5. Recently more attention to ethical issues in this sector is evident with the formation by the INDEPENDENT SECTOR of an ethics committee and the nonprofit work of the Joseph and Edna Josephson Institute for the Advancement of Ethics.

6. John Nason, *Foundation Trusteeship: Service in the Public Interest*. New York: Foundation Center 1989, pp. 51–62.

7. Virginia Hodgkinson and Murray S. Weitzman, *Dimensions of the Independent Sector*. Washington D.C.: INDEPENDENT SECTOR, 1986.

8. "Telemarketing: Developing a Code of Ethics and Business Practices." *Philanthropy Monthly*, Apr. 1986, pp. 10–18.

9. Henry Hansmann, "The Two Independent Sectors." In *Working Papers from the 1988 Spring Research Forum*. Washington D.C.: INDEPENDENT SECTOR, 1988, pp. 15–24.

10. "Cause Related Marketing" is a phrase that was copywritten by American Express during its support of the renovation of the Statue of Liberty. The concept has provoked editorials, op-ed pieces, special reports, and some reexamination of corporate philanthropy. See, for example: Peter Goldberg, "A Dangerous Trend in Corporate Giving." *New York Times*, Mar. 29, 1987; Maurice G. Gurin, "Phony Philanthropy?" *Foundation News*, May/June 1989, pp. 32–35; Peter Hutchinson, "Whose Interest." *Foundation News*, Jan./Feb. 1987, pp. 74–75; Marge Salewic, "Charities in the Marketplace: A Look at Joint Venture Marketing," Parts I and II. In *Insight*. Rosslyn, Va.: Philanthropic Advisory Service Council of Better Business Bureaus, 1987; Leslie Savan, "Plastic Charity." *Village Voice*, Dec. 8, 1987, p. 70; and Philip J. Webster, "The Case for Cause Related Marketing." *Foundation News*, Jan./Feb. 1989, pp. 30–32.

11. Gurin.

12. Webster.

Chapter 9   *Bruce R. Hopkins*

Legal Issues
in Fund Raising
and Philanthropy

In the United States, philanthropy and the law have had a long relationship. Today, that relationship is largely expressed in the field of federal taxation, simply because of the importance of the charitable contribution deduction and the tax exemption for charitable (philanthropic) organizations. But it also manifests itself elsewhere, at both the state level (again, by means of charitable deductions and tax exemptions and in the area of fund-raising regulation) and the federal level (for example, in terms of exemptions in the postal and securities laws).

Contemporary American laws relating to the concept of philanthropy—as found in statutes, court opinions, and administrative agency rules and regulations—are founded on common law principles that come mainly from centuries-old rulings of the courts of England. Many of the pronouncements on philanthropy articulated weekly by the Internal Revenue Service echo the sentiments of judges who decided trust and property cases hundreds of years ago.

For most of United States history, the law and philanthropy lived in peaceful coexistence. Indeed, the common law generated a variety of presumptions in favor of philanthropic ends, from the standpoint of both the philanthropic organizations and those who financially supported them. This favoritism spilled over into the twentieth century, as the United States developed an income tax structure.

As the income tax system evolved, it generously accommo-
dated the philanthropic impulse by means of exemptions and deductions. State income tax systems followed suit, as did other
federal, state, and local laws that provided a variety of other exemptions and exceptions for charitable groups.

Over time, however, somewhere around the mid-1900s,
things began to change, at first barely perceptibly. The states started
to regulate fund raising for charity more stringently. Congress began to worry about the relationship between tax-exempt organizations and business enterprises, and it created the unrelated business
income tax. Charities became more sophisticated and organized,
and instituted aggressive lobbying and innovative fund raising.

More recently, the process that led to the enactment of the
Tax Reform Act of 1986 brought pressures for tax reform as expressed in terms of fairness and simplicity, forcing a flattening of
the income tax base and eliminating, reducing, and threatening all
deductions, exemptions, and other tax preferences. Mounting federal deficits are today causing Congress to look everywhere for revenue. Philanthropic organizations are finding themselves the
subjects of greater scrutiny, much like everyone else. For philanthropy and the law, the bloom is off the rose.

This, then, is the legal climate in which organized philanthropy currently finds itself. All that has been achieved, that is
cherished, that has been taken for granted by the philanthropic
community is under examination, challenge, and threat. There are
many, in and out of government, who believe that nonprofit organizations are largely anachronisms and that features such as tax
exemptions and the charitable deduction should yield to the dictates
of a flatter tax system.

Although philanthropy flourishes today despite these loom-
ing constraints, without offensive action by those determined to
protect and enhance this nation's independent sector, coming federal and state regulatory policies are likely to erode philanthropy's
legal base in the United States. Today's custodians of American
philanthropy cannot responsibly operate on the assumption that
present law in regard to this field will be tomorrow's law.

The principal legal issues that confront philanthropy include (1) the definition of the term *philanthropy* in the face of

charges of "commercial" and "unfairly competitive" practices, (2) potential revision of the unrelated-business rules, (3) challenges to the charitable contribution deduction, (4) fund-raising disclosure requirements, (5) the impact of new fund-raising techniques, and (6) the future of government regulation of fund raising.

Defining the "Philanthropic" Organization

No more fundamental and pressing issue of law faces philanthropic and many other tax-exempt organizations today than the matter of their definition under basic American legal doctrines, principally the federal tax law. This does not entail an academic perusal of the meaning of the term *philanthropy* (or *benevolence* or *eleemosynary*) or the more commonly used counterpart term *charity*. Instead, it pertains to the role of nonprofit organizations in contemporary United States society. Most of these organizations are exempt from taxation, and many of these tax-exempt organizations are philanthropic ones. Therefore, this issue directly affects institutions such as universities, colleges, hospitals, museums, and other charitable, educational, health care, arts, and scientific organizations—in short, the "501(c)(3)" community.

At present, certain forces are at play that are causing a reexamination of the appropriate functions of nonprofit organizations in our culture. In large part, this phenomenon is focusing on the proper undertakings of nonprofit organizations in relation to the other two general sectors of United States organizational structure: the business sector and the government sector.

A recent report of the President's Commission on Privatization opened with this observation: "The United States is experiencing a renewed interest in the systematic examination of the boundary between public and private delivery of goods and services." The same sorting out process is occurring between the nonprofit sector and the for-profit sector of American society.

The reexamination of the functions of nonprofit organizations has been stimulated in recent years by a subset of the for-profit sector, the "small business" community. Essentially, the complaint of this community against philanthropic and other nonprofit organizations is that they have become "unfairly competitive" with the nation's small businesses. The charges of small business in this regard, while wide ranging, can be distilled to three: (1) nonprofits are doing things that should be done only by for-profits (the "competition" part), (2) nonprofits are capturing a meaningful segment of the market because of their positive public image (a portion of the "unfair" part), and (3) nonprofits, particularly philanthropic ones, have access to capital—in the form of accumulated funds, including gifts, sheltered by tax exemption—denied to for-profits (the rest of the "unfair" part). For good measure, the small business community contends that nonprofit organizations, not being beholden to shareholders, are able to lower prices and undercut the for-profit competition.

This crusade by small business was given form and financial support by the United States government, through the Office of Advocacy of the Small Business Administration, which issued some stirring reports on the subject. Organizations such as the Business Coalition for Fair Competition gave the movement structure and direction, and the 1987 White House Conference on Small Business gave it prominence. Many states, through legislative committees and special commissions, launched investigations of the "unfair competition" allegations.

However, the small business community concentrated its efforts on Congress, largely in the tax context. These efforts were rewarded with a five-day hearing, in June 1987, by the House Subcommittee on Oversight on the subject of the current effectiveness of the unrelated-business income taxation rules. The specifics of the resulting proposed changes are discussed below in a different setting.

For purposes of this cutting-edge issue, however, it is necessary to view these developments from the broadest of perspectives. The hearings led to a draft set of recommendations made public on March 31, 1988, recommendations that were the subject of still another hearing on May 9, 1988. Because of a lack of consensus within the subcommittee, it failed to issue its proposals to its parent body, the House Ways and Means Committee, because the 100th Congress adjourned in October 1988. Nonetheless, it is the implicit position underlying the subcommittee's initial recommendations that is of concern.

The draft recommendations do not explicitly address the matter of alleged "unfair competition." Rather, although they started out as an embodiment of a variety of proposed law changes predicated upon the view that the activities involved are "inherently commercial," the draft recommendations evolved to specific proposals that were not tied together into a unified philosophy. Nonetheless, it is this "commerciality" doctrine that is the foundation for the most crucial legal issue confronting philanthropic organizations.

The commerciality doctrine is not addressed in the draft recommendations. Instead, the unstated principle seems to be twofold: (1) if the service or product is available in the for-profit sector, the activity providing the service or product is a "commercial" one, and (2) a commercial activity translates to an "unrelated" and thus taxable business. Thus, the underlying assumption seems to be that if the activity is available in the for-profit sector, it is a taxable activity when found in the nonprofit sector.

This entire subject is currently woefully unappreciated by nonprofit organizations across the country and certainly is misunderstood by many. Indeed, existing law only awkwardly responds to the "competition" issue.

All too many believe that this is an "unrelated-income" matter, a belief that is somewhat understandable inasmuch as the unrelated trade or business rules presently in the law were instituted as the result of charges of "unfair competition." However, today's allegations of unfair competition are complaints about activities that, under existing law, are related to the tax-exempt organization's function. As a result, much of the coming debate will quickly shift the discussion to the matter of overall qualification for tax exemption.

Underlying the struggle to define the term *philanthropy* for legal (primarily tax) purposes are the criteria (existing and emerging) for defining the terms *nonprofit* and *tax-exempt*.

Under existing law, what distinguishes a "nonprofit" from a "for-profit" entity? Despite common belief, this has nothing to do with whether the entity enjoys a "profit" in the sense of income exceeding outgo. Rather, the difference is largely structural: a for-profit has owners of equity (such as stock) and the net earnings flow to the owners (such as dividends to stockholders). By contrast, a nonprofit organization does not have equity owners and its net earnings may not inure to private individuals.

The legal concept of tax exemption is built upon the concept of the nonprofit entity but goes beyond it, particularly in the case of philanthropic (charitable) organizations. Thus, not only may there not be "private inurement" or "private benefit" emanating from tax-exempt organizations but these entities must affirmatively engage in exempt functions.

Existing law is relatively explicit about what constitutes an "unrelated" activity. It is the scope of what is "related" activity that is rather murky—and the source of much of today's unhappiness and confusion over the matter of "unfair competition" between nonprofits and for-profits (the latter particularly referring to "small business").

If the philanthropic world is to escape severe statutory law changes in this area, it must become more adept at explaining what it means to be "nonprofit" and "tax-exempt," why that differs from being "for profit," and why the present law of tax exemption, tax deductions, postal privileges, and the like should remain. At the other extreme, if "abuses" of tax-exempt status are occurring—particularly any that cannot be corrected under existing law, assuming proper enforcement—the nonprofit community should be forthright about it.

Thus, as noted, it is important that the rationale for being "nonprofit" and "tax-exempt" be articulated. Part of the distinction between nonprofits and for-profits lies in the differences in their structure, that is, the absence of owners and net earnings flowing to them in the case of nonprofits. This is an irrefutable difference.

Another part of the distinction rests in what philanthropic organizations do. But, again, this is where troubles loom. Nonprofit hospitals say that they provide health care delivery; for-profit (proprietary) hospitals say that they do, too. The same holds true in regard to the distinction between nonprofit and for-profit schools, colleges, universities, libraries, theaters, museums, and the like.

Still another distinction is the fact that the many nonprofits work to better the conditions of the "poor" (a term embracing impoverishment, destitution, economic insecurity, and more). This is not the only definition of what it means to be "charitable," although all too many believe that it is. The function of many charitable entities today is to enhance the quality of life for a broader aggregation of individuals than just the impoverished—perhaps to benefit the "general public." Of course, most if not all for-profits presume that they are advancing the needs and interests of the general public. So that is unlikely to be the sole rationale for the difference.

Under existing law principles, the meaning of tax exemption for philanthropic organizations goes far beyond betterment of the conditions of the indigent. But how far beyond? Is the rationale for tax exemption going to turn on more than structure? If so (and there surely is more), on what terms? Is the basis to be the activities that are performed, or how they are performed, or the quality of the performance, or the manner in which the activities are funded, a combination of these factors, or some other criteria?

Although the structural differences cannot be overstressed and the intent of the founders of an organization is also important (though admittedly this can disappear or change over time), the focus—in the political context—will probably be on what nonprofit organizations do and how this differs from what for-profits do.

It is this last factor that will cause nonprofit organizations the greatest stress because, as noted earlier, in many fields, nonprofits and for-profits do the same thing: provide education, render health care services, engage in research, sponsor seminars, sell products and services, and publish materials. As to this element, then, there cannot be a precise line of demarcation.

Nor is there a clear line of differentiation as to whom nonprofit versus for-profit organizations provide service. If only the poor are being served, the activity is likely to be considered "charitable." Today, however, most charitable activities are provided to classes of individuals (perhaps the entire "public") that are far broader than the impoverished.

Another aspect of differentiation may lie in how nonprofit organizations are funded. Those organizations that rely primarily on gifts and grants are, despite any shifts in tax law policy, likely to continue to be considered charitable. Those organizations that are principally funded with "exempt function revenue" (namely, funds from the sale of products or services, where the business activity is in furtherance of exempt functions), however, are certain to be the target of future inquiries.

A battle is shaping up, and philanthropic and other nonprofit organizations have to date assumed only a defensive position—seemingly believing that the best they can hope for is to maintain the status quo. The big test is whether they can do better than that. Given this attitude, there is little wonder that legislators, regulators, and the general public are having difficulty understanding the contemporary philanthropic organization and its functions in relation to the private (business) and government sectors. Indeed, within the nonprofit community itself, there appears to be an identity crisis, an uncertainty over appropriate roles.

Many nonprofit organizations are engaging in activities that were previously the sole domain of for-profit businesses. A variety of fee-for-service activities is disturbing the traditional view of "donative" charities—those philanthropic groups that are funded largely or wholly by gifts and grants. Both the general public and the policymakers are becoming confused and uncertain as to what nonprofit organizations are in relation to for-profit entities.

There is no question but that a certain measure of self-restraint on the part of philanthropic and other nonprofit organizations would have spared them some of their current difficulties. Activities such as controversial sale-leaseback transactions gave rise to the tax-exempt entity leasing rules. Even fund raising plays a role in this setting, as innovation transforms the development process. The recent and evolving law with respect to affinity card programs, cause-related marketing, and commercial coventuring bears this out.

While policymakers in Congress, the Treasury Department, and the independent sector grapple with these issues, another branch of government is frequently overlooked: the judicial branch. The courts are heavily involved in the issue of what constitutes philanthropy and are busily churning out opinions that find nonprofit organizations not to be tax-exempt, as charities or otherwise, because of their engagement in activities that can be characterized as "commercial," "competitive," or both.

Revisions of the Unrelated-Business Income Rules

A second and related issue in the law that philanthropy faces today involves revision of the rules by which nonprofit organizations are taxed on their unrelated-business taxable income. As noted above, these rules are currently under review as chiefly manifested in the specifics of the draft recommendations prepared for the House Subcommittee on Oversight, and most of them have been influenced by the assumption that certain activities being conducted by nonprofit organizations today are "inherently commercial," even though this has not been proposed as a test for unrelatedness. Thus, the draft proposals identify several such activities and propose to tax them as unrelated businesses.

Among the revenue-producing activities of philanthropic organizations identified are catalogue sales by museums; bookstore sales by colleges and universities; provision of testing services by hospitals; sale of hearing aids, tours, and advertising by nonprofits; affinity card programs of membership groups; and health, fitness, and similar programs.

The subcommittee proposes to affect adversely the use of for-profit subsidiaries by imputing the activities of the subsidiaries to the exempt parent organizations for the purpose of assessing the ongoing tax-exempt status of the parent organizations. Other potential law revisions in this area include significant revisions of the exception for royalties, the introduction of cost-allocation rules, and the expansion of annual reporting requirements.

The draft recommendations also include a range of proposed studies, among them an analysis of philanthropic and other types of nonprofit organizations that participate in joint ventures and other partnerships and the hospital reorganization phenomenon, and a study of the impact of changes in law in this area after five years' experience with them.

These studies could lead to still more statutory revisions in the federal tax law pertaining to the unrelated-business issue, and such revisions could, in turn, affect the statutory law on this subject at the state level. Certainly, the courts will continue to create new rules in the unrelated-business field, expanding upon the doctrines of "commerciality" and "competition." Indeed, several of the legislative proposals to revise the law of unrelated-income taxation would be codifications of court-made (or IRS-made) law.

As touched on earlier, still another factor that is driving the process of revising the law in this area is the federal government's need for revenue to reduce the deficit. This factor will lead to serious consideration of proposals such as a 5 percent tax on the net investment income of all tax-exempt organizations, including philanthropic ones.

The philanthropic community's response to the evolution of these proposals could have a dramatic impact on the attitude of Congress in subsequent legislation with respect to philanthropic organizations. This is also true in terms of the development of the various studies that are likely to be undertaken in the wake of revision of the unrelated-income tax law. Of lesser consequence, but nonetheless important, is the ongoing relationship between the various subsectors of the independent sector.

Retention of the Charitable Contribution Deduction

The third major legal issue facing philanthropy is retention of the federal income tax charitable contribution deduction. (At issue also is the federal estate and gift tax charitable contribution deduction, but the principal focus here is on the income tax deduction.)

Probably most people in the philanthropic community take the charitable deduction for granted, assuming that it will always exist. This is dangerous and ignorant thinking, however, because a number of people in government and academia are opposed to the income tax charitable deduction. Some take this stance because they are pushing for a "flatter" income tax base—a system with fewer (perhaps no) deductions, credits, or other tax preferences—in an attempt to "democratize" the federal income tax structure or in the name of tax simplification. These individuals made great progress in bringing about the enactment of the Tax Reform Act of 1986. That is why there is such pressure today on the mortgage interest deduction; if that is done away with, the charitable deduction is just about all that separates today's tax base from a much flatter one.

Others are pushing for new restrictions on the charitable deduction because they do not like it. Of this group, some believe that many of the functions being undertaken today by nonprofit organizations are more properly the province of government. Others dislike the charitable deduction because they find it "unfair," as a tax preference favoring the wealthy. Still others (as noted above) envision substantial amounts of tax revenue to be found in the world of philanthropy.

Simply put, then, the charitable contribution deduction is endangered because of the ongoing push for a simpler tax system and more tax revenue. The political process being what it is, however, it is highly unlikely that Congress will one day soon just repeal the deduction. Instead, its opponents will chip away at it, achieving slowly and incrementally what they cannot achieve directly.

For example, one proposal that will be seriously pondered in the coming months is the thought that all deductions (including the charitable one) should be subject to a floor: a percentage of adjusted gross income that must be exceeded before the charitable deduction becomes available. This proposal alone would raise billions of dollars without directly affecting the charitable deduction rules. It would do so by cutting back deductible charitable giving because of the floor itself or because of the number of taxpayers that would be converted into nonitemizers (those that lack any tax incentive for giving). Another idea that routinely resurfaces is a trimming of the appreciated property charitable deduction. Other proposals would repeal or eliminate other deductions, such as those for mortgage interest and for state and local taxes. These moves, also, would raise revenue and create additional nonitemizers.

As the focus on the deficit intensifies, we will see attempts to increase tax revenues by increasing tax rates. A general tax increase, by raising the individual and/or corporate marginal tax rates, is likely. Another possibility is an income tax surtax, as well as an increase in the alternative minimum tax rate. These would make the income tax charitable contribution deduction, however computed, "worth more."

Of course, philanthropy will be in sad shape if the charitable deduction is of utility only because the wealthy class of taxpayers uses it to help defray taxation. The charitable community and those it serves will be enhanced to the extent that access to tax incentives for giving is broadened.

Viewing this cutting-edge issue more expansively, if Congress decides to go to a value-added or national sales tax, the philanthropic community will have to struggle to create law-providing exemptions and deductions for charity in relation to that tax.

Charitable Fund-Raising Disclosure

When Congress adopted the Revenue Act of 1987, it enacted a rule that requires noncharitable organizations to disclose the nondeductibility of contributions to them. At the time this rule was made a part of the House of Representatives' version of the Tax Reform Act of 1986, the House Ways and Means Committee included a discussion in its report on the legislation about the nondeductibility of a variety of payments to charitable organizations, warning that there will likely be law revisions in this area as well if the charitable community does not police itself more on the point. Since there is little evidence that any organization within the philanthropic community is about to assume a major leadership role in this area, the fourth major issue facing philanthropy is the coming new law on disclosure of the nondeductibility of payments to charitable organizations.

In mid-1988, the commissioner of the Internal Revenue Service took the unusual step of sending an announcement to the nation's charities, requesting them to aid the IRS in ensuring that the requisite disclosure of nondeductibility be made. This pronouncement also strongly suggested that in the absence of fairly immediate voluntary compliance with the requirements, Congress may act.

All of this is based upon the fact that not all transfers of funds to philanthropic organizations are deductible gifts. The most obvious of these nondeductible transfers are tuition payments to schools and payments to hospitals for health care services. There are situations, nonetheless, where payments to philanthropic organizations are thought by the payers to be deductible gifts or, regrettably, where the recipient organizations induce, knowingly or not, the payers to believe that the payments are deductible gifts. This situation arises most frequently in instances of dues payments or payments in connection with auctions, sweepstakes, lotteries, raffles, and other forms of special-event fund raising.

Closely associated with the disclosure rule is the concept of a "gift." Despite the complexity of law surrounding deductible charitable giving, there is a rather startling paucity of law that defines just what a "gift" is. In general, a gift is the result of a transaction in which the donor does not receive anything of consequence in return. Yet, in practice, the rule is frequently difficult to apply.

New Fund-Raising Techniques

One of the great difficulties with which philanthropic organizations were faced in the 1980s was that even as they were asked to provide more services because of more need, their ability to raise deductible contributions and receive federal funding was being eroded. Not surprisingly, these organizations have turned to other ways of acquiring funds, in the process placing more emphasis on fee-for-service revenue. (Part of this phenomenon is also the result of the greater sophistication of the management of nonprofit organizations.) In some instances, this development has exacerbated the problems perceived by the small business community as "unfair competition" (see above).

Aside from the impact of all of this on the development of the unrelated-business income rules, the philanthropic community's increasing reliance on fee-based revenue is causing considerable confusion as to what, exactly, "fund raising" is and how it is distinguished from "business" activity. This is a separate major issue, although it also impacts upon developments in the areas of fund-raising disclosure (discussed above) and fund-raising regulation (discussed below).

Related to this issue is the seeming increase in use of traditional fund-raising techniques by nonprofit organizations, which is bound to create new debates in the fields of federal tax law and federal and state regulation of fund raising.

Two examples of this development will suffice. One is the expansion of the use of "planned giving" techniques. Once largely the province of universities, major hospitals, and national philanthropies, planned giving is now becoming a staple throughout the charitable world. Since a properly administered planned giving program can be bountiful, this development is all to the good for philanthropic organizations—as long as it is permitted by accompanying law.

Nearly any philanthropic organization can be the beneficiary of a charitable remainder trust or a charitable gift annuity. More organizations are establishing pooled income funds, and greater uses of life insurance in the charitable giving context are readily apparent. The use of other techniques, such as charitable lead trusts, is probably on the rise as well.

Not only is the use of planned giving techniques on the increase, the contexts in which they are being utilized are expanding. Philanthropic groups are finding new uses for planned giving, such as substitution of pooled income funds for involvement in partnerships, use of planned giving in designing fringe benefit and retirement income programs, and ways of producing current income for charity as the result of planned giving techniques. However beneficial to the philanthropic community, these techniques could lead to law changes to restrict their use.

The second example of the expansion of traditional fund raising is the greater use of the charitable deduction by noncharitable organizations. Most commonly, this is done by means of a "foundation" associated with a noncharitable, tax-exempt organization, such as a trade or professional association. Another growing practice is the use of related charitable foundations by for-profit organizations. Moreover, there is an increase in the use of the "conduit" gift, whereby a gift is made to a noncharitable, tax-exempt organization for a charitable purpose or is flowed through the organization for ultimate use by a charitable organization; the IRS is demonstrating a greater proclivity to allow a charitable deduction for this type of gift.

State Regulation of Fund Raising

Probably the "sleeper" legal issue for philanthropy is the rapid increase in the regulation of charitable fund raising by the states. It is by no means certain where this will lead, but it is clear that many states that lack a charitable solicitation act are writing one, that many states that have such a law are making it tougher, and that philanthropic organizations are either unaware of such laws or blatantly ignore them, more so than any other applicable law. Were it not for recent Supreme Court decisions, this area of the law would be even more draconian than it now is. Nonetheless, state regulation of fund raising is experiencing another great surge.

Originally designed to protect citizens against abuses in the form of extraction of the charitable dollar for flim-flam purposes, this body of law—and its enforcement—have become something else indeed. It is one of the most stringent and onerous bodies of law confounding the philanthropic process.

These state laws require compliance by charitable organizations that engage in fund raising. They apply to these charities, by the law of the state in which the organization is located and by the law of each of the other states in which the organization solicits contributions. Moreover, these laws directly impact charities by reason of the regulation of those who help them raise funds, namely, professional fund raisers, paid solicitors, and commercial co-venturers.

There is no parade of abuses that warrants the attention being focused by state governments on fund raising for charitable purposes. There is too little sensitivity by the regulatory officials as to the fragility of the institution that they are purportedly endeavoring to protect—the philanthropic sector of American society. Other than the tendency of politicians to criticize charity and the staffs of the regulatory agencies to multiply (like nature, government abhors a vacuum), it is difficult to explain the spate of regulations applied to charitable fund raising in the modern era.

Another explanation for this growth is the explosion in the consumer protection field. As the federal government experiments with deregulation, the state attorneys general are expanding their domain over consumer issues. Once acting within their own states, the attorneys general have gone interstate, by means of a massive networking system spearheaded by the National Association of Attorneys General.

There is, obviously, nothing wrong with protecting the rights of consumers, and that includes protection against fraudulent fund-raising appeals. Fund-raising abuses are taking place, and the public needs and deserves a place to lodge complaints and be assured that those perpetrating the frauds are prosecuted and punished. However, the zeal of unelected officials and/or the underlying bureaucracy in regulating charities and fund raising for them is continuing unabated, and many fear that the cure is worse than the disease.

The typical contemporary state charitable solicitation act is a monster. Its laws are unnecessarily complex and burdensome. They are often written by a legislator or regulator with a motive to curb the practices of some person or are otherwise ill conceived. These laws are frequently authored by individuals with a dim view of what they are doing and administered by bureaucrats with a negative view toward philanthropy. In too many cases, the zeal to control fund raising is leading to the creation of regulatory empires staffed at taxpayers' expense by lawyers and investigators whose skills are sorely needed elsewhere in government service. The paperwork and the costs imposed upon charities and their professional consultants exceed any value these overreaching laws may provide.

The shame of it all is that the legislatures and regulators have lost perspective on what it is they are regulating. Philanthropy contributes importantly to the sustenance of the American pluralistic system. Billions of dollars are annually provided for services and other benefits that government will not and cannot supply. Giving to charity is, obviously, what fuels this machine. But fund-raising regulation is damaging the legitimate gift solicitation process—a constitutionally protected act of free speech.

Most of the fund-raising regulation zealotry is being directed at the quickie promotors, those who roll into town for a weekend with a circus or some like attraction and roll out of town with most of the money. Yet the statute writers cannot seem to find the ability to develop law regulating these types. It is a virtual scandal that all of fund raising, be it capital, annual giving, direct mail, or planned giving programs, is heavily regulated so that purveyors of tickets to vaudeville acts can be monitored.

The impending worsening of the situation is compounded by the inability or unwillingness of the nonprofit sector to stand up to the onslaught of governmental regulation. The question is Will that inability and unwillingness persist?

Federal Regulation of Fund Raising

In recent years, Congress has shown no interest in developing a federal charitable solicitation act, either in addition to state law or preemptive of state law. This does not mean, however, that the federal law of fund-raising regulation is not on the increase. Indeed, this body of law is rapidly expanding, although the fact seems to be a secret to many philanthropic groups. The likely expansion and shape of this type of law is another part of the government regulation issue facing the philanthropic community.

Most of this body of law will not come from Congress, although as noted above, the legislature is demonstrating interest in the field of fund-raising disclosure. Rather, the law change will come from the courts, as they increase application of the unrelated-income rules in the fund-raising context, and from the IRS, as it presides over an increase in the extent of annual reporting by tax-exempt organizations.

Other Issues

There are, of course, many other legal issues confronting the nation's philanthropic organizations. These include lobbying and political campaign activities, trustee liability, and charitable contribution deduction substantiation, to name just a few. However, none of these can be termed "cutting-edge" issues, as important as they may be.

Conclusion

Despite the foregoing, it is not the intent of this chapter to posit only gloom and doom for philanthropy in terms of impending changes in the law. It is this writer's belief (and certainly hope) that philanthropy as we know it in this country will continue to thrive and grow and be undertaken in other countries of the world. Nonetheless, there is no question that, law-wise, tough times lie ahead for philanthropy. This need not be a time of despair and surrender but, instead, a time of challenge, for it is the task of today's managers of the philanthropic establishment to preserve and improve philanthropy in the United States in the face of massive efforts to dismantle it.

Chapter 10   *Robert D. Herman*
                                                Stephen R. Block

The Board's Crucial Role in Fund Raising

The punchline is this: Raising dollars is a crucial survival activity
for the boards and staffs of most nonprofit organizations.

Unlike their for-profit counterparts, nonprofit organizations
are founded not to generate cash profits but rather to solve a social
problem, advance a cause, or preserve or express a point of view.
The initial formation of a nonprofit organization is a time of great
enthusiasm. The founders' enthusiasm is soon confronted by the
stark realities of running a business, albeit a social improvement
business. In order to survive, the nonprofit organization now requires leadership and management control, planning, and money.

These needs never cease for the nonprofit organization. Unfortunately, many nonprofits focus their attention primarily on delivering program services rather than solidifying the organization's
decision-making structure, which would consequently provide a
stronger base for programming support. The emphasis on program
delivery at the expense of integrating effective management principles into the operation is understandable. Many nonprofit organizations are rarely, if ever, founded or directed with the aid of
business plans, working plans, or operational plans. Also common
to many nonprofit organizations is the fact that their "leaders" are
cause-specific, excellent clinicians or practitioners, perhaps, but not
necessarily trained or savvy in the operation of organizations.

Sorting out the roles of paid staff and volunteer board members is perplexing to most nonprofit organizational players. The stakes are high and often include the success or survival of the organization. As in the frequently cited complaints about troubled marriages, finances in the nonprofit organization also tend to strain the relations of board members and staff. Describing and analyzing the roles of and relationships between volunteer board members and paid staff in carrying out fund-raising activities may shed light on these complex issues and thus provide the opportunity for both understanding and problem solving.

Toward these ends, this chapter begins with a brief assessment of what historical evidence tells us about the roles and relations of board and staff in earlier times. The second section turns to a review of the current prescriptive literature to discover what is recommended in terms of appropriate roles and relationships. The third section considers what descriptive studies reveal about actual roles and relationships. The final section presents our reconciliation of the prescriptive and descriptive, offering conclusions about desirable board-staff roles and relationships in fund raising and strategies for progressing toward the desirable.

Historical Perspective—Was There Innocence to Lose?

It is tempting to conjure up a picture of charitable fund raising in the past as an activity directly and completely undertaken by voluntary amateurs. Such a picture could serve to show how far fund raising has advanced as it has become more specialized and professional and to reaffirm the continuity of contemporary fund raising, which emphasizes the crucial *leadership* role of volunteers, within historic roots. However, the evidence available in highly regarded histories of U.S. philanthropy and fund raising suggests that "paid staff" have long been a part of fund raising. For instance, Cutlip observes that the first systematic fund-raising effort in North America occurred in 1641, when the Massachusetts Bay Colony sent three (presumably salaried) clergymen to England to solicit money for Harvard College.[1] The first, unsuccessful, attempt at a U.S. federated fund drive was organized by Matthew Carey in Philadelphia in 1829 and was conducted with paid agents.[2]

Certainly there is evidence that in many early charities, fund raising, as well as myriad other duties, was solely a volunteer activity. McCarthy reports that the Chicago Orphan Asylum, founded in 1849, had in its first years a high turnover among its paid matrons and as a consequence "the board members made the clothes and bedding themselves, purchased supplies, investigated and admitted inmates, hired and fired staff, . . . and canvassed relentlessly to raise the necessary funds to keep the Home open, staging fairs and benefits as well."[3] Similarly, at the Chicago Home for the Friendless, established in 1858, the "directresses did much of the work themselves. The supply committee solicited funds and provisions."[4]

Concurrent with the settlement house movement in the United States, the English invention of the Charity Organization Society movement took hold. The advocates of this movement were committed to an effective system of private charity.[5] The movement's framers argued against indiscriminate almsgiving and advanced a rationalized approach in which conscientious thought was given to long-term consequences and outcomes. Indeed, this movement appears to have been the forerunner of the modern philanthropic foundation or corporate giving program based on a rationale of purpose to achieve a prescribed outcome. A feature of this movement was the attempt to be scientific both by collecting data about charitable agencies and by coordinating the effects of several of the charities. Members of a Charitable Organization Society, like the modern foundation, would review applications for financial assistance. In addition to providing cash relief, the society might also arrange for a host of in-kind contributions and services.

Support for the organized charity movement grew after the turn of the century with the financial support of the business sector. Business donors expected that private charities would be better administered than public charities. Following from this expectation, business donors pushed for the development of a federated organization of charities that would regulate fund-raising efforts and the distribution of monies. In addition, the federation would be able to monitor the quality of management of the charitable organizations. The creation of the Cleveland Federation for Charity and Philanthropy in 1913 was one such example and was also a pioneering model for financial federations in other cities.[6] The development of federations was another critical step toward the creation of paid staff positions to oversee the donor collection and expenditure process.

By the early twentieth century other distinct approaches to fund raising were being tested and developed. For example, Bishop Lawrence Williams, as president of the Harvard Alumni Association, in 1904–05 created the alumni appeal, which raised $2.4 million to support faculty salaries.[7] Among other interesting advances was the first commercial fund-raising firm, established by Frederick C. Barker in 1915.[8] Barker had worked with Charles S. Ward in an effort to raise money for the University of Pittsburgh. Ward and Lyman L. Pierce, both of whom worked for the YMCA at the turn of the century, are credited with developing the short-term intensive fund-raising campaign.[9] Many of the early independent fund-raising firms were started by men who had worked with Ward, Pierce, or Barker. Fund raising was becoming more varied and demanding of specialized knowledge and skills, thus creating a need for the independent fund-raising consultant. Bremner reports that by the end of the 1920s there were twenty fund-raising firms in New York City.[10]

Neither additional examples of all-volunteer or paid-employee fund raising from various times nor further review of the development of the fund-raising profession will lead to an unequivocal conclusion about the undoubtedly varied relationships between volunteer board members and paid employees or consultants in earlier times. Reading the histories inclines us to conclude that, on the whole, in the nineteenth century volunteers were largely instrumental in directing fund-raising efforts and frequently in carrying out the day-to-day detailed activities. Paid employees were probably substantially under the direction of volunteers. In the early twentieth century as the concept of "professionalism" was enhanced in many fields, fund raising was also emerging as a field of specialized knowledge and skills, thus shifting the general relationship between volunteers and paid fund raisers. Though volunteer board members continued to have formal responsibility for fund raising, the view that fund raising was a profession (or at least a specialized trade) led volunteer board members to a greater deference toward and reliance on fund raisers. Because asking others for money appears to be a universally uncomfortable task, many volun-

teer board members were probably quite content to delegate responsibility for fund raising to the professionals. At the risk of overstate-
ment, we suggest that this view became widespread during the
middle part of this century.

We are not implying that the wealthy ceased giving or soliciting gifts from others in their circles. Rather, we are suggesting that
even in those established organizations that have long depended on
the financial support of the wealthy, organizing and implementing
fund raising has been the de facto responsibility of paid professionals. Whether we are in the midst of another shift is a question we
will explore shortly. With the expansion of the number of nonprofit
charities during the 1960s and 1970s and the reduction in governmental funding for programs delivered by such nonprofit organizations in the early 1980s, many are apparently searching for ways
of using volunteer board members to enhance fund raising in the
private sector.

How It's Supposed to Be: Prescriptive Perspectives

Though the standards of conduct applicable to individual nonprofit boards are sometimes vague,[11] virtually all authorities agree
that boards that steward nonprofit incorporated entities are ultimately legally responsible for the sound conduct of their organizations' affairs. From this starting point has come a widely
disseminated prescriptive model of what a nonprofit board should
be and do. The prescriptive ideal, which one of us has labeled a
"heroic model" of nonprofit boards, includes the following
standards.[12]

First, the nonprofit board has and uses a systematic process
for assessing the strengths and weaknesses of the composition of the
current board. Strengths and weaknesses are usually assessed in
terms of demographic characteristics, expertise, and skills, and the
result is a board profile.

Second, the board profile is used to identify the personal
characteristics and expertise/skills desired in new recruits to the
board.

Third, recruitment of potential board members is systematic
and rigorous in that potential members are thoroughly informed as

to the mission and goals of the organization; its financial condition; and the time, effort, level of contributions, and fund-raising activities expected of them. Potential members are interviewed by a board committee (and perhaps the full board) as to their motives and interests in volunteering for board service.

Fourth, new board members receive additional, thorough training and orientation beyond that provided during recruitment and selection.

Fifth, board members commit significant time to board duties, not only attending board and committee meetings but also preparing for meetings and undertaking other assignments, perhaps including fund-raising activities.

Sixth, board meetings are characterized by a process through which all are encouraged to participate and disagreement is welcomed, while relationships are collegial and consensual. The board works as a team.

Seventh, the board uses processes of assessing the performance of the board as a whole and the performance of individual members. The board has and follows standards of removing members who do not perform.

Eighth, the board's chief tasks are to (a) select, evaluate, and, if necessary, dismiss the chief executive; (b) define and periodically reevaluate the organization's mission and major goals, develop a strategic plan, and approve budgets and policy statements consistent with the plan; and (c) ensure that the organization obtains the resources necessary to meet the plan.

As implied in the description of the "heroic model," the board of directors is responsible for the overall policy and program management of the nonprofit organization, whether members participate on an operational level or delegate their responsibility to a management staff. Even if the board delegates its management responsibility to an executive director, the board cannot divorce itself from its fiduciary responsibility; thereby it always remains responsible for funding both policy and program decisions.

Exactly how board or staff responsibilities should translate into functional activities and tasks is a murky area. Some guidance is offered by Block, Leduc, and Carroccio, who contend that the role of the board member in fund raising is in part determined by the

maturity of the organization. In the earlier phases of the organization's life cycle, board members' involvement might be indistin-
guishable from that of the staff. In later phases, the board's hands-
on role would be replaced by a staff who could devote the appropriate concentration of time that is required, such as the day-to-day
mechanics of prospecting, proposal writing, and plan implementation. The board, however, would still be required to participate in
special events and community networking and serve as organizational representatives before foundations and corporate giving
directors.[13]

Block, Leduc, and Carroccio also argue that successful resource development is an extension of the effective practice of nonprofit organization management. Accordingly, fund raising is an
outgrowth of strategic directional planning, a process that examines and seeks an understanding of the management and program
strengths and weaknesses contributed by both staff and volunteers;
an understanding of the service needs of the organization's constituents; an understanding of the organization's attraction to existing
and potential stakeholders; and familiarity with the organization's
competition. Using the collected information as a data base allows
for sound judgments about how the organization will generate its
revenues. The board and staff can then responsibly delegate which
role a board member or staff member may play.[14]

Although it is unclear who should receive credit for the concept of the three W's, many board advisers attempt to reason the
board's role within the boundaries of providing wisdom and knowledge, doing work on committees and special assignments, and sharing wealth through their cash contributions and access to other
prospects. While some may debate the need to discourage board
members' enthusiasm in thinking that "work" means participating
in the daily operations of the organization's business, the tension
is certainly more evident around the notion of sharing one's wealth
as dictated through a board policy.

That board members *must* make a cash contribution to the
organization in which they serve is an unsettled issue that is receiving more attention these days. There has been some attempt to
cushion the tone of the debate by suggesting that a board member's
giving is a demonstrated expression of leadership that also encour-

ages giving by others. According to Stephen Wertheimer, "The role of trustees/directors is clear and unavoidable: they must set an exemplary pace to all prospective donors by giving the finest gift of which they're capable."[15]

During recent Institute for Nonprofit Organization Management training programs on resource development, we have also heard arguments from volunteer board members and staff who take a more modified position on mandatory board giving. They view the time and efforts of the volunteer board as satisfying contribution requirements to the organization. Others admittedly frame the argument this way because they are embarrassed to ask volunteers to give cash beyond the valuable time that they are already giving, especially volunteers with modest economic means. We are reminded, however, that board members with modest economic means are no less responsible as organizational leaders, and therefore their financial contribution, at whatever level, represents an important message about their commitment. Furthermore, when a board of directors gives, its request for funds from outside sources is more credible. Indeed, as part of the decision-making process, many foundation directors will query fund seekers about the giving pattern of their board of directors.

This fact, coupled with the leadership function of the board, has led to more specific guidelines on the responsibility of boards for fund raising and the roles of and relationships between boards and paid staff in fund raising. For instance, Michael Seltzer tells us, "[W]hile it has always been expected among the charitable endeavors supported by wealthy patrons in a community that board members would also be donors, the notion only recently is becoming accepted among organizations with less privileged constituents. . . . The bottom line is, if a board member asks others to give money, shouldn't he or she be willing to do the same?"[16] Fred Setterberg and Kary Schulman are more direct: "*Every* Board member, in accordance with his or her means, should contribute annually to the organization."[17] O'Connell affirms the expectation that every member contribute, and he suggests that every member should also be expected to solicit. He further places the fund-raising leadership responsibility on the board, observing that "one of the greatest problems with fundraising and within nonprofit organizations generally is the confusion between the fundraising roles for board and staff. In terms of accountability, it is a board function . . . and the board leads."[18]

Interestingly, one prescriptive source that does *not* assert that all board members should be givers and getters was published in 1980. Connors's treatment of the nonprofit board includes all the usual roles for the board except fund raising. In addition, Connors notes that nonprofit boards were then undergoing a significant metamorphosis, with board membership becoming increasingly more representative of the total community. He further suggests that the more diverse boards, in conjunction with the fiscal management practices required of those organizations receiving governmental grants, frequently led to substantial management (that is, staff) control of the organization. He later warns that boards must, nonetheless, carefully monitor the policies and practices formulated and initiated by staff, though without clear guidance as to how such monitoring could be achieved in the circumstances.[19]

Though Connors does not ignore the reality that boards are often involved in fund raising, that he did not explicitly include fund raising as a board responsibility, when writing in the late 1970s, suggests that fund raising was a less critical issue in those times than it is now. Or it may be that Connors sidestepped the potentially inflammatory position, especially with more broadly representative and diverse boards who, until recently, were not prepared to examine their own cash-giving role.

If nearly all agree that every board member should personally give and participate in other fund-raising activities, who should be responsible for seeing that such expectations are achieved? On this issue, the answer is much less clear, excepting O'Connell, who unambiguously puts the responsibility on the board, especially the board chair. Thomas Broce agrees but is even more specific about the chair's role in board solicitation. He states that the "first major task" of the chair is to "make his gift." "Once the steering or development committee of the governing board is selected, . . . the chairman . . . solicits each member personally . . . ideally . . . at the time the members are invited to serve."[20] Broce also advances an interesting twist on the staff's role in the board soliciting process. Speaking about the board chair's giving, Broce further delineates that "Since he is the top volunteer, it usually falls to the institution's chief executive officer to solicit his gift."[21] Another author who tackles the issue, Paul Firstenberg, recommends that a nonprofit board "must be supported intelligently and indeed 'managed' by the organization's staff."[22] Firstenberg argues that boards work best when they can react to specific management proposals. Likewise, Conrad and Glenn state that "Board volunteers are only as effective as staff wishes or helps them to be."[23] Unfortunately, neither source elaborates on how management staff should manage the board's role in fund raising, although Conrad and Glenn offer general advice about the board volunteers' expectations of the staff role. They write, "Board volunteers expect from their staff competence and personal integrity; they expect performance to keep pace with promises; they expect satisfaction with both direction and pace."[24]

In summary, there seems widespread agreement that all board members should give to their organization and take on other fund-raising tasks. The question of who should see that such expectations are met is much less frequently raised or answered. One authority holds the board responsible for managing itself. Others suggest that the staff, especially the chief executive, must manage the board.

How It Is: Descriptive Evidence

Surprisingly little research has been conducted on the extent of board involvement in fund raising. Dan H. Fenn, in a 1971 study of 400 business executives who were board members of nonprofit organizations, reports that 68 percent had undertaken fund raising.[25] Unfortunately, the data do not tell us whether the 68 percent refers to the proportion of executives who had engaged in volunteer fund raising at any time for any organization or the proportion who had raised funds for a specific organization within a specific period. The presentation suggests the former. Thus, "68 percent" may overstate the proportion who raised funds for a particular organization. Fenn also reports that when asked what tasks the executives preferred, only 11 percent responded with fund raising.[26]

In a study of board-staff relations, Herman and Tulipana

surveyed ninety-six board members of seven nonprofit organizations (all United Way affiliates) in one southern city. When members were asked whether they had participated in fund raising for their organization, 58 percent reported that they had. When asked about whether and how they contributed to their organization, 38 percent said that they contributed to their organization as well as to the local United Way, 9 percent contributed to their organization instead of the United Way, 43 percent contributed only through the United Way, and 11 percent did not contribute in any fashion.[27]

Kathleeen Brown studied fund-raising attitudes and behavior of board members of ten nonprofit organizations in Marin County, California. Of seventy-one board members who responded, nearly 48 percent indicated that they found fund raising either "somewhat distasteful" or "distasteful." However, nearly 75 percent said that they would ask for money if requested, with only 9 percent refusing to ask for money. Most of the board members had participated in one or more fund-raising activities during the previous year; only 10 percent said that they had performed no fund-raising activity. When asked about their own contributions to their organization during the previous year, only 12 percent reported that they had given nothing, while 48 percent had given $100 or more.[28]

The available evidence, limited though it is, strongly suggests that many, perhaps most, boards fail to meet the prescriptive expectations. Although we have no systematic evidence, our experience leads us to believe that the extent of board fund-raising involvement is closely related to either one of two factors. One factor is the extent to which the nonprofit organization has integrated effective nonprofit management practices that focus on improvement in such areas as governance, planning, evaluation, and leadership and human resource development (including the paid employee and the volunteer). The second factor relates to the composition of the board of directors and the community prestige of the organization. In every city, some nonprofit organizations, typically including art museums, symphonies, private universities, and some hospitals, are regarded as more prestigious than others. As such, they are better able to attract a community's elite to board service. Our experience is that elite boards are more likely to honor the fund-raising expectation of giving to their organization. The elite board's fulfillment of this expectation does not, however, preclude the need to raise funds from additional outside sources; nor does it suggest that elite board members would actively pursue donor contributions.

On the issue of who actually manages the board's involvement in fund raising, there is no direct systematic evidence. Those who have studied board-executive relations agree that usually the chief executive plays the major leadership role, initiating activities for the board. Fenn offers as one of the conclusions of his study that the business executive "turns out to be a follower instead of a leader, an implementer rather than an innovator. He reacts to the initiatives of the paid staff of the voluntary organization, rather than managing it."[29] On the basis of a study of 103 nonprofit organizations, Unterman and Davis assert that "time limitations encourage the executive director to control the strategic decision process. Although in theory both director [for example, corporate business] and trustee boards should make policy decisions, it is of interest to note that CEOs and executive directors have control of strategic management even though their power is derived differently."[30] Similarly, Middleton concludes: "[M]ost of the data indicate that boards do not formulate policy but rather ratify policy presented to them by staff."[31]

If it is generally true that boards react rather than lead, does it follow that board-executive relations with respect to fund raising follow the same pattern? We think not. Because fund raising is widely recognized as a key board function and because board members often dislike fund raising, board decisions, collectively and individually, about board participation in fund raising cannot be avoided. Boards and individual board members ultimately decide whether, how, and to what extent they will undertake fund raising for their organization. The chief executive cannot decide for them. Certainly, in some organizations whose revenues are derived almost entirely from governmental contracts or third-party payers, chief executives and board members have frequently "decided" (by default) that fund raising is not a board function, and this decision is a difficult one to change. A chief executive cannot decide that the board will become a fund-raising board and then expect it to happen immediately. Even in organizations where the board is fully involved in giving and fund raising, such is the case because the board and its members have decided it will be so. The chief executive's role is to facilitate and support the activities that encourage such board behavior.

Our experience leads us to believe that behind successful fund-raising boards are chief executives and other staff who have taken an unobtrusive leadership role in developing board and organizational processes that promote effective board fund raising. Included in those processes are (1) the establishment of an effective nominating or board development committee, (2) peer recruitment of potential board members and complete disclosure of expectations, and (3) a great deal of staff support in fund-raising activities, ranging from drafting letters to scheduling appointments to preparing board members for solicitation visits.

Conclusions

The two preceding sections convince us that in many nonprofit organizations there is often a gap between what should be and what is. In this section we offer an analysis of why such a gap often exists and suggest some steps boards and chief executives can take to close the gap.

In another piece, one of us has presented an argument about why board practices often fall short of the heroic ideal (presented in the section on prescriptions).[32] There Herman argues that the gap is typically the result of two realities: the ownership issue and the structure of incentives for board participation and performance. We believe the same realities create the frequent board fund-raising gap.

First, unlike in business firms, no one in a nonprofit organization has an equity interest. While board members may, in some circumstances, be held personally liable for the actions of a nonprofit organization and thus be exposed to some financial risk, they have no corresponding financial incentive. The economic-legal ownership reality in nonprofit organizations has very significant implications for psychological ownership. Though there are important exceptions, our judgment is that for a majority of established nonprofit organizations, the paid staff, especially the chief executive, has the greater sense of ownership of and responsibility for the success of the organization. Assuming the responsibility for generating revenues for the organization is the type of emotional and behavioral commitment that would be expected of individuals who want some assurance of their continued employment. Indeed, the investment of time, its impact on career advancement or stabilization, and financial security are the types of issues that can be powerful motivators for staff involvement and leadership in the fund-raising role.

While the evidence for this assertion is mostly impressionistic, recently completed research provides more rigorous and systematic evidence.[33] The study, which used a sample of fifty-one nonprofit organizations, first asked chief executives to describe one recent event that was especially successful and another that was unsuccessful. Each executive was then asked to complete a short questionnaire assessing the extent to which each of eight different factors contributed to the successful or unsuccessful outcome of the event. The eight factors assessed were these:

1. Your personal skills and abilities
2. Your personal board work and effort
3. The skills and abilities of your subordinates
4. The hard work and effort of your subordinates
5. The skills and abilities of your board
6. The hard work and effort of your board
7. Positive circumstances beyond anyone's control
8. Negative circumstances beyond anyone's control

Similar questionnaires, appropriately modified to fit their roles, were sent to three subordinates who had been involved in each event and the board president (or presidents) at the time of the two events. These individuals assessed the same eight factors.

Analysis of the responses provides some very revealing evidence about who takes responsibility and gets assigned responsibility for both success and failure in nonprofit organizations. Chief executives assign themselves (through their skills and abilities and hard work and effort) greater responsibility for success *and failure.*

In contrast to both subordinates and volunteer board presidents/ chairs, chief executives take responsibility for unsuccessful events, assigning higher responsibility to themselves than to others or to circumstances. Both subordinates and board chairs assign the responsibility for unsuccessful events to others and to bad luck more than to themselves. In both successful and unsuccessful events, chief executives are credited by themselves, their subordinates, and board presidents/chairs as contributing the most to outcomes. On the other hand, board presidents assign themselves relatively little responsibility for either success or failure. That is not especially surprising. What happens in nonprofit organizations occupies a much less central part of the lives of board presidents than the same events do for chief executives.

Second, as a number of recent studies[34] demonstrate, those who participate on nonprofit boards usually have multiple motives or incentives, though the relative importance of the motives or incentives varies substantially among individuals. The literature on work motivation has long distinguished between incentives that induce participation in or joining an organization and incentives that induce varying levels of performance. We believe this distinction is very useful in understanding the behavior of nonprofit board members.

Many of the incentives most people look for in board service are achieved primarily through membership and attendance at meetings. For example, if board membership is thought to confer some prestige, or is valued by one's employer, or is likely to provide useful business contacts, such incentives will motivate people to join and do enough—attend meetings—to maintain membership. However, such incentives are unlikely, by themselves, to motivate high levels of performance on board tasks, including fund raising. Nonprofit organizations have been very inventive in designing incentives scaled to differing levels of contributions. Many organizations have developed a series of labels recognizing differing dollar amounts of contributions, as well as differentiated social events for differing levels of giving. Thus, some of the "rewards" for giving are sensitive to differing levels of giving performance.

When it comes to varying levels of soliciting performance, the recognition is more likely to be informal and generated within

the fund-raising group. Indeed, as Galaskiewicz's research in Minneapolis–St. Paul demonstrated, among those who are part of or
aspire to be part of a community's elite, the importance of peer
pressure, reciprocity, and the maintaining or gaining of status from
the elite circle strongly affects giving and soliciting. As Galaskiewicz notes, "refusing to cooperate [in reciprocal giving and solic-
iting] jeopardizes one's status in the business community, which for
all practical purposes seems equivalent to a civic culture. . . . One
is excluded from groundbreaking ceremonies, receptions for visiting artists, parties on opening day at the Metrodome, task forces,
and fundraising events."[35] At least for those nonprofit organizations
that are well connected to a community's elite, the performance of
board members in both giving and soliciting is often linked to
variable and valued incentives. For organizations not connected to
the elite, board giving and soliciting is less often connected to variable or valued incentives.

If this analysis of why there is often a gap between prescriptive ideals and actual practice is valid, what can be done—either to
move practice closer to the ideal or to change the ideal? We believe
some modification of the ideal is necessary, as outlined below.

First, if an organization asks others, whether individuals,
foundations, or businesses, to contribute, it is desirable and practically useful that the board members also contribute. Such an expectation and its rationale should be clearly communicated during
recruitment and accepted by all potential board members.

Second, all board members should accept a role in at least
one fund-raising activity each year. Some might solicit, others organize an event, and still others stuff envelopes. These expectations
also need to be communicated to and accepted by all members, and
careful records of participation should be kept.

Third, more and more nonprofit organizations are attempting to recruit the community elite. This is, apparently, an often
frustrating and unsuccessful experience. We suggest that one of the
greatest priorities be given to a person's commitment to the organization's mission. We are not suggesting that organizations set
aside attempts to achieve greater social diversity or that recruiting
board members who have needed expertise, skills, or connections is
undesirable. Rather, we believe that the most important criterion is

a potential member's willingness to share the talents and skills that she or he has, including the characteristics of loyalty and dedication. Because such members share in the vision of the organization, they are more likely to find the rewards of board service, especially in nonelite organizations, related to performance rather than to mere membership. Additionally, individuals who demonstrate an abiding respect for the work of the chief executive or board chair are likely to make personal concessions to the organization more readily than individuals who are recruited to fulfill a model board profile.

Where these prescriptions are not being achieved, what can be done and by whom to move toward them? While there may be occasions where a member (or members) of a board will initiate changes in the board's fund-raising practices, our experience is that generally the chief executive must carefully lead the process. Such leadership may take many different paths including the following:

1. An informal board education process whereby selected articles are sent to board members as informational items.
2. Use of a nonprofit management consultant who can focus on clarifying the roles and responsibilities of the board of directors. Generally, board directors are more willing to accept the "difficult" role demands of their board position when they are argued by a consultant rather than their own chief executive.
3. Use of a fund-raising consultant who designs a fund-raising activity in conjunction with a board or a board committee "sounding out" the willingness of the board chair and other key board members to introduce new fund-raising expectations for the board.
4. The chief executive or a consultant can participate in the work of the board development committee and guide the recruitment of potential board members who have experience in and commitment to fund raising.

As the board's norms and expectations about fund raising begin to change, the chief executive and other staff members must provide a great deal of detailed support work.

Though a chief executive will probably have to assume the

responsibility for turning around a board's fund-raising norms and practices, the executive's actions will need to be directed at building the board's capacity to function as an effective fund-raising body. The board's capacity for fund raising depends on communicated and accepted expectations, relationship-building skills, confidence, recognitions and celebrations of fund-raising achievements, and a commitment to the organization characterized by a strong feeling of psychological ownership toward it. All that a chief executive can do to strengthen her or his management skills while enhancing the board's governance capacity will not only improve the fund-raising performance of the board but also the board's overall performance.

Notes

1. Scott M. Cutlip, *Fundraising in the United States: Its Role in America's Philanthropy.* New Brunswick, N.J.: Rutgers University Press, 1965, pp. 3–4.
2. Cutlip, pp. 7–8.
3. Kathleen D. McCarthy, *Noblesse Oblige.* Chicago: University of Chicago Press, 1982, p. 8.
4. McCarthy, p. 10.
5. J. Leiby, *A History of Social Welfare and Social Work in the United States.* New York: Columbia University Press, 1978.
6. F. T. Waite, *A Warm Friend for the Spirit.* Cleveland, Ohio: Family Service Association of Cleveland, 1960.
7. Cutlip, pp. 51–53.
8. Cutlip, p. 87.
9. Cutlip, pp. 40–50.
10. Robert H. Bremner, *American Philanthropy.* Chicago: University of Chicago Press, 1960, p. 140.
11. Melissa Middleton, "Nonprofit Board of Directors: Beyond the Governance Function." In W. W. Power (ed.), *The Nonprofit Sector: A Research Handbook.* New Haven, Conn.: Yale University Press, 1987. Middleton notes that the legal status of public charity boards "falls between the law of trusts and the law of business corporations" (p. 142). She concludes that the legal status of charitable boards is "ambiguous and contributes to the vagueness surrounding their explicit functions and

status in organizations. With minimal guidance board members are left to answer those questions for themselves, assuming they raise them at all" (p. 143).

12. The standards associated with the heroic model are from Robert D. Herman, "Concluding Thoughts on Closing the Board Gap." In Robert D. Herman and Jon Van Til (eds.), *Nonprofit Boards of Directors: Analyses and Applications*. New Brunswick, N.J.: Transaction Books, 1989.

13. Stephen R. Block, Robert F. Leduc, and Jean M. Carroccio, *Getting in Shape for Fundraising*. (Manuscript in progress.)

14. Block, Leduc, and Carroccio.

15. Stephen Wertheimer, "Resource Development: A Manager's Approach to Fundraising." In Stephen R. Block, Robert F. Leduc, and Jon Van Til (eds.), *The Effective Practice of Nonprofit Management*. (Manuscript in progress.)

16. Michael Seltzer, *Securing Your Organization's Future: A Complete Guide to Fundraising Strategies*. New York: Foundation Center, 1987, p. 41.

17. Fred Setterberg and Kary Schulman, *Beyond Profit: The Complete Guide to Managing the Nonprofit Organization*. New York: Harper & Row, 1985, p. 13.

18. Brian O'Connell, *The Board Member's Book*. New York: Foundation Center, 1985, p. 124.

19. Tracy D. Connors, "The Board of Directors." In Tracy D. Connors (ed.), *The Nonprofit Organization Handbook*. New York: McGraw-Hill, 1980.

20. Thomas Broce, *Fund Raising*. Norman: University of Oklahoma Press, 1979, p. 48.

21. Broce, p. 48.

22. Paul B. Firstenberg, *Managing for Profit in the Nonprofit World*. New York: Foundation Center, 1986, p. 205.

23. William R. Conrad and William R. Glenn, *The Effective Voluntary Board of Directors*. Chicago: Swallow Press, 1976, p. 25.

24. Conrad and Glenn, p. 27.

25. Dan H. Fenn, Jr., "Executives as Community Volunteers." *Harvard Business Review*, Mar./Apr. 1981, p. 12.

26. Fenn, p. 14.

27. Robert D. Herman and F. Peter Tulipana, "Board-Staff Relations and Perceived Effectiveness in Nonprofit Organizations." *Journal of Voluntary Action Research*, 1985, *14* (4), 48–59.
28. Kathleen M. Brown, "Board Involvement in Fund Raising in Marin County, CA: A Study of Ten Nonprofit Human Service Agencies." Unpublished M.P.A. thesis, University of San Francisco, 1986.
29. Fenn, p. 4.
30. Israel Unterman and Richard H. Davis, "The Strategy Gap in Not-for-Profits." *Harvard Business Review*, May/June 1982, p. 36.
31. Middleton, p. 152.
32. The following discussion is based on Herman (1989).
33. Robert D. Herman and Richard D. Heimovics, "Critical Events in the Management of Nonprofit Organizations: Initial Evidence." *Nonprofit and Voluntary Sector Quarterly* 1989, *18*, 119–132.
34. See Candace Widmer, "Why Board Members Participate." *Journal of Voluntary Action Research*, 1985, *14* (4), 8–23. See also Melissa Middleton, "The Characteristics and Influence of Intraboard Networks," and Justin Fink, "Community Agency Boards of Directors: Viability and Vestigality, Substance and Symbol." In Robert D. Herman and Jon Van Til (eds.), *Nonprofit Boards of Directors: Analyses and Applications*. New Brunswick, N.J.: Transaction Books, 1989.
35. Joseph Galaskiewicz, *Social Organization of an Urban Grants Economy*. Orlando, Fla.: Academic Press, 1985, p. 75.

Chapter 11   *Peter Dobkin Hall*

The Dilemmas of Research on Philanthropy

When a special-interest group seeks to promote academic research about itself, difficult dilemmas crop up—both for the interest group and for those who do research on it. On the one hand, such involvement is an essential component of the process through which groups—be they industries, political causes, or social movements—achieve public recognition and legitimacy. On the other hand, such involvement inevitably threatens the integrity and credibility of the research process itself.

Since the 1950s, research has become increasingly important in the efforts of charitable tax-exempt organizations to formulate guidelines for self-regulation, to build their case for tax and other special forms of public consideration, and to protect themselves from outbursts of regulatory enthusiasm. As it has grown more

Note: The research on which this chapter is based was supported by grants from the American Council of Learned Societies, the Lilly Endowment, the Rockefeller Archive Center, and the Program on Non-Profit Organizations, Yale University. I am grateful to Anne Lowrey Bailey, Robert Bothwell, Charles Clotfelter, Harvey Dale, Pablo Eisenberg, Carol Estes, Bradford Gray, Barry Karl, Stanley N. Katz, Charles E. Lindblom, Richard Lyman, Robert Wood Lynn, Richard Magat, Carl Milofsky, Waldemar Nielsen, Brian O'Connell, Robert L. Payton, Terry Odendahl, Gabe Rudney, David Horton Smith, Hayden Smith, Henry Suhrke, Jon Van Til, and Dennis Young for sharing their recollections and for their responses to earlier versions of this chapter. Portions of the text have appeared in *Philanthropy Monthly*.

central to the activities of these organizations, research has come to reflect the tensions between the various stakeholders in its findings. These include charitable donors, grant-making and grant-receiving institutions, trustees and professional staffs of these institutions, constituencies served by these institutions, and regulatory agencies—as well as the scholars themselves.

As long as these tensions remained in the background of the research process, scholars were relatively unconcerned about them. Indeed, the diversity of stakes and stakeholders seemed to present "many doors to knock on," as one researcher put it—a variety of sources of funding and alternative agendas. Over the past decade, however, charitable tax-exempt organizations, however diverse their activities, have succeeded in recognizing their common interests. This growing unity of purpose has expressed itself institutionally in the form of increasingly well-defined expectations of the research process.

Some scholars have found this troubling. Reviewing the first major collection of research on nonprofit organizations in 1987, historian Barry Karl expressed deep disquiet about this confusion of research and advocacy. Substituting the term *nonprofit* for *philanthropy* and *charity*, he argued, served to enhance philanthropy's public character and obscure its ties to private interests by suggesting an organizational conception that was "presumably efficient, subject to cost-accounting standards of performance and principles of effective management." Similarly, he asserted, the use of the term *research* was "an umbrella that would cover the various aspects of advocacy without drawing critical attention to the process," a process that used the rhetoric of open-ended scholarly enquiry but that was in fact committed "to arguing the fundamental effectiveness of philanthropy."[1]

Examining the development of research on the "nonprofit sector," as well as the origins of the term itself, permits us to view the tensions between the various stakeholders in the research process and to understand how, at various points, they have encountered and attempted to resolve creatively the dilemmas inherent in research on special-interest groups.

Inventing the Nonprofit Sector

The term *nonprofit sector* as a category encompassing the complex domain of voluntary, philanthropic, and charitable organizations was coined barely two decades ago. As Barry Karl has suggested, the term is more than descriptive. It involves powerful prescriptive assumptions about the management, funding, regulation, and responsibilities of these institutions. Disregarding vast differences of scope and scale, kinds of goods and services produced, sources of support and clientage, it posits a single characteristic—tax-exempt status under the federal tax code—as the criterion for inclusion in the sector. This suggests a more than coincidental linkage between scholarship and public policy.

Scholars did not begin writing about the nonprofit sector simply "because it was there." While there was a vast literature on particular kinds of nonprofits—charities, educational institutions, hospitals, museums, social welfare organizations, and so on—no effort was made before the 1970s to treat these as part of a unified "sector" of activity. Indeed, the Department of Commerce's national income accounts, which originated the concept of a sectored economy after the Second World War, had no "nonprofits" category until a decade ago. The terms *nonprofit, third,* and *independent* sector entered scholarly usage in the 1970s, and their appearance was specifically linked to organized philanthropy's efforts to defend itself from government regulation and oversight.[2]

To understand how this happened, it is worth reviewing the origins of philanthropy's interest in creating a body of literature about itself. Before the 1950s, foundations were indifferent or hostile to scholarly inquiries into their activities. Even the friendly efforts of the Russell Sage Foundation's F. Emerson Andrews to compile what became the *Foundation Directory* (which first appeared in 1960) were met with endless obstacles.[3] But in 1955 there was a major turnaround. Key funders suddenly became enthusiastic about generating information about themselves.

The chronology of congressional interest in organized philanthropy seems to suggest the motive for this sudden turnaround. The foundations had, almost miraculously, escaped congressional attention during the Temporary National Economic Committee (TNEC) hearings in the late 1930s, though a number of officials, including the Carnegie Corporation's Frederick W. Keppel, worried privately that the foundations' failure to "recognize their responsibility to the public enjoying exemption from taxation" by creating a public record of their activities would endanger "public confidence in the foundation as a social instrument."[4] Philanthropy's immunity from congressional inquiry ended with the advent of the Cold War. The 1948 House Committee on Un-American Activities investigation of Alger Hiss, president of the Carnegie Endowment for International Peace, was only the beginning of steadily broadening political and regulatory challenge to the autonomy of grant-making foundations. By 1955, foundations had been the subject of two major congressional investigations, each of which produced more stringent oversight through the federal tax code.

Not surprisingly, the initiative for creating "a public record" of foundation activities came not from scholars but from the foundations, which were finally heeding Keppel's warnings of a decade and a half before. In 1955, the Ford Foundation made its first grants to encourage the scholarly investigation of the role of philanthropy in American life, which produced pioneering volumes by University of Wisconsin historian Merle Curti and his associates.[5] In 1956, the Carnegie Corporation underwrote the establishment of "a new organization [that] would be a strategic gathering place for compiling and using knowledge about foundations," the Foundation Center Library. Not content merely to gather information, the library also propagated it, first through the publication of the *Foundation Directory*, which first appeared in 1960 (though work on it had begun in 1957), and later through the publication of *Foundation News*, which began publication in the fall of 1960.

Events of the tumultuous 1960s showed how much more needed to be done. On May 2, 1961, Congressman Wright Patman delivered the first of what would prove to be a protracted series of attacks on foundations. Patman's efforts struck a chord among his colleagues, who were increasingly besieged by constituents unhappy with their mounting tax liabilities and unhappier still with the prospect that the wealthy were using charity to get a free ride. In response to this, the Department of the Treasury in 1965 issued its *Report on Private Foundations*, which, while far more moderate than Patman's recommendations, still pointed to the need for significant government intervention in what had heretofore been a virtually unregulated domain.

Though the 1969 Tax Reform Act (TRA69) was passed after

lengthy, well-publicized, and sometimes acrimonious hearings, it was, despite the lamentations of many friends of foundations, far less draconian than it might have been. Still, its passage made it unmistakably clear not that the foundations would never again enjoy immunity from public oversight and regulation, but that they, in effect, existed on congressional sufferance. If the foundations hoped to survive the next outburst of regulatory enthusiasm, they would have to justify themselves to a public that was increasingly skeptical about the capacity of private wealth to act in the public interest and increasingly inclined to look to government as the prime actor.

Even before the passage of TRA69, there were major disagreements about how the charitable community should defend itself. One group, led by Emerson Andrews and Manning Patillo of the Foundation Center, had been calling for a system of self-policing, complete with a formal system of accreditation. Another, representing the largest national foundations and social service agencies, was willing to "stonewall" Congress, using moralistic arguments about the essential Americanness of philanthropy and the necessity for it to be free of onerous regulation. A third group, convened by John D. Rockefeller 3rd and calling itself the Commission on Foundations and Private Philanthropy (better known as the Peterson Commission, after its chairman), advocated a more moderate course that would recognize the public obligations of tax-exempt enterprises, while also seeking to preserve and enhance the tax incentives that Rockefeller and his associates viewed as essential to strengthening this aspect of the free enterprise system.[6]

It was this awareness, combined with fears of further congressional action in the early 1970s, that led to the establishment of the Commission on Private Philanthropy and Public Needs (Filer Commission). The commission was a unique hybrid: though nominally a public body operating under the authority of the Department of the Treasury, it was privately funded by over $2 million in donations from individuals, foundations, and corporations. Strategically, the Filer Commission represented a considerable risk for charitable tax-exempt organizations. Unlike previous task forces, it was, relatively speaking, a representative body with an ambitious and apparently open-ended research program. There was no way of predicting what its conclusions might be. Further, it was unique in that its scope of enquiry included not only foundations, but the whole realm of 501(c)(3) organizations: community chests, hospitals, museums, libraries, churches, neighborhood associations, and "associations of a thousand other kinds." For the first time, all charitable tax-exempt agencies, from giant grant makers through grass-roots activist organizations, were treated as part of a unified "nonprofit sector." More than merely reporting on the current state of American philanthropy and voluntarism, the Filer Commission succeeded in creating a new language and a new conceptual framework that would profoundly shape all subsequent research on voluntary, philanthropic, and charitable activity.[7]

Beyond the Filer Commission, 1975–1980

When the Filer Commission issued its report in the fall of 1975, many of its members and consultants realized that their work raised more questions than it answered. For that reason, the majority urged that the federal government establish a "permanent national commission on the nonprofit sector" to collect data on the sector's sources and resources, to explore and propose ways of strengthening private giving and nonprofit activity, to provide a forum for public discussion of issues affecting the nonprofit sector, to study its relationship to government, and to act as an ombudsman in protecting the sector's interests.[8] Commission members would be jointly appointed by Congress and the president, and funds for its support would come half from government and half from private sources.[9]

This proposal also aroused sharply worded dissent from the commission's most conservative members: "the functions proposed . . . to be performed by a 'permanent national commission for the nonprofit sector' could be better executed by a recognized and supported private instrument. Indeed, the creation of this 'national commission' by Congress is likely to lead to governmental intervention in the private nonprofit sector that will weaken it rather than strengthen it."[10]

The more radical Donee Group, which generally favored greater federal regulation of tax-exempt organizations, gave the proposal only lukewarm endorsement, fearing that such an agency would quickly become the captive of larger and better organized interests.[11] But the final blow came from President Carter's new Treasury secretary, Michael Blumenthal, who expressed skepticism about the ability of such a body to simultaneously represent the public interest and defend a private one.[12]

Had the Filer Commission's recommendation for a "Federal Bureau of Philanthropy" been followed, the development of the nonprofits research community would have followed a very different course, and the kinds of dilemmas facing nonprofit research would have been of a very different sort. By privatizing nonprofits research, the Carter administration ensured that research would become the instrument of the various groups that were contending for leadership of the "nonprofit sector" and, ultimately, of whichever emerged as the dominant one.

Even before the dismissal of the national commission early in 1977, an assortment of private groups, most of them led by former members of the Filer Commission, were scurrying to take its place. These included the Joint Committee on Research in Philanthropy, the Coalition of National Voluntary Organizations (CONVO), the Council on Foundations, the Foundation Center, the American Association of Fund-Raising Counsel, the National Council on Philanthropy (NCOP), the National Committee for Responsive Philanthropy, and the Association of Voluntary Action Scholars (AVAS). All acknowledged the need for further research, and some were prepared to do it themselves, though none had the financial resources to undertake a major research program and all seem to have understood that as advocacy organizations, their research might lack credibility. Ultimately, the failure of any of these entities to inherit the research mantle of the Filer Commission was due to their close ties to one or another of the factions that had divided Filer Commission members.[13]

The Beginnings of Nonprofits Research

The plan to establish a nonprofits research center at Yale first surfaced in 1975, with a lengthy "Proposal for a Study of Independent Institutions" coauthored by university president Kingman Brewster, law school professor John Simon, and political scientist Charles

E. Lindblom.[14] The original impetus for what would become the Program on Non-Profit Organizations (PONPO) came from Kingman Brewster, who, by the early 1970s, had grown increasingly alarmed about the impact of federal funding—and the "strings" attached to it—on the autonomy of private universities. Simon's interest stemmed not only from his role as Yale Law School's specialist on charities but from the fact that he was president of the innovative Taconic Foundation and trustee of the Council on Foundations and the Foundation Center, and had served as special consultant to the Filer Commission. Lindblom's involvement was based on his scholarly interest in promoting multidisciplinary and policy relevant social science research. By 1975, he had taken charge of Yale's Institution for Social and Policy Studies, which contained within it centers for the study of education, health care, and urban problems.

"It was a somewhat odd way to begin a research program," Simon would say in 1980, two years after PONPO had finally begun its work: "Most programs begin with a group of scholars who have ongoing work they want to finance. Or a program sometimes begins with a donor—a foundation or a government agency—that has money it wants to devote to meet some of its informational needs. Scholars or dollars launch most programs. Our program began without many scholars, without any dollars—with only an idea. Accordingly, it took some time to start up—to collect the financing and the personnel to get going."[15]

That the Yale program should have lacked scholars is hardly surprising. Despite the fact that many of Yale's faculty had done work on one or another kind of activity supported by private philanthropy, the idea of a "nonprofit sector" that treated all of these as a unified and coherent entity was simply too new and strange. Indeed, even Lindblom, who was enthusiastic about creating the center, regarded its fundamental task as one of defining what was meant by the term.[16]

But it is surprising that the proposal also lacked dollars, given Yale's wealth and prestige and the evident post-Filer interest in creating a research center. Despite its reputation, Yale, like so many other institutions during those inflationary years, was hemorrhaging financially. In addition, Brewster's controversial political stances had alienated many potential contributors to its fund drives.[17] Because the university could not give the program direct support, PONPO had to turn to the entities that the program was proposing to study.

There was no great rush to underwrite the Yale program, despite John D. Rockefeller 3rd's personal pledge of a quarter-million dollars. The primary reason for this was summed up in the response of the Ford Foundation to its appeals for support. The program's research agenda, Ford officials felt, put "too much emphasis . . . on theory and not enough on quantitative measures" and that, as a result, "the research results would be of little relevance in the formulation of policy with regard to non-profit institutions."[18] As John Simon would put it 1980, "some third sector admirers . . . have to be prepared for research outcomes we might not find emotionally satisfying."[19] But at this stage of the game, they were not so prepared.

Finally, PONPO was only one of several research efforts seeking support.[20] Others included the Committee for the Third Sector (which emerged in 1978 from the Aspen Institute and included among its backers John Gardner, Walter McNerney, Porter McKeever, and other Filer Commission notables) and the National Center for Charitable Statistics (established in 1979 by Filer Commission veterans Jack Schwartz of the American Association of Fund-Raising Counsel and Bayard Ewing of United Way). It was far from clear which would best serve the interests of the various and often conflicting groups that comprised the "sector."

The situation began to change late in 1979, as various organized factions began to overcome their differences. Efforts were under way to merge CONVO, NCOP, and several lesser advocacy groups into INDEPENDENT SECTOR, a national organization that would represent the interests of all charitable tax-exempt organizations. As this occurred, the leaders of the philanthropic community were able to agree on the kind of research product they wanted and, as a result, were able to allocate the task of examining "the philosophical basis and the long-term societal aspects of the third sector" to the Yale program, while assigning to INDEPENDENT SECTOR the task of "focusing attention, in hopefully an objective way, on near and medium-term issues in both a research and convening role."[21] By the end of 1980, the Yale program had garnered over a million dollars in commitments.

Despite the hope that the Yale program would be left free to pursue a relatively unconstrained academic research effort, pressures to pursue a more focused agenda—one that would yield "useful" results and contribute to the sector's advocacy concerns—were unremitting. It proved to be far easier to raise funds for special projects than for general support, and this inevitably drew the academic research effort away from unfundable basic research toward the "near and medium-term issues" that funders were more willing to underwrite.

INDEPENDENT SECTOR and Nonprofits Research

From the beginning, INDEPENDENT SECTOR (IS) had a stated commitment to fostering the development of "a body of knowledge necessary to accurately define, describe, chart, and otherwise understand the sector and the ways it can be of greater service to society." It pledged neither to do the research itself nor to be a significant funder of it; it would seek to "facilitate, encourage, and stimulate the work of others."[22] IS was as good as its word. After 1980, funding became more abundant as the audience for serious research on nonprofits grew. At the same time, IS's commitment to an arm's-length relationship reassured many of those who feared that industry sponsorship would impair the credibility of their work.

The conception of the diverse and complex universe of charitable tax-exempt organizations as a unified and coherent "sector" grew easier to accept as these entities, working through INDEPENDENT SECTOR, overcame their differences and suspicions of one another. As their policy interests converged, so too did their willingness to agree on their common stake in research. In 1983, when IS's Research Committee was first convened, its members, who included scholars as well as representatives of donor and donee organizations, were willing to commit themselves to sustaining both applied and basic research, cautioning, however, the necessity of establishing a balance between the two.[23]

By 1985, the committee, encouraged by the success of its early initiatives, began to assume a far more proactive stance.[24] "Research

252 Critical Issues in American Philanthropy

agendas or priority research topics," the committee declared, have
"become more necessary." It urged, moreover, that more attention
be given to "supporting research institutions where the capacity can
be built to accomplish and sustain such research."[25] Once again, the
efforts were successful. By 1987, twelve research centers had been
established in various universities; by 1988, a total of twenty were
in operation. In addition, by 1986, the American Association of
Fund-Raising Counsel's Trust for Philanthropy, through the Association of American Colleges, both IS member organizations, underwrote courses on philanthropy in colleges and universities
around the country, and the AAFRC Trust supported the research
and writing reported in the present volume.[26]

The Growth of Nonprofits Research
and the Crisis of Credibility

The proliferation of research centers after 1985 fundamentally transformed the relationship between funders and researchers. More centers created increased demands for greater and more sustained
support. This vastly complicated the decision-making process for
grant makers, who now not only had to consider what kind of
research was most worthwhile but also to decide which of twenty
research institutions were most worthy of their benevolence. In addition to the university-based programs, mainstream industry
groups like IS, the Council on Foundations, and the Foundation
Center, as well as others such as the National Committee for Responsive Philanthropy and the Center for Community Change,
were requesting funds to underwrite their own in-house research.
By this time, IS, for one, had demonstrated the ability to attract
major support to conduct its own interpretive studies of the sector.[27]

As demands for funding increased, so too did pressures from
funders for further rationalization of the research infrastructure:
delineating agendas outlining the important topics, ranking researchers and research centers in terms of their reliability and quality, and informally dividing obligations between the major funders.
Believing that it had the confidence both of the funders and of the
research community, INDEPENDENT SECTOR began to formal-
ize its brokerage role.

As IS and its Research Committee moved forward in their plans to further institutionalize the research effort, differences of opinion began to be heard with regard to its direction. In a keynote address to the 1987 Spring Research Forum, Kettering Foundation president and Research Committee founding member David Mathews worried that the organizations of INDEPENDENT SECTOR had failed to come to grips with their "larger political function" and that this "misreading of their history" threatened to "undermine the efforts of the sector to develop a comprehensive strategy for responding to current political challenges." Concerned that nonprofits research had become narrowly preoccupied with short- and medium-range issues, he proposed that the Research Committee "encourage studies to enrich the *concept* of the Sector: Ultimately, . . . the purpose of a richer self concept in the Sector is not for tactical self defense. It is to inform what the Sector tries to do. Civic organizations have real political responsibilities that go beyond lobbying and providing services. They are basic, elemental political functions. . . . How people understand participation, how they come to join with one another, how they learn to talk with one another for public purposes, how public leadership is defined and developed—those are the overarching and common responsibilities of the Sector. There is a political environment that is just as real and just as important as the natural environment. And no group is more able to ensure its well-being than the organizations of the Independent Sector."[28]

Mathews's concern that IS's research focus had slipped into a trade association mode, focusing on institutional interests rather than the public good, was echoed a few months later by Lance Buhl, a corporate contributions manager, who in reviewing the first phase of post-Filer research complained that researchers had failed to look at the "large ideas—equity, justice, service, leadership—that relate to public purpose."[29]

The concerns of these funders paralleled those of certain veteran nonprofits researchers. In 1986, political scientist Lester Salamon, in a paper to the annual meeting of the Association of Voluntary Action Scholars, argued that nonprofits research, in casting the charitable tax-exempt domain as an "independent" sector, had distorted its capacity to perceive the reality of its interdependence. This, he believed was "a product of the limitations of the conceptual lenses through which this reality is being perceived. Both the theory of the 'welfare state' and the theory of the voluntary sector, moreover, leave much conceptual room for a flourishing government-nonprofit partnership. To the contrary, both suggest quite strongly that such cooperation could not, and should not, exist. Equipped with such theories, it is no wonder that observers have tended to overlook such cooperation when it appears."[30]

Though Salamon was circumspect in identifying the source of the "limitations of the conceptual lenses" to which he pointed, others were not. Historian Barry Karl's review of the Yale handbook for the May 1987 issue of *Science* placed the blame squarely on those who had an interest in enhancing philanthropy's public character and obscuring its ties to private interests by using "research" as "an umbrella that would cover the various aspects of advocacy without drawing critical attention to the process." Scholarship that represented itself as dispassionate and open-ended enquiry had become, thanks to its close ties to the industry it studied, committed "to arguing the fundamental effectiveness of philanthropy."[31]

Coming to Terms with the Dilemmas of Nonprofits Research

Not surprisingly, IS's initial response to these criticisms was defensive. Some leaders worried that critical research would engender "outbursts of regulatory enthusiasm."[32] Nevertheless, events of 1988 and 1989 brought into the foreground of concern the dilemmas that faced both researchers and the industry that had a vital stake in research. Most importantly, it had become increasingly clear that the kinds of relationships appropriate to the first phase of developing nonprofits research would have to be reevaluated.

In the decade after the Filer Commission, the ability of scholars to do sustained work on nonprofits had depended on the willingness of funders to underwrite such work. Unlike other research funding arenas, where the grant-making process was highly institutionalized and peer review mechanisms gave the appearance of objective appraisal, the funding of nonprofits research had been highly personalized and dependent on powerful and well-connected sponsorship. Though IS's involvement in the research opened the process in important ways, particularly by enlarging opportunities for scholars interested in the field, the fact that IS represented the industry rather than scholars presented an additional set of problems.

The forums, workshops, committees, and retreats and access to funding made possible by IS's investment in knowledge development succeeded in creating a community of scholars drawn from many fields. At the same time, this community's dependence on IS ran the risk of isolating it from the academic mainstream, which tended to be suspicious of industry-sponsored research. Further, researchers themselves, troubled by this growing dependence, began to question their own motives: how self-serving had they been in offering opinions about the work of others? How far had they bent their thinking to suit the requirements of a funder or research center? Were they special pleaders who had traded away their commitment to objective scholarship?

The industry, of course, faced a matching set of dilemmas. On the one hand, it had a vital stake in research: research of the right kind could enormously enhance both its effectiveness and its public image. Research of the wrong kind could have a devastating impact. Moreover, funders felt that they were accountable for how research grants were used—how could they justify advancing funds to researchers without assurances that they would be used appropriately? On the other hand, however, subjecting the research process to oversight and control posed its own problems as far as the credibility of the research was concerned.

By September 1988, when the *Chronicle of Higher Education* featured a story on nonprofits research's "built-in conflict," it was no longer possible to avoid coming to terms with these dilemmas.[33] This article may have had an influence on IS's decision to restructure the Research Committee, placing a well-known scholar, Stanley Katz, in its chair and increasing the number of scholar members. This reshuffling coincided with the announcement of the creation of a "superfund" to centralize support for nonprofits research and to place it under the control of scholarly peer review committees.[34] Discussions also were initiated with regard to creating a separate (that is, separate from IS) scholarly organization that would become the basis for constituting "philanthropy studies" as a field.[35] Ac-

companying these initiatives were efforts to create a formal scholarly apparatus through the establishment of journals and the formation of a program committee to consider proposed sessions for
future IS research meetings.[36]

These efforts were inevitably controversial. Some feared that
IS had strayed far from its original intention not "to do the research
or even be a significant funder of it" and worried that its involvement in the research process was diminishing "the very pluralism
[that IS was] created to serve and enhance."[37] Others felt that IS had
confronted the dilemmas and was struggling to find creative solutions to them.[38]

It may be that the dialectic of successive dissents, defenses,
confrontations, and justifications is as characteristic of philanthropy as it is of the broader democratic political culture of which
it is a part.[39] While there are pressures that confuse research and
advocacy, there are also counterpressures. These may prevent nonprofits scholarship from following the course of other fields that
have developed "in a special atmosphere of professional purpose,"
isolated from the major influences and shaping minds of the academic mainstream, its parochialism rendering it incapable of at-
tracting the kinds of scholars "who could give it broad relevance
and bring it back to the public domain."[40]

Notes

1. Barry Karl, "Nonprofit Institutions." *Science*, May 22, 1987,
    pp. 984–985.
2. The best introduction to the conceptual framework of sector-
    ing can be found in Carolyn Webber and Aaron Wildavsky,
    A History of Taxation and Expenditure in the Western World.
    New York: Simon & Schuster, 1986, pp. 476–559. On the im-
    plementation of these concepts, see National Income Division,
    U.S. Department of Commerce, *National Income, 1954 Edi-
    tion.* Washington, D.C.: U.S. Government Printing Office,
    1954. On the reformulation of the national income accounts
    to include a nonprofit sector, see Richard Ruggles and Nancy
    D. Ruggles, "Integrated Economic Accounts of the United

States." Working Paper no. 841, Institution for Social and Policy Studies, Yale University, 1980, pp. 4-30.

3. Emerson Andrews's account of the difficulties encountered in assembling the first *Foundation Directory* are to be found in his autobiography, *The Foundation Watcher*. Lancaster, Pa.: Franklin & Marshall College, 1973, pp.156-158, 201-202, 217-219.

4. Quoted in Horace Coon, *Money to Burn: What the Great American Philanthropic Foundations Do with Their Money.* London and New York: Longmans, Green and Company, 1938, pp. 334-335.

5. These volumes, most of them now out of print, include Merle Curti, *American Philanthropy Abroad.* New Brunswick, N.J.: Rutgers University Press, 1963; Merle Curti and Roderick Nash, *Philanthropy in the Shaping of American Higher Education.* New Brunswick, N.J.: Rutgers University Press, 1965; Scott M. Cutlip, *Fundraising in the United States.* New Brunswick, N.J.: Rutgers University Press, 1965; Howard S. Miller, *The Legal Foundations of American Philanthropy.* Madison: State Historical Society of Wisconsin, 1961; and Daniel M. Fox, *Engines of Culture: Philanthropy and Art Museums.* Madison: Department of History, University of Wisconsin, 1963.

6. The most easily available, though necessarily partisan, overview of TRA69-era strategizing is Andrews, *The Foundation Watcher* (note 3). Detailed, critical, and gossipy reporting by Richard Fitzgerald on the congressional hearings in *Non-Profit Report* (now *Philanthropy Monthly*) are invaluable. The most comprehensive files of unpublished materials on TRA69 lobbying are to be found in the Rockefeller Archive Center's collections in the papers of John D. Rockefeller 3rd and his associate Datus Smith and in the recently donated files of the Council on Foundations.

7. To date, there is no written history of the Filer Commission. The best published sources on its composition, methods, and impact can be found in *Non-Profit Report/Philanthropy Monthly*, Nov. 1973, July 1974, Aug. 1974, June 1975, Dec. 1975, Nov. 1976, and Jan. 1977. The John D. Rockefeller 3rd,

Datus Smith, Porter McKeever, and Council on Foundations papers at the Rockefeller Archive Center provide detailed information on every aspect of the commission's activities. The commission's own files, donated by its executive director Leonard Silverstein to INDEPENDENT SECTOR, are not available to researchers.

8.   National Commission on Private Philanthropy and Public Needs, *Giving in America: Toward a Stronger Voluntary Sector.* Washington, D.C.: National Commission on Private Philanthropy and Public Needs, p. 26.

9.   "A National Commission on Philanthropy—An Excerpt of Donald R. Spuehler's Report to the Filer Commission." *Philanthropy Monthly,* June 1975, pp. 10-16.

10. National Commission on Private Philanthropy and Public Needs, pp. 221-222.

11. "Private Philanthropy: Vital and Innovative or Passive and Irrelevant—The Donee Group Report and Recommendations." In National Commission on Private Philanthropy and Public Needs, *Research Papers.* Washington, D.C.: Department of the Treasury, 1977, p. 84.

12. Following the issuance of its report, the Filer Commission's members were able to persuade Treasury Secretary William Simon to establish an advisory committee on philanthropy in the Department of the Treasury. It was hoped that this would become the nucleus of the "permanent national commission" (Pablo Eisenberg, telephone interview, Mar. 21, 1989; *Philanthropy Monthly,* Mar. 1977, p. 4). On the fate of this plan once the Carter administration took office, see Leonard Silverstein, "Memorandum to Commission Members." *Treasury News,* Apr. 18, 1977; and "Treasury Secretary Blumenthal Cuts Advisory Committees." *Treasury News,* Mar. 15, 1977 (Rockefeller Archive Center, RG-17, Porter McKeever Papers, Filer Commission folder).

13. "Organizing Charity." *Philanthropy Monthly,* Nov. 1976, pp. 7-11, gives an excellent overview of the groups vying for the national commission's mantle. See also *Journal of Voluntary Action Research,* Winter 1972. I am grateful to Jon Van Til, David Horton Smith, and Pablo Eisenberg, who shared

their recollections of this period in telephone interviews on Mar. 21, 1989. Once again, the papers of John D. Rockefeller 3rd and Porter McKeever contain invaluable information both on the groups themselves and on the concerns of funders with regard to the research problem.

14. Kingman Brewster, John G. Simon, and Charles E. Lindblom, "Proposal for a Study of Independent Institutions." Unpublished grant proposal dated Oct. 1975, author's collection. On how this proposal was regarded, see "Organizing Charity." *Philanthropy Monthly*, Nov. 1976, pp. 9–10.

15. John G. Simon, "Research on Philanthropy." Speech given at the twenty-fifth anniversary conference of the National Council on Philanthropy, Denver, Colo., Nov. 8, 1979. The text of this speech was published as an INDEPENDENT SECTOR research report in July 1980.

16. Lindblom's ideas about the purposes of the program are scattered through the minutes of the 1978–79 workshop on nonprofit organizations. Minutes of these meetings, taken by John Simon's student Bob Boisture, are in the author's collection.

17. On Brewster's precarious position at Yale by 1976–77, see his obituary in the *New York Times* of Nov. 9, 1988.

18. Comments of Richard Sharpe, Ford Foundation program officer to the Yale nonprofits workshop, seminar minutes, Jan. 16, 1979.

19. John G. Simon, p. 13.

20. *Philanthropy Monthly*, Oct. 1978, p. 3; June 1979, p. 3; and Mar. 1981, pp. 18–19.

21. Memorandum of Porter McKeever to John D. Rockefeller 3rd, "Re: Meetings with John Gardner and Walter McNerney in Washington, May 12" (May 16, 1978) and McKeever's letter to Wayne Thompson, Feb. 16, 1979 (Rockefeller Archive Center, RG-17S, Box 1). For background on political tensions within IS during this formative stage, see Henry C. Suhrke, "Independent Sector, Inc.—The 'How' and 'Why' of a Proposed Organization." *Philanthropy Monthly*, Oct. 1979, pp. 5–9; and "Who Speaks for Philanthropy." *Philanthropy Monthly*, Oct. 1984, pp. 13–17.

22. INDEPENDENT SECTOR, *Program Plan* (as amended and

approved by the membership, Oct. 24, 1980). Washington, D.C.: INDEPENDENT SECTOR, p. 37.

23. Independent Research Committee minutes, Sept. 13, 1983. See also *"IS* Research Plan: A Program for the Development of Knowledge in the Independent Sector." Internal document of INDEPENDENT SECTOR, Sept. 1984, p. 1.

24. "Research Program Plan, 1985–86–First Working Draft." Internal document of INDEPENDENT SECTOR, Sept. 1985.

25. "Seminars, Colloquia, Workshops—A Plan to Stimulate the Development of Knowledge on the Independent Sector." Internal document of INDEPENDENT SECTOR, Sept. 1984, p. 2.

26. On these, see Virginia Hodgkinson, *Academic Centers and Research Institutes Focusing on the Study of Philanthropy, Voluntarism, and Not-for-Profit Activity—A Progress Report.* Washington, D.C.: INDEPENDENT SECTOR, 1988; and "Research on the Independent Sector: A Progress Report." Unpublished manuscript, Aug. 1987. On IS's understanding of the significance of its work in knowledge development, see David Johnston, "Nonprofit Pied Piper." *Foundation News,* Mar./Apr. 1989, pp. 67–69.

27. IS's expenditures for research went from $354,664 in 1985 to $658,270 in 1986, increasing to $825,554 by the end of 1987. Part of this can be accounted for by the merger of IS and the National Center for Charitable Statistics, but an increasing proportion was being devoted to interpretive work done in-house. The first product of this in-house research effort was Virginia A. Hodgkinson, Murray S. Weitzman, and Arthur D. Kirsch, *From Belief to Commitment: The Activities and Finances of Religious Congregations in the United States— Findings from a National Survey.* Washington, D.C.: INDEPENDENT SECTOR, 1988.

28. David Mathews, "The Independent Sector and the Political Responsibilities of the Public." Keynote address delivered to the IS Spring Research Forum, New York City, Mar. 1987. In delivering the speech, Mathews referred to those pushing for an enlarged view of the sector as "an embattled minority" on the Research Committee, suggesting that there was some unhappiness within IS about the tendency of research to focus on "near- and medium-term issues."

29. Lance Buhl, "As We're Seen by Social Scientists." *Foundation News*, Jan./Feb. 1988, pp. 71–72. (Review of W. W. Powell [ed.], *The Nonprofit Sector: A Research Handbook*.)

30. Salamon's paper "Of Market Failure, Voluntary Failure, and Third-Party Government: Toward a Theory of Government-Nonprofit Relations in the Modern Welfare State" was originally presented at the AVAS annual meeting, New York City, in 1986. It was later published in *Journal of Voluntary Action Research*, Jan./June 1987; and in Susan A. Ostrander, Stuart Langton, and Jon Van Til (eds.), *Shifting the Debate: Public/Private Sector Relations in the Modern Welfare State*. New Brunswick, N.J.: Transaction Books, 1987, p. 32.

31. Karl, pp. 984–987.

32. See the text of Richard Lyman's keynote address to the 1988 IS Spring Research Forum, "Looking Forward to the Year 2000: Public Policy and Philanthropy," particularly his comments on the work of Robert Bothwell and Teresa Odendahl (p. 16). In a luncheon speech presented at the same meeting, John G. Simon responded forcefully to Barry Karl's review in *Science* (a tape recording of this speech is in the author's possession).

33. Anne Lowrey Bailey, "Philanthropy Research's Built-In Conflict." *Chronicle of Higher Education*, Sept. 21, 1988, p. A36.

34. David Arnold, "Concept Paper—National Fund for Research on Philanthropy and the Nonprofit Sector." Unpublished paper, 1988. David Arnold was kind enough to provide me with a copy of this paper.

35. On efforts to a field of "philanthropy studies," see Robert L. Payton to author, Apr. 3, 1988; and Payton, "The Emergence of a Field." Unpublished essay, Apr. 1988.

36. On the move of the *Journal of Voluntary Action Research* from Transaction Books to Jossey-Bass, where it was renamed the *Nonprofit and Voluntary Sector Quarterly*, see Jon Van Til, "Publishing About the Management of Voluntary Organizations." In Mel Moyer (ed.), *Managing Voluntary Organizations: An Agenda for the Future*. Proceedings of a conference held at York University, Toronto, Oct. 18–20, 1989, pp. 113–127. Correspondence with Jossey-Bass editor Alan Shrader has also assisted me in understanding the ties between

AVAS, IS, and Jossey-Bass, which also publishes the journal *Nonprofit Management and Leadership* and has published as well an anthology of papers presented at IS meetings (Richard Lyman, Virginia Hodgkinson, and Associates, *The Future of the Nonprofit Sector: Challenges, Changes, and Policy Considerations*. San Francisco: Jossey-Bass, 1989). Jon Van Til and Dennis Young have provided me with information about IS use of a program committee apparatus in designing its research meetings.

37. Peter Dobkin Hall, "Obstacles to Nonprofit Teaching and Research." Unpublished paper presented to the IS Academic Retreat, June 7-8, 1988; and the six-part series "Dilemmas of Nonprofits Research," which appeared in *Philanthropy Monthly*, Jan.-June 1989.

38. Responses to the series, particularly letters from Stanley N. Katz, Harvey Dale, Robert L. Payton, Richard Magat, and Brian O'Connell, have effectively presented IS's view of these dilemmas and its efforts to deal with them. That such dilemmas inescapably confront developing fields of applied social science is suggested by Jon Van Til, "On the Independence of Research on Nonprofit Organizations and Voluntary Action." *Nonprofit and Voluntary Sector Quarterly*, Summer 1989, pp. 95-99. The most extensive public discussion of these issues occurred at the IS Academic Retreat and Professional Forum in Durham, N.C., in July of 1989. Portions of statements from this meeting are contained in Peter Dobkin Hall, "Who Speaks for the Research Community?" *Philanthropy Monthly*, June 1989, pp. 9-13.

39. This was the substance of an unpublished letter written by Barry Karl to the editor of the *Chronicle of Higher Education* in response to Anne Lowrey Bailey's "built-in conflict" article of Sept. 21, 1988.

40. Bernard Bailyn, *Education in the Forming of American Society*. New York: Vintage Books, 1960, pp. 8-9. Bailyn's analysis of the relation between scholarship, the institutional interests of education, and the professionalization of educators presents a paradigm of the dilemmas of special-interest research.

Chapter 12   *Jon Van Til*

Preparing for Philanthropy's Future

Philanthropy, like any other organized human activity, faces a future that no one can predict with certainty. And yet the future of philanthropy merits our careful consideration. Why? Because we will live that future. Indeed, we will help create it by our responses, in whatever mix of passive and active we may choose.

What We Know About the Future

To be sure, the future is not precisely knowable. As a result, it is tempting to take things one day at a time, coping with surprises as they present themselves. Such pragmatism characterizes much of current corporate, governmental, and philanthropic practice. But however common it may be largely to ignore the future, one does so at some considerable risk, for day by day, the future becomes the present and, with similar inexorability, the past. The first fact we know about the future, then, is that it is always there. It cannot be denied; it cannot be halted; it *will* arrive.

We are also beginning to learn a second fact about the future: some people seem to understand it better than others. Thus, while nowhere demonstrated yet by rigorous test, it is nonetheless the case that many corporations find it profitable to scan their futures rigorously in search of new markets. Similarly, some governmental organizations have begun to be served by futures committees that seek to identify the problems to be raised by constituents yet to reach voting age.[1]

Fact number three asserts that there may indeed be patterns in the way some futures unfurl. Following on the observations of the eighteenth-century theorist of social change Giambattista Vico, who saw recurrent cycles to history, the economist Kondratieff has in our own time sought to identify economic cycles of fifty-year duration. Even more compelling to the American experience are the observations of two generations of Arthur M. Schlesingers[2] that a powerful thirty-year cycle may be discerned. Thus cycles of conservatism (early 1890s, 1920s, 1950s, 1980s) can be seen alternating with cycles of liberalism (late 1890s, 1930s, 1960s). These cycles can be paired with recurrent economic dislocations that appear in close relation with the political cycles, as attested to by the depressions of 1893 and 1929 and the rediscovery of poverty in the early 1960s.

From these observations flows a fourth fact: it is worth our effort to admit the study of the future to the wide range of interdisciplinary fields deemed appropriate for consideration and study. The future is important; it is real; and it can be studied intelligently.

The "Four-Futures" Approach

Many futurists, including the present writer, have found that it is most useful in thinking about the future to imagine four possible ways that it may develop.[3]

It is probably easiest to think of the future as being continuous with the present and the recent past. It is certainly possible that the future will offer "more of the same," with some problems unresolved and subject to gradual improvement or decline. This is one possible future, and I identify it as the "continuity future."

It is also possible that the future will not be as tractable as the present and the recent past. As Yeats put it, it is possible that the center will not hold and "mere anarchy" will be loosed upon the world. We moderns have a keen sense of such cataclysm, whether occasioned by nuclear conflict, economic disintegration, world terrorism, AIDS, or dozens of other potential disasters. The possibility of what I call the "hard luck future" is real, and its potential forms are manifold.

Happily, a third possible future finds human affairs less constrained than painted in either the continuity or hard luck scenarios. It is possible that the future will find almost everything working more smoothly and productively than it is at present. Ancient scourges of humankind may begin to be lifted: among them poverty, distrust, racism, and war. The future dawns as a time of fellowship, peace, and progress. This is the "good luck future."

The fourth possible future, which I term the "transformational future," involves a common determination on the part of human beings to transcend the limits of the past and the present. Such "transformational" images of the future posit either a decisive structural shift in society (for example, a shift to a viable social democratic policy and practice) or a widespread acceptance of beliefs and practices of common caring and concern replacing those of narcissism and privatism. Whatever transformational future one may choose to envision, it will involve a replacement of current practices with those more fully consistent with the autonomy and growth of the individual and the patterned justice of the social order.[4]

These four possible futures may each be specified in considerable detail by means of the development of scenarios relating to their emergence and characteristics. As futurists construct such scenarios, they also begin to view them in terms of the probability of their emergence and their various levels of desirability.

The three P's of futuring—possibility, probability, and preferability—make the study of the future not just an intellectual pastime but a crucial aspect of any effective strategic planning process. Let us recall that the really intriguing aspect of the futuring process is that the future, because it has not yet occurred, is subject to some degree to our own influence. It follows, then, that futuring is not merely a passive activity but rather one in which we may both reflect on and build images of the kind of future we wish to inhabit. The process of futuring is thereby a particularly important and empowering sort of human activity. It would appear to be well suited to the study of philanthropy, another form of human activity seen by many as important and empowering itself.

Four Futures for Philanthropy

Applying the four-futures approach to philanthropy, imagine, if you will, the "Anthropy" family, which is comprised of two reasonably normal parents and (the now unusual number of) four children. Of course, Phil is one of the children; the other three are Polly (or Pol), Missy (known as Mis), and Neut. Each child in the Anthropy family holds a different image of the future:

> *Future 1:* Phil Anthropy envisions a future in which the love of fellow beings flourishes and is supported by a creative blend of individual voluntarism, organized voluntary action, generous giving, and effective governmental provision of human and social services.

> *Future 2:* Pol Anthropy imagines a future in which the political sphere expands its commitment to human and social services and people come to rely more and more on government for the provision of those services.

> *Future 3:* Mis Anthropy foresees a future in which the forces of privatism and self-absorption continue to develop, and the unfortunate are left to fend largely for themselves.

> *Future 4:* Neut Anthropy envisions a future in which little changes in the way of love of humankind, and the poor and unfortunate are cared for by a significant minority of individuals, organizations, and government programs.

Looking at these futures, we can see that Future 1 (philanthropy) is transformational in that it involves considerable changes in both values and structures. Future 2 (polanthropy) may involve good luck, but it is certainly not transformational. Future 3 (misanthropy) is a classic hard luck scenario. And Future 4 (neutanthropy) seems to represent an image of the future as continous with the recent past, or the continuity scenario.

What prevents us from achieving philanthropy? To answer this question, we must look at the set of ordinary conditions that keep us from creating better futures.

The Usual Pitfalls

We live in a world that, at best, finds it difficult to take account of the future. At worst, it is a world that identifies the future as a dumping ground for problems it does not wish to face. Examples abound:

- The federal government annually spends nearly 15 percent more money than it receives. Who is to pay for this profligacy? Those who will live in the future.
- One-third of the world's population is cutting firewood faster than trees can grow.[5] Who will fail to cook their food and heat their homes and possess arable land and ample oxygen? Those who will live in the future.
- American business continues to fail to produce products that can compete in world markets.[6] Whose standard of living will suffer as a result of this failure? Those who will live in the future.
- Recent studies show that people in rural parts of Iowa, Nebraska, and Illinois have higher-than-normal rates of leukemia, lymphoma, and other cancers because of pesticide pollution of the Farm Belt's water supplies.[7] Who will drink the water we presently poison with our myriad toxic wastes? Those who will live in the future.
- Sales of war toys in the United States increased by 600 percent between 1982 and 1986, and federal military spending exceeded inflation by 61 percent from 1981 to 1986.[8] Who will be predisposed to kill when they reach adulthood? Those who will live in the future.
- Three-fourths (some 3,000) of the participants in the annual National Religious Broadcasters Convention are "dispensationalists," believing that only a nuclear holocaust can bring Christ

back to earth. Sixty-one million Americans regularly listen to their broadcasts.[9] Who will die in that holocaust so many Americans so fervently await? Those who will live, at least for a while, in the future.

I was struck during the endless 1988 presidential campaign with the general absence of futures awareness in the various candidacies. Who a candidate slept with last night, whether he really was an "outsider," whether his campaign director really knew about that nasty TV spot—these were the real issues of the moment.[10] What the candidates would do to make life more secure for the twenty-first century—come on, who's interested in that kind of issue?

Politics, even after an election, takes as its time perspective the years or months until the next election. And business, even after many decades of documented experience with the business cycle, finds its executives and even the economists who study it uncertain about whether the next turn of the cycle will actually develop. Everywhere in modern life, it seems, the focus is on the "here and now" of pop psychology, the "bottom line" of the corporation (profit or nonprofit), the next election. . . .

Within the confines of this "present-oriented" organizational culture, futures, if we think of them at all, become the short-sighted and short-termed "investments" of the commodities market and even the stock market itself, among myriad other forms of legalized gambling in our society. If Edward Banfield was correct in assuming that the essence of being "lower class" is to fail to appreciate the blessings of deferred gratification,[11] then we are decidely people of the lower class in a lower-class society. Pull out the plastic, snap your MAC, and give not a thought to the final bill. Tomorrow never comes. . . .

Some Good Solutions

If what is conventionally done about the future in our time is to deny it, what can we do if we choose to act more responsibly? In this section, I will describe three vehicles by which we can proceed:

the search conference, futuring as strategic planning, and modeling the study of the future for the topic at hand, philanthropy.

The Search Conference. Thomas Gilmore and his colleagues at the Wharton Center for Applied Research in Philadelphia have described the search conferences they conduct for business, governmental, and nonprofit organizations.[12] In a search conference, a group of twenty to thirty people work together for two or three days surveying trends and considering issues facing their organization. During the conference, participants diagnose the external and internal environments of the organization, define a desirable future for the organization, and develop an action plan.

Among the powerful concepts introduced in the search conference is that of "ideas in good currency." Such ideas dominate an era, emerging slowly and then bursting upon our consciousness as they assume a period of ascendancy, which precedes their inevitable decline from prominence. Examples of ideas in good currency include science and technology in the late 1950s, poverty and civil rights in the mid-1960s, energy in the 1970s, and privatization in the 1980s.

The search conference permits its participants to identify issues and problems that will confront their organization in the years ahead and to position themselves to cope with these challenges successfully. It is difficult to understand why any organization would not wish to be in the position of meeting its future needs; as such, futuring becomes a critical element of any strategic planning process.

Futuring as Part of Strategic Planning. Few ideas have gained such currency in our management-dominated age than that of strategic planning, or strategic management. Central to any effective practice of strategic planning is the capacity to envision and elaborate images of potential futures. As the search conference indicates, only after these futures are articulated can one begin to develop an action, or strategic, plan. Insofar as organizations adopt strategic planning processes as part of their routines, futuring will come to be a more widely accepted aspect of the way we think and act in modern society.

Modeling the Study of the Future. Let us consider specifically the future of philanthropy. The expert authors whose work is presented in this volume, as well as a surrounding group of their supporters, completed two rounds of a Delphi study in late 1987 and early 1988. The experts were asked to score each item on a long list of world problems defined by futurist Michael Marien as particularly important.[13] The problems were categorized under a scheme developed by Brian O'Connell, a scheme that identifies nine major areas of philanthropic concern.[14] Then each problem was scored for the degree to which it had received philanthropic attention and the expectation that it required philanthropic concern in the years ahead.

From this process, it is possible to identify five sets of societal problems: (1) those that have been important to philanthropy in the past but may be of lesser importance in its future; (2) those that have been important to philanthropy in the past and will continue to be of roughly similar importance in the future; (3) those that have been important to philanthropy in the past and will be of even greater importance in the future; (4) those that have been of lesser importance to philanthropy in the past but will be of critical importance in the future; and (5) those "sleeper" problems that are certainly growing in importance even though they are not yet highly significant. The five sets of problems are listed below, grouped under their principal categories.

IMPORTANT IN PAST, LESS SO IN FUTURE

Nourishing the Spirit
  Religion
  Encouraging the "performing arts"

IMPORTANT IN BOTH PAST AND FUTURE

Discovering Knowledge
  Education
  New thinking (for example, futures research)
Relieving Misery
  Disaster relief

Nourishing the Spirit
    Public arts and delights

IMPORTANT IN PAST, MORE SO IN FUTURE

Enhancing Human Potential
    Inequality
    Children in crisis
    Teenage pregnancy
    Drug abuse
Relieving Misery
    Health care
    Health costs
    Poverty
    Hunger

LESS IMPORTANT IN PAST, HIGHLY IMPORTANT IN FUTURE

Relieving Misery
    AIDS
    Unemployment
Nourishing the Spirit
    Preserving open spaces
Preserving Democracy
    Justice system and crime
    Generational equity
    Nonprofit/for-profit competition
Developing Community
    Urban decline
    Homelessness
    Regenerating local economies
Creating Understanding
    Better U.S.–U.S.S.R. relations
    Nuclear war
    Mexican instability
    Africa in reverse
    Environmental concerns

Water-quality concerns
Discovering Knowledge
Agricultural technology
Energy and resources
Communications
Supporting Excellence
Building economic capacity
Conditions of work

NOT YET OF IMPORTANCE, BUT GROWING

Outer space
Public works and infrastructure
Corporate restructuring

What is most apparent from examining this list is the degree to which the emerging problems outnumber the traditional ones. Philanthropists have in the past specialized in a number of difficult problems, such as education, the arts, and the relief of misery. But what the twenty-first century seems likely to present to them is a much wider set of challenges—from AIDS and homelessness to the very survival of the physical environment that sustains us.

"Guess who's coming to college?" is the question Harold Hodgkinson asks educational leaders in his demographic presentation of the role of minority group members in the American twenty-first century. "Guess what philanthropists will be asked to do?" is the question we must ask ourselves. And the answer is "Much, much more than has been asked of us or accomplished by us in the past." The range and complexity of the problems that will be presented to philanthropy in the years ahead surely outweigh anything that has emerged in either the past or the present. The most significant aspect of philanthropy's cutting edge may rest as much in its length as in the sharpness of its honing.

A Possible Future for Philanthropy. It is possible, even likely, that the future of philanthropy will emerge according to a pattern that may be described as follows:

1. The range and complexity of problems brought to philanthropy for amelioration and resolution will steadily and insistently increase.
2. The capacity of first- and second-sector organizations (corporations and businesses) to resolve these problems will continue to be restrained by resource limitations and the multiple constraints imposed on them to provide other services (such as products in consumer demand and military readiness, respectively).
3. In recognition of the critical role philanthropy can ensure in creating a societal "commons" (a place where people can come together to resolve pressing human problems), a long-term growth in the size of giving will occur; by the year 2025 this will approach the 5 percent goal set in the 1980s by corporate "5 percent clubs" and the "Give Five" program of INDEPENDENT SECTOR.
4. As philanthropy becomes recognized as a "major player" in the struggle for humanity's survival, its leaders will come to accept the appropriateness and productivity of a puissant societal role in the public examination and evaluation of philanthropy's process and activity. Philanthropy will adopt "standards and goals" processes in which the broader society participates in assessing and redirecting the contribution of philanthropy to the resolution of common human concerns and problems.

Although it is possible, even likely, that philanthropy will emerge along such lines, it is also possible that its devolution will occur and follow other patterns. It is of course up to those who choose and care to shape such forces to act, or not act, so as to influence the future that we and our children will share. If we do choose to commit ourselves to this fateful enterprise, however, we might wish to commit ourselves to a set of principles for practice that will give us as good a chance as possible to prevail. Hence, this volume concludes with a beginning sketch of such principles.

Notes

1. Consider, for example, the work of the Congressional Institute for the Future (218 D Street S.E., Washington, D.C. 20003).

2. Arthur M. Schlesinger, Jr., *The Cycles of American History.* New York: Houghton Mifflin, 1986.

3. Jon Van Til, *Living with Energy Shortfall: A Future for American Towns and Cities.* Boulder, Colo.: Westview Press, 1982.

4. Willis W. Harman, *An Incomplete Guide to the Future.* New York: Norton, 1979; see the same author's *Global Mind Change: The Promise of the Last Years of the Twentieth Century.* Indianapolis: Knowledge Systems, 1988; and Marilyn Ferguson, *The Aquarian Conspiracy: Personal and Social Transformation in Our Time.* (2nd ed.) Los Angeles: J. P. Tarcher, 1987.

5. Peter H. Raven, "We're Killing Our World: Preservation of Biological Diversity." *Vital Speeches of the Day,* May 15, 1987, pp. 472-478.

6. Ian I. Mitroff, *Business Not as Usual: Rethinking Our Individual, Corporate, and Industrial Strategies for Global Competition.* San Francisco: Jossey-Bass, 1987.

7. Thomas J. Knudson, "Experts Say Chemicals Peril Farm Belt's Water." *New York Times,* Sept. 6, 1986, p. 8.

8. Center for Defense Information, "Militarism in America." *Defense Monitor,* 1986, *15* (3).

9. Grace Halsell, *Prophecy and Politics: Militant Evangelists on the Road to Nuclear War.* Westport, Conn.: Lawrence Hill, 1986.

10. Columnist George Will exemplifies the abysmal level of contemporary political concern in his column of Apr. 22, 1988, which I first located in the *Columbus Dispatch* (page 13a). Will writes of George Bush and Michael Dukakis: "Many people believe Bush resembles a willow, not an oak. Dukakis calls to mind Henry James' dessicated characters who 'never make lusty love, never go to angry war, never shout at an election or perspire at poker.'" Prescinding from the presidentiality of provoking angry war, or one's behavior at poker, the admission of bedroom behavior more intimate than the mere selection of a partner (marital or not) stands as an indicator of the depths to which our current dirty-minded politics have sunk. Would the yellow journalist of an earlier generation have even

thought to apply the Jamesian criteria to a Herbert Hoover or a Franklin Delano Roosevelt?

11. Edward Banfield, *The Unheavenly City*. Boston: Little, Brown, 1968.
12. Thomas North Gilmore, "Overcoming Crisis and Uncertainty: The Search Conference." In Larry Hirschhorn and Associates, *Cutting Back: Retrenchment and Redevelopment in Human and Community Services*. San Francisco: Jossey-Bass, 1983, pp. 70–90.
13. See Michael Marien (ed.), *Future Survey Annual 1986: A Guide to the Recent Literature of Trends, Forecasts, and Policy Proposals*. Bethesda, Md.: World Future Society, 1987, p. vii.
14. Brian O'Connell, *Philanthropy in Action*. New York: Foundation Center, 1987.

Conclusion   *Jon Van Til*

Toward Guidelines
for Effective
Philanthropic Practice

≈≈≈≈≈≈≈≈≈≈≈≈≈≈≈≈≈≈≈≈

Eleven guidelines for philanthropic practice may be drawn from this study.

First Guideline: A sophisticated understanding of the theory and practice of philanthropy is required if effective professional practice is to be sustained.

This is surely the master guideline to emerge from the present study. It challenges the reader to draw other guidelines for her or his personal practice of philanthropy from the various chapters of this volume and others. It challenges teachers, students, parents, administrators, and citizens to see in the philanthropic endeavor a subject for school and college curricula. And it challenges those with careers in philanthropy to recognize the need for a continuing process of reflective education as part of an emerging professionalism.

Second Guideline: Philanthropy is no longer a matter of purely "private" action and behavior: those active in the field should recognize that it is a field of lively public policy and concern, and quite likely to remain such.

Philanthropy, the authors of this study assert, is a matter of public concern surrounded by an active public policy interest. Lawyer

Bruce Hopkins shows that while such policy review may be uncomfortable to those accustomed to viewing philanthropy as essentially private, it has become a fact of contemporary life. Those who practice in the world of philanthropy are well advised to recognize John Dewey's 1927 observation that in a democracy, the realm of the public extends to the many actions that are public in their ramifications.[1]

Third Guideline: Philanthropy is most appropriately seen as a relationship between donors and recipients mediated by varying images of the public good.

The "relational" aspect of philanthropy is described by several authors in this volume. Recipients and their needs are, and surely ought to be, as central to the philanthropic world as are the resources and preferences of donors. If philanthropy is to be seen as centrally involved in serving the public good (as Robert Payton, in particular, asserts), it follows directly that its practice should be held to tests beyond a donor's simple assertion that an action meets a public goal.

Fourth Guideline: Engaged donors and need-centered recipients will keep philanthropy centered on its truest goals.

If philanthropy involves a relationship between donor and recipient for the public good, then it follows that donors should be as fully aware as possible of their options and activities, and recipients should be aware of needs that require giving. A vital philanthropy will resist those powerful forces of current society (such as bureaucratization) that tend to separate need from resource and will seek to keep alive the connection between the giver and the receiver. Perhaps the best example of this guideline is found in the work of philanthropist Eugene Lang and his philanthropic colleagues, the "Dreamers," who commit themselves to achieving a college degree and living a life of useful service as a condition of receiving philanthropic support in the "I Have a Dream" program.

Fifth Guideline: The time has come to admit religion to full membership in the world of philanthropy, while recognizing that

*the philanthropic world will thereby become even more diverse
than it was previously.*

Although it is surely the case that some of what passes for religion
is more nearly the manipulation of lonely and anxious individuals
(and their donations), the core of religious practice belongs in the
philanthropic realm. Even though supporting the liturgical structure of a religious institution involves a different kind of philanthropy than supporting a church's social or political outreach
activity, both are philanthropic actions. Philanthropy is by no
means unitary in form, content, or structure. And including religion in this category extends the pluralism of philanthropy. No
other great social institution reflects as centrally on the relations
between giving and receiving than does religion. For that reason
alone, it seems appropriate, as James Wood and James Hougland
assert, to bring religion fully into the arena of philanthropic analysis and practice.

*Sixth Guideline: Philanthropy, while it cannot fully escape the
temptations of individualism and commercialism so rampant in
society, should nonetheless struggle bravely to preserve altruism
and solidarity as core values.*

As those who have focused on philanthropic ethics in this study
have shown, philanthropic practice does not always conform to the
kinds of standards one might wish. Philanthropic practice is also
subject to the same blandishments of "bottom-line" enhancement
that lead many corporate and governmental organizations to focus
on short-term gains at the price of long-term losses. A recurrent
theme among the authors of the present volume involves the validity of core philanthropic values in the building of a caring and
democratic society. It is not gratuitous to note the importance of
these values or the degree to which they are imperiled in contemporary life. If philanthropy can assist in keeping lighted the flames
of altruism, humane caring, and active participation in a dark time
of narcissistic self-absorption, it will have served humankind well
enough.

Seventh Guideline: There is more than enough work for dedicated board members, effective administrative staffers, and productive providers of technical assistance in the nonprofit world: An important task is to assure the most effective articulation of these roles.

We live in an age of management, and effective management is important. In the world of philanthropy, innovation and organizational change are required to assure that as much of what is needed gets accomplished as effectively as possible. This is not, however, a time to replace volunteers with paid staff, or vice versa. Neither is it a time to propogate any other management fad and offer it as a panacea for an overstretched organizational sector. The essence of effective nonprofit management requires a strong contribution from each major group of actors: board, staff (paid and volunteer), and providers of technical assistance alike.

Eighth Guideline: Philanthropy rests, like all other social institutions, in the cusp of global economic, political, and social forces: its leaders should address those forces with the confidence that they can be shaped, at least in part.

It is all too easy, in a world dominated by megainstitutions, to conclude that one cannot make a difference. Consumerism and exaggerated individualism reflect this malaise, and those who seek to advance philanthropy are as subject to it as anyone else. But if any human profession should be proactive and committed to the struggle for human advancement whatever the odds, it should be philanthropy. Why? Because the essence of the core values of the philanthropic endeavor assert that the individual can make a difference, that the world can be made better by the caring acts of individuals and the organizations they join with others to create.

Ninth Guideline: Philanthropists should be sophisticated futurists as well.

It is astounding how often those of us in organizations act without concern and regard for the future. There are few things to be known certainly about tomorrow, but one is that it will certainly arrive. It would seem appropriate for philanthropic organizations to commit themselves to act upon this elementary truth and to seek to orient themselves intelligently toward the future.

The effective practice of futuring is represented by an increasingly large literature and body of practice. With a commitment of time and resources, any philanthropic organization can avail itself of the emerging wisdom of the futures field to address its own image of proactivity in the complexities of the emerging future. Within the third sector, the United Way of America has taken the lead in demonstrating the utility of this approach. Another place to begin is with the World Futures Society or with one of a set of authors who have contributed importantly to our understanding of the methods and possible contents of the future.[2]

There are many ways to think about and to plan for the future. What seems most important is that we actually do that thinking and planning.

Tenth Guideline: Philanthropy should be seen as a key to the future.

This guideline is a kind of internal pep talk. We hear so much about the powers of the transnational corporation and the national state these days (not to mention that our own sector comes in only third) that we may not always remember just how important philanthropy is as a societal force. Obviously, there is no assurance that our work will prevail or even that we will make a dent in the kinds of challenges we will confront in the future. What is important, however, is to remember that it is possible that we can make that difference,[2] and to act upon that possibility.

Eleventh Guideline: The future of philanthropy is ours to create: let us be about the task.

This guideline reinforces the eighth, but it is important enough to warrant standing as the conclusion to this work.

We live in a world in which the gods, John Calvin notwithstanding, give few if any guarantees that our interventions, wise or otherwise, will actually succeed. But neither does the known structure of our world foredoom or foretell any other future. Intelligent action, whatever its chances of success, is always an option the true philanthropist will wish to consider, for the possibility that such action will make a difference is part of the very essence of the philanthropic vision.

It may be time for all philanthropists, as well as the leaders of the foundations they endow, to address more directly the scanning, evalution, and selection of priority actions on the basis of as full an awareness of the future as we can reasonably achieve. A process of "futuring philanthropy" might both clarify the future needs the field will be called upon to address and simultaneously attract the new contributions such new priorities will require.

Elliot Liebow concludes his brilliant study of black streetcorner life, *Tally's Corner,* by repeating Auden's celebrated observation: "We must love each other or die."[3] Philanthropy, which is a major way in which human beings organize their love of each other and blend that love with their own respect for themselves, may never be more important than in the years ahead.

Notes

1. John Dewey, *The Public and Its Problems.* Denver, Colo.: Alan Swallow, 1927.
2. Brian O'Connell, *Philanthropy in Action.* New York: Foundation Center, 1987.
3. Elliot Liebow, *Tally's Corner.* Boston: Little, Brown, 1967. In regard to the eleventh guideline, see also William Van Til, *My Way of Looking at It: An Autobiography.* Terre Haute, Ind.: Lake Lure Press, 1983.

Name Index

Subject Index

AAFRC Trust for Philanthropy, The, 7, 126, 252

Accountability: and corporate giving, 107–108; ethical issues of, 200–202; and religious fund raising, 114–116

ACORN, 153

Adoptive philanthropy, personal engagement in, 79–80

Adult Social Service Block Grant, 156

Affective demand, in social relation, 72

Affinity cards: for fund raising, 51, 53; and legal issues, 211, 212

Africa: missionaries to, 167, 168; relief to, 182, 185–186

Agenda-based strategy, of recipients, 90–92, 94

Alliance Marketing, 51

Altruism: and self-interest, 36–37, 46, 59–60; and solidarity, 121, 278

American Association of Fund-Raising Counsel, 62, 160, 161; and research, 248, 250; standards of, 199; Trust of, 7, 126, 252

American Baptists, in Congress, 109

American Council of Learned Societies, 242*n*

American Express, and marketing, 117–118, 203

American Indian Movement, 154

American Institute of Certified Public Accountants, 55

American Red Cross, fund-raising sales by, 52

Amnesty International, 182

Asian-Americans: and community organizations, 142, 150; and philanthropy, 42

Aspen Institute, 250

Associated Charities of Denver, 15

Association of American Colleges, 252

Association of Voluntary Action Scholars (AVAS), 248, 253, 262

AT&T, giving by, 46

Bangladesh concert, 182

Baptists, in Congress, 109

Bear Stearns, giving required at, 59

Big Brothers and Big Sisters: adoptive philanthropy in, 79; students in, 171

Black United Fund: donor and recipient roles of, 69; and special-interest philanthropy, 151

Blacks, and community organizations, 142, 150, 151

288